"This is an important book. This book changes everything."
—Joe Scarborough

"This is a book with an important message. It is also one that brims with intelligence, erudition, and—best of all—common sense. I found myself nodding in agreement on almost every page."
—Fareed Zakaria, author of *The Post American World*

"This brilliant and courageous book is also a gripping read. At a time when most politicians and pundits on the left and the right look back to past golden ages, the *Economist*'s John Micklethwait and Adrian Wooldridge dare to ask what must be done to make democracy work again. Their answers point beyond the dull nostrums of conventional politics, toward new ideas and reforms that could renew the democratic systems in both the U.S. and Europe. This is a landmark study of a vital subject, told with great verve and dash, and it is a book that no one who cares about the future of politics can afford to miss."
—Walter Russell Mead, James Clarke Chace Professor of Foreign Affairs and Humanities at Bard College

"[*The Fourth Revolution*'s] case is elegantly made, with big-picture philosophy and political economy punctuated by colorful detours into the world's rising economies."
—*Financial Times*

"Clever and sharply argued."
—G. John Ikenberry, *Foreign Affairs*

"*The Fourth Revolution* is a lively book."
—*The New York Times Book Review*

"Micklethwait and Wooldridge do an outstanding job of describing Asia's modernizing autocracies. In some ways, these governments look more progressive than the Western model; in some ways, more conservative."
—David Brooks, *The New York Times*

"This book's message is simple but severe: if the state promises too much to too many, cynicism grows, and democracy is damaged."
—*The Wall Street Journal*

"*The Fourth Revolution* has . . . an insatiable curiosity and an enthusiasm for reform."
—Michael Ignatieff, *The New York Review of Books*

"A different, provocative view of the challenge emerging in Asia."
—*Kirkus Reviews*

"There is much to praise in Micklethwait and Wooldridge's account, and it has been lauded widely. The bloat they take aim at is undeniable. Also the need for technological and managerial innovation. Truly government has overreached in a way that is deeply intrusive in our lives. What is more, Micklethwait and Wooldridge are deeply right to insist that beyond technological innovation, we need to think about ideas: namely, the idea of what we want our government to be."
—Roger Berkowitz, Hannah Arendt Center for Politics and Humanities blog

"Superb . . . Micklethwait and Wooldridge's must-read manifesto is a plea for more reform, inspired this time by successful reforms in other countries and the harnessing of the digital revolution."   —*The Telegraph* (UK)

"The basic argument of this well-written, intelligent book is twofold. First reform [of the state] is essential. Second, reform is possible because it is happening all over the world and because new technology is available. By the end of reading *The Fourth Revolution* it is hard to deny either of these points."
—*The Times* (London)

"This book's success is rooted in its case studies that prove something beyond doubt: government can be made slimmer and better. Facing aging populations and an entitlement-born disaster, this book offers an alternative to partisan 'theaterocracy' and a call to much-needed revolution."
—*The Washington Times*

"[The authors] offer thoughtful proposals. . . . It is a useful look at America from the outside in."   —*The Seattle Times*

"It is . . . refreshing to read a contemporary analysis that advocates for the importance of ideas—and which understands that, in the case of how to improve governance, the ideas that matter are not just found in developed countries. The ability to make comparisons—to share ideas for smarter governance across borders—is a key aspect of the ongoing fourth revolution."
—Formar Hub

"This is a big and important idea whose time has come. The great failing of American politics is not that the Tea Party wants to shrink the government or that the Democrats want to keep every single entitlement in place. The great failing is that the country's leaders can't seem to have a real debate on what kinds of things a twenty-first-century American government should or should not do. Instead they argue about cutting the whole thing down or they argue about protecting every last nickel. And in the interstices of that non-debate, rent seekers of all sorts from Medicare scammers to Wall Street gamblers are sucking the legitimacy out of the government. We should heed the call of *The Fourth Revolution*." —Elaine Kamarck, Brookings Institution

PENGUIN BOOKS

THE FOURTH REVOLUTION

John Micklethwait is the editor in chief of *Bloomberg News*. After studying history at Magdalen College, Oxford, he worked as a banker at Chase Manhattan before joining *The Economist* as a finance correspondent in 1987. He served as *The Economist*'s editor in chief from 2006 to 2015 and was named an Editors' Editor by the British Society of Magazine Editors in 2010.

Adrian Wooldridge is *The Economist*'s management editor and writes the Schumpeter column. He was previously based in Washington, D.C., as the Washington bureau chief. Together they are the authors of five previous books: *The Witch Doctors*, *A Future Perfect*, *The Company*, *The Right Nation*, and *God Is Back*.

THE FOURTH
REVOLUTION

THE GLOBAL
RACE TO REINVENT
THE STATE

**JOHN MICKLETHWAIT
& ADRIAN WOOLDRIDGE**

PENGUIN BOOKS

PENGUIN BOOKS

Published by the Penguin Group
Penguin Group (USA) LLC
375 Hudson Street
New York, New York 10014

USA | Canada | UK | Ireland | Australia
New Zealand | India | South Africa | China
penguin.com
A Penguin Random House Company

First published in the United States by The Penguin Press,
a member of Penguin Group (USA) LLC, 2014
Published in Penguin Books 2015

Copyright © 2014 by John Micklethwait and Adrian Wooldridge
Penguin supports copyright. Copyright fuels creativity, encourages diverse voices,
promotes free speech, and creates a vibrant culture. Thank you for buying an authorized
edition of this book and for complying with copyright laws by not reproducing, scanning,
or distributing any part of it in any form without permission. You are supporting writers
and allowing Penguin to continue to publish books for every reader.

THE LIBRARY OF CONGRESS HAS CATALOGED THE HARDCOVER EDITION AS FOLLOWS:
Micklethwait, John.
The fourth revolution : the global race to reinvent the state / John Micklethwait, Adrian Wooldridge.
pages cm
Includes bibliographical references and index.
ISBN 978-1-59420-539-2 (hc.)
ISBN 978-0-14-312760-4 (pbk.)
1. World politics—1989– 2. Nation-state. 3. Social change. 4. East and West. 5. Crisis management
in government. 6. Political science—History. 7. Hobbes, Thomas, 1588–1679—Political and social views.
8. Mill, John Stuart, 1806–1873—Political and social views. 9. Webb, Beatrice, 1858–1943—Political and
social views. 10. United States—Politics and government—1989– I. Wooldridge, Adrian. II. Title.
D860.M525 2014
320.1—dc23   2014005396

Printed in the United States of America
1 3 5 7 9 10 8 6 4 2

Designed by Marysarah Quinn

While the author has made every effort to provide accurate telephone numbers, Internet
addresses, and other contact information at the time of publication, neither the publisher nor
the author assumes any responsibility for errors, or for changes that occur after publication.
Further, publisher does not have any control over and does not assume any responsibility for
author or third-party Web sites or their content.

For:

Tom, Guy, and Edward

Ella and Dora

CONTENTS

PART THREE
THE WINDS OF CHANGE

THE FOURTH REVOLUTION

INTRODUCTION

BURIED IN A SHANGHAI SUBURB, close to the city's smoggy Inner Ring Road, the China Executive Leadership Academy in Pudong appears to have a military purpose. There is razor wire on the fences around the huge compound and guards at the gate. But drive into the campus from the curiously named Future Expectations Street and you enter Harvard, as redesigned by Dr. No. In the middle stands a huge bright red building in the shape of a desk, with an equally monumental scarlet inkwell beside it. Around this, spread across some forty-two hectares, are lakes and trees, libraries, tennis courts, a sports center (with a gym, a swimming pool, and table-tennis tables), and a series of low brown dormitory buildings, all designed to look like open books. CELAP calls all this a "campus" but the organization is too disciplined, hierarchical, and businesslike to be a university. The locals are closer to the mark when they call it a "cadre training school": This is an organization bent on world domination.

The students at the leadership academy are China's future rulers. The egalitarian-looking sleeping quarters mask a strict pecking order, with suites for the more senior visitors from Beijing. And as with other attempts at global supremacy, there is an element of revenge. Thirteen hundred years ago, CELAP's staff remind you, China set up an imperial exam system to find the best young people to become civil servants. For centuries these "mandarins" ran the world's most advanced government, but in the nineteenth century the British and the French (and eventually the Americans) stole their system—and improved it. Since then better government has been one of the West's great advantages. Now the Chinese want that advantage back.

When the leadership academy was established in 2005, President Hu Jintao spelled out its purpose: "To build China into a modern and prosperous society in an all-round way and to develop socialism with Chinese characteristics, it is urgent for us to launch large-scale training programs to significantly improve the quality of our leaders." Rather than focus on indoctrination like the party schools, CELAP and its two smaller sisters in Jinggangshan (CELAJ) and Yan'an (CELAY) have been designed to be practical places. The talk is of leveraging your skills, strengthening your global mind-set, and improving your presentation abilities. It is all meant to complement what goes on in the party schools. But the fact that CELAP is based in Shanghai while the central party school is in Beijing adds a competitive frisson. When one trainee in Pudong explains that the party school focuses on "why," while CELAP looks at "how," there is no mistaking which question he thinks is more important to China's future. If CELAP had a motto, it might be Alexander Pope's couplet, "For forms of government let fools contest/What'er is best administer'd is best."

Driven by the desire to "best administer," about ten thousand people a year attend courses at the school, nine hundred for the first time. Some arrive ex officio: If you are a bureaucrat who has just been put in charge of a state-owned company, a governor who has been given a province to run, or an ambassador en route to a new posting, you are sent to Pudong for a refresher course. (As a thank-you, the ambassadors are supposed to send the library a book to symbolize their new posting. The man who sent *The Rough Guide to Nepal* has some explaining to do.) More generally, a course at the leadership academy has become a prize to be pocketed by any ambitious bureaucrat. Every Chinese civil servant is expected to have clocked three months of training every five years, or about 133 hours a year. Courses at CELAP are oversubscribed by a factor of three, with most of the candidates drawn from the ranks of deputy director generals, the fourth-highest rung in the Chinese system.

The two most common questions, says one teacher, are "What works best?" and "Can it be applied here?" A typical course is divided into three parts, with lectures soon giving way first to fieldwork, with the mandarins sent out to study something that could be useful, and then to discussion about how to apply it. The subjects vary from the relatively small, such as the most convenient way to demolish houses for infrastructure projects, to the monumental, such as designing the most equitable pension system. The appetite for ideas is rapacious: ideas from local businesses (there are two hundred field-study centers in the Yangtze River delta, including a mini CELAP campus in Kunshan city); ideas from various national universities; ideas from Western management thinkers.

When the Chinese modernized their economy, they turned to the West for inspiration, and the leadership academy still sends people to Silicon Valley to look at innovation. Government is a different story. There is talk of CELAP being "China's Kennedy School," and Joseph Nye, the former dean of Harvard's Kennedy School of Government, has given a talk there. But there are also hints that Harvard is a little too theoretical for what China needs now. Historical examples are not what is called for, let alone historical examples that celebrate the virtues of democracy or soft power. CELAP is about delivering efficient government in the here and now, about providing cheap health care and disciplined schools. And from that point of view there are better places to look than gridlocked America—most notably Singapore.

The city-state may be tiny, but it has delivered most of the things that the Chinese want from government—world-class schools, efficient hospitals, law and order, industrial planning—with a public sector that is proportionately half the size of America's. For the Chinese, it is the Silicon Valley of government. Even the idea at the heart of CELAP—training an elite civil-service cadre—is based on a Singaporean model, though the Chinese boast that their requirements are more onerous. So it is not surprising that the leadership academy proudly features pictures of its senior figures attending meetings in Singapore and of Singapore's creator, Lee Kuan Yew, visiting the campus.

The leadership academy can sometimes look a bit comical. Officials tie themselves in knots trying to explain why some governmental ideas that work well abroad, like democracy and free speech, will not work in China for "cultural reasons." A teacher quotes a proverb about some orange trees tasting sweet "only on the south bank of the river." Corruption in Washington is denounced in ringing terms regardless of the fact that the published wealth of the fifty richest members of Beijing's National People's Congress is $95 billion—sixty times the combined wealth of the fifty richest members of America's rather more strictly monitored Congress.[1] The local Web sites in Shanghai are full of tales of inefficiency and graft. Indeed, the reason CELAP exists is that the Chinese know they have to do better.

Yet taken as a whole, the correct response of any Western politician visiting CELAP is similar to that of a Western manufacturer visiting a Shanghai factory two decades ago: awe, and perhaps a degree of fear. Just as China deliberately set out to remaster the art of capitalism a couple of decades ago, it is now trying to remaster the art of government. The main difference is that the Chinese believe that nowadays there is far less to be gained from studying Western government than they did from studying Western capitalism.

LEVIATHAN AND ITS DISCONTENTS

CELAP may be extraordinary, but it is hardly unique. Around the world, from Santiago to Stockholm, the cleverer politicians and bureaucrats are also scouring the world for ideas. The reason is simple: The main political challenge of the next decade will be fixing government. In The Federalist Papers Alexander Hamilton urged his fellow Americans to decide "whether societies of men are really capable or not of establishing good government from reflection and choice, or whether they are forever destined to depend for their political constitutions on accident and force."[2] His words are just as true today. Countries that can establish "good government" will stand a fair chance of providing their citizens with a decent standard of life. Countries that cannot will be condemned to decline and dysfunction, in much the same way the Chinese once were.

For the state is about to change. A revolution is in the air, driven partly by the necessity of diminishing resources, partly by the logic of renewed competition among nation-states, and partly by the opportunity to do things better. This Fourth Revolution in government will change the world.

Why call it a *fourth* revolution? Not least as a reminder that the state can change dramatically. Most of us in the West only know one model—the ever-expanding democratic state that has dominated our lives since the Second World War. However, history before then tells a different story. Indeed, Europe and America surged ahead precisely because they kept changing: Government was engaged in a continual process of improvement. Looking back, others might identify dozens of small revolutions, such as Thomas Cromwell's "revolution in government" in Tudor England or Otto von Bismarck's pension reforms in nineteenth-century Germany. In this book we simplify and argue that the Western state has been through three and a half great revolutions in modern times.

The first took place in the seventeenth century, when Europe's princes constructed centralized states that began to pull ahead of the rest of the world. In the 1640s, when a middle-aged royalist on the run called Thomas Hobbes produced his anatomy of the state against the background of the English Civil War there were good reasons to believe that the future lay with China or Turkey. Hobbes decided to name the state, which he regarded as the only answer to the nastiness, brutality, and brevity of human life, after a biblical monster, Leviathan. But what a successful monster it proved to be! Europe's network of competing monsters threw up a system of ever-improving government: Nation-states became trading empires, then entrepreneurial liberal democracies. The struggle for political and economic prowess was often bloody and messy—Britain has waged war on virtually every Western European country—but that contest has also ensured that the West left other regions of the world behind.

The second revolution took place in the late eighteenth and nineteenth centuries. It began with the American and French revolutions and eventually spread across Europe, as liberal reformers replaced regal patronage systems—"Old Corruption," as it was known in England—with more meritocratic and accountable government. We focus on the British manifestation of this revolution partly because its better-known twins have more distractions—the French Revolution degenerated into a bloodbath while the American one had the peculiar virtue of having a continent-sized country to work on—and partly because it is the Victorian one that seems to be most relevant today. English liberals took a decrepit old system and reformed it from within by stressing efficiency and freedom. They "stole" China's idea of a professional civil service selected by exam, attacked cronyism, opened up markets, and restricted the state's rights to subvert liberty. The "night-watchman state," advanced by the likes of John Stuart Mill, was both smaller and more competent. Even though the size of the British population rose by nearly 50 percent from 1816 to 1846 and the Victorians improved plenty of services (including setting up the first modern police force), the state's tax revenues fell from £80 million to £60 million.[3] And later reformers like William Gladstone kept on looking for ways to "save candle-ends and cheese-parings in the cause of the country."

However, as often happens, one revolution set up another. Throughout the second half of the nineteenth century, liberalism began to question its small-government roots: What good, wondered Mill and his followers, was liberty for a workingman who had no schooling or health care? And if that man (and eventually woman) deserved the right to vote, and it would be illiberal to think otherwise, then that schooling needed to be broad and ambitious. And if governments were in competition with one another—and that was increasingly the view as Bismarck welded Prussia into a Great Power—then surely those who educated their workers best would triumph.

Thus an improved life for every citizen became part of the contract with Leviathan. That paved the way for the aberration of communism but also for the third great revolution: the invention of the modern welfare state. That too has changed a great deal from what its founders, like Beatrice and Sidney Webb, imagined; but it is what we in the West live with today. In Western Europe and America it has ruled unchallenged since the Second World War—except for during the 1980s, when Margaret Thatcher and Ronald Reagan, inspired by classical liberal thinkers like Milton Friedman, temporarily halted the expansion of the state and privatized the commanding heights of the economy. We dub this a half revolution because, although it harked back to some of the founding ideas of the second "liberal" revolution, it failed in the end to do anything to reverse the size of the state.

The twists and turns of each revolution, as we shall see, have been significant. What is clear, however, is that for the past five hundred years Europe and America have been the font of new ideas about government. Not all of them worked, but even in its more grotesque deviations of fascism and communism, the West was still striving, at least in theory, to forge the future. The rest of the world followed. The Chinese and the Russians followed Marxism. India, when it became independent in 1947, embraced British Fabianism even as it put a torch to British imperialism. In Latin America, despite their citizens' love-hate relationship with the gringos in *el norte*, the region's economies lurched forward two decades ago when most of them embraced "the Washington consensus" (a phrase invented by John Williamson to mean a combination of open markets and prudent economic management). Even in Pudong there is a recognition that, until recently, the Western model represented the gold standard of modernity.

Freedom and democracy have been central to that. The rise of the Western state was not just a matter of setting up a competent civil service. Even Hobbes's monster, as we shall see, was a dangerously liberal one for a royalist to propose, because Leviathan relied on the notion of a social contract between the ruler and the ruled. The Victorian liberals saw a well-run state as a prerequisite for individual emancipation. Their Fabian successors saw a welfare state as a prerequisite for individual fulfillment. As it has expanded, the Western state has tended to give people more rights—the right to vote, the right to education and health care and welfare. Things like a university education that a century ago were regarded as a white, male, wealthy privilege are now seen as a public service, in some cases a free entitlement, for everybody.

Yet the Western state is now associated with another trait: bloat. The statistics tell part of the story. In America government spending increased from 7.5 percent of GDP in 1913 to 19.7 percent in 1937, to 27 percent in 1960, to 34 percent in 2000, and to 41 percent in 2011. In Britain it rose from 13 percent in 1913 to 48 percent in 2011, and the average share in thirteen rich countries has climbed from 10 percent to around 47 percent.[4] But these figures do not fully capture the way that government has become part of the fabric of our lives. America's Leviathan claims the right to tell you how long you need to study to become a hairdresser in Florida (two years) and the right to monitor your e-mails. It also obliges American hospitals to follow 140,000 codes for ailments they treat, including one for injuries from being hit by a turtle. Government used to be an occasional partner in life, the contractor on the other side of Hobbes's deal, the night watchman looking over us in Mill's. Today it is an omnipresent nanny. Back in 1914 "a sensible, law-abiding Englishman could pass through life and hardly notice the existence of the state, beyond the post office and the policeman," the historian A.J.P. Taylor once observed. "He could live where he liked and as he liked. . . . Broadly speaking, the state acted only to help those who could not help themselves. It left the adult citizen alone." Today the sensible, law-abiding Englishman cannot pass through an hour, let alone a lifetime, without noticing the existence of the state.

There have been periodic attempts to stop the supersizing of the state. In 1944 Friedrich Hayek warned that the state was in danger of crushing the society that gave it life in *The Road to Serfdom*. This provided an important theme for conservative politicians from then onward. In 1975 California's current governor, Jerry Brown, in an earlier incarnation, declared an "era of limits." This worry about "limits" profoundly reshaped thinking about the state for the next decade and a half. In the 1990s people on both the Left and the Right assumed that globalization would trim the state: Bill Clinton professed the age of big government to be over. In fact, Leviathan had merely paused for breath. Government quickly resumed its growth. George W. Bush increased the size of the U.S. government by more than any president since Lyndon Johnson, while globalization only increased people's desire for a safety net. Even allowing for its recent setbacks, the modern Western state is mightier than any state in history and mightier, by far, than any private company. Walmart may have the world's most efficient supply chain, but it does not have the power to imprison or tax people—or to listen to their phone calls. The modern state can kill people on the other side of the world at the touch of a button—and watch it in real time.

There are powerful demographic and economic reasons why many people think that the state will continue to grow. Entitlements grow as populations age. Governments dominate areas of the economy, like health and education, that are resistant to productivity improvements. But the other reason for the state's sprawl has been political. Both the Left and the Right have indulged its appetites, the former singing the praises of hospitals and schools, the latter serenading prisons, armies, and police forces, and both creating regulations like confetti. The call that "something must be done," i.e., that yet another rule or department must be created, comes as often from Fox News or the *Daily*

Mail as it does from the BBC or the *New York Times*. For all the worries about "benefit scroungers" and "welfare queens," most state spending is sucked up by the middle classes, many of them conservatives. Voters have always voted for more services; some people just resent having to pay for them more than others. The apocryphal sign at a Tea Party rally warning "big government" to "keep its hands off my Medicare" sums up many Americans' hypocrisy about the state.

For better or worse, democracy and elephantiasis have gone hand in hand. Our politicians have been in the business of giving us more of what we want—more education, more health care, more prisons, more pensions, more security, more entitlements. And yet—here is the paradox—we are not happy.

Having overloaded the state with their demands, voters are furious that it works so badly. From Seattle to Salzburg the worry is that the system that has served the West so well has become dysfunctional, that, to borrow a phrase from polling organizations, things are "on the wrong track," that our children will live more cramped lives than we have. In America the federal government has less support than George III did at the time of the American Revolution: Just 17 percent of Americans say that they have confidence in the federal government, less than half of the 36 percent found in 1990 and a quarter of the 70 percent found in the 1960s.[5] Congress regularly scores an approval rating of 10 percent. Membership in political parties has collapsed. In Britain less than 1 percent of the population is a member of a political party. The number of card-carrying Tories has declined from 3,000,000 in the 1950s to 134,000 today, a performance that would have put a private company into receivership. In America more people now identify themselves as independents than they do as Republicans or Democrats. The only politicians with fire in their bellies seem to be on the extremes—people who either want no state at all, refuse to countenance reform, or blame the whole thing on immigrants or bankers or the European Union.

The drift to the extremes is not surprising given the center's inability to face up to reality. Take the two biggest crises in Western government, America's fiscal mess and the euro debacle, and you find mainstream politicians behaving like ostriches. With the first, most economists agree that the solution requires a combination of spending cuts and tax rises. The economists might disagree about the proportion. In most successful "fiscal adjustments" in other countries spending cuts have done most of the work, but never all of it. Yet in the last presidential election every single Republican candidate rejected the idea of any tax rises whatsoever. "Not a penny more" was the universal refrain. The Democrats were only a little less deranged in their adamant refusal to consider reducing entitlements.

Perhaps, you might argue, Americans have a little time to avoid fiscal reality; the euro crisis, by contrast, is already graphically real. Yet look at the elections in the eurozone's three biggest economies. France's contest in 2012 was an exercise in denial, with neither Nicolas Sarkozy nor François Hollande entertaining the idea of cuts to what has become the continent's most bloated government. In 2013, despite their country enduring its worst crisis since the war, one in four Italians could not be bothered to vote—and over half of those who did chose either Beppe Grillo, a former comedian, or Silvio Berlusconi, a congenital clown. Nobody would accuse Angela Merkel of clownishness, but even her easy victory in Germany in 2013 was a national refusal to face reality, where the euro crisis was a southern European problem, with the thrifty Germans having to save the day. Nobody discussed the fact that Germany's banks were still standing only because their borrowers in the south had been bailed out.

There are some mechanical reasons for this lurch to the edges of reason. In America gerrymandering has left many congressional districts in the hands of hard-liners, while the European Union's governance system is a maze of unaccountability. But the plain fact is that voters—be they Bavarians furious at lazy Italians living *la dolce vita* on their euros or Greeks furious at Mrs. Merkel's austerity—are frustrated with the system. They are mad as hell. They cannot take it anymore. The West has lost confidence in the way that it is governed.

The same can be said of the emerging world. After a decade of spectacular growth in the emerging markets, many now have their own debate about government. China's princelings realize that further progress now relies on improving the state, not just opening up markets. And, like their peers in India, they are confronted by the consequence of those freer markets—an educated middle class, increasingly fed up with an outdated, often corrupt state.[6] In Brazil protesters have focused on corruption: One in four Brazilians say that they have paid bribes. In Turkey the complaint is high-handedness on the part of a prime minister, Recep Tayyip Erdogan, who acts more like a sultan than a democrat. Gurcharan Das, an astute Indian commentator, points out that, not that long ago, his countrymen were willing to argue that "India grows at night while the government sleeps": Now they realize that India cannot continue to grow so long as its schools are substandard and its roads are full of holes.[7] Even China has not been immune: You can feel the frustration with lousy schools in Guangzhou as surely as you can in Tahrir Square or the favelas of São Paulo.

So in both the West and the emerging world the state is in trouble. The mystery is why so many people assume that radical change is unlikely. The status quo in fact is the least likely option. As an American economist, Herbert Stein, once drily observed, "If something cannot go on for ever, it will stop." Government will have to change shape dramatically over the coming decades. In the emerging world the era of growing by night is over. In the West the era of more is coming to an end. It is time for the Fourth Revolution.

WHY IT HAS TO CHANGE

Why should this time be different? Bringing Leviathan under control will be the heart of global politics because of a confluence of three forces: failure, competition, and opportunity. The West has to change because it is going broke. The emerging world needs to reform to keep forging ahead. There is a global contest, but one based on promise as much as fear: Government can be done better.

Debt and demography mean that government in the rich world has to change. Even before Lehman Brothers collapsed, Western governments were spending more than they raised. The U.S. government has run a surplus only five times since 1960; France has not had one since 1974–75. The crunch has only increased the debt, as governments rightly have borrowed. By March 2012 there were some $43 trillion of government bonds in issue,[8] compared with only $11 trillion at the end of 2001. That is only a fraction of Western governments' true liabilities, once you factor in pensions and health care. The numbers for many cities are even worse: San Bernardino in California and Detroit in Michigan both filed for bankruptcy because of these off-balance sheet obligations.

And who will pay for all this? In "old Europe," for instance, the working-age population peaked in 2012 at 308 million—and is set to decline to 265 million by 2060. These will have to support ever more old people: The old-age dependency ratio (the number of over-sixty-fives as a proportion of the number of twenty-to-sixty-four-year-olds) will rise from 28 percent to 58 percent—and that is assuming that the EU lets in more than a million young immigrants a year.[9] Across the Atlantic, America continues to tax itself like a small-government country and spend like a big-government one while hiding its true liabilities by using tactics that would have made Bernie Madoff blush. With the baby boomers aging, the Congressional Budget Office reckons the bill for medical benefits alone will rise by 60 percent over the next decade—its deficit may be manageable now, but the United States faces a choice: Rein in those entitlements, raise taxes to extraordinary levels, or stagger from crisis to crisis.

Every six months the International Monetary Fund publishes its fiscal monitor, in which Statistical Table 13a has the exciting title "Advanced Economies: Illustrative Adjustment Needs Based on Long-Term Debt Targets"; its final column makes a guess, once age-related spending has been factored in, about how much governments need to cut costs or raise revenues in order to bring down their debt to reasonable levels by 2030. In America the figure is 11.7 percent of GDP, in Japan it is 16.8 percent, and across the G20 advanced countries as a whole it averages out at 9.3 percent. You can quibble about some of the IMF's requirements for particular countries. Some economists think it is much too hard on America, for example: They argue that the Fund sets an unnecessarily ambitious target for reducing government debt (60 percent of GDP) and they point out that a small change in either growth numbers or tax revenues would make a big difference to America's prospects.[10] But the past two decades of America's political history suggest that it would be foolish to bet on the country's ability to raise its taxes. And even if the numbers can somehow be made to balance, without serious reforms of its public sector America will turn into "an insurance conglomerate protected by a large, standing army,"[11] with all the money going to entitlements and defense and none left for education or anything else.

For the foreseeable future the Western state will be in the business of taking things away—far more things than most people realize. In some places, where governments have managed their finances spectacularly badly, such as Greece and some American cities, that taking away has already been dramatic: In San Bernardino the city attorney advised people "to lock their doors and load their guns" because the city could no longer afford police. Even Europe's most consensus-minded politicians recognize that something has got to change: Angela Merkel's favorite statistic is that the European Union accounts for 7 percent of the world's population, 25 percent of its GDP, and 50 percent of its social spending.[12] But the politics of introducing change will be bloody, pitting cash-strapped governments that have to trim services against disgruntled voters who want to maintain their social rights, and taxpayers who want more value for their money against powerful public-sector unions that want to preserve their privileges. If millions of French people took to the streets when President Nicolas Sarkozy raised the pension age from sixty to sixty-two, heaven knows what will happen when François Hollande or his successor is eventually forced to push it up to seventy.

This battle will go straight to the heart of democracy. Western politicians love to boast about the virtues of democracy and urge errant countries, from Egypt to Pakistan, to embrace it. They argue that one person, one vote holds the cure to everything from poverty to terrorism. But the practice of democracy in the West is diverging ever more from the ideal, with the U.S. Congress polluted by money and partisanship, European parliaments plagued by drift, and the general public increasingly disgruntled. The unedifying truth is that Western democracy got rather flabby and shabby when it was mostly giving things away. Interest groups (including many people who work for the state) have proved remarkably successful at hijacking government. The example of Japan is a frightening one: For decades it failed to fix its sclerotic political system, even as its economy withered. The European Union seems to be following a similar trajectory.

If failure is the first prompt for change in the West, competition is the second. For all its frustrations with government, the emerging world is beginning to produce some striking new ideas, eroding the West's competitive advantage in the process. If you are looking for the future of health care, then India's attempt to apply mass-production techniques to hospitals is part of the answer, just as Brazil's system of conditional cash transfers is part of the future of welfare. But it goes deeper than that. Chinese-oriented Asia offers a new model of government that challenges two of the West's most cherished values: universal suffrage and top-down generosity. This "Asian alternative" is an odd mixture of authoritarianism and small government, best symbolized by Singapore's long-term ruler, Lee Kuan Yew. He has been a stern critic of the West's unfettered democracy but also of the West's welfare state, which he compares to an all-you-can-eat buffet: Things that should have been targeted at the poor, such as free university tuition and health care for the elderly, have become middle-class rights, bloated and unaffordable. And China is trying to follow Singapore rather than the West when it comes to welfare as well as democracy: It has extended pension coverage to an additional 240 million rural people in the past two years, far more than the total number of people covered by America's public-pension system, but it also plainly wants to avoid America's excesses.

It is easy to poke holes in the Asian model—and we poke a lot of them in this book. Singapore is very small. China's governmental efficiency falls apart at the local level. So far the emerging world has not seized the opportunity to leapfrog ahead that technology has presented it with. Brazil is heading toward a pension crisis that could dwarf even those in Greece and Detroit. India may have a few of the most innovative hospitals in the world, but it has some of the lousiest roads and laziest politicians. But do not be fooled into thinking that the emerging world is miles behind. The bureaucrats at CELAP are right: The days when the West had a monopoly on clever government are long gone.

This points to the third force: the opportunity to "do government" better. The crisis of the Western state and the expansion of the emerging state are both coming at an auspicious time: New technologies offer a chance to improve government dramatically, but so does asking old questions such as the most basic question of all: "What is the state for?" As with the previous revolutions, the threat is plain: bankruptcy, extremism, drift. But so is the opportunity: the chance to modernize an institution that we have overloaded with responsibilities.

WHY IDEAS MATTER

How should the state be changed? We think that any answer has to involve two things—one rooted in pragmatism and the other in political principles.

The pragmatic answer, which people of all persuasions should seize upon, relies on improving management and harnessing technology, particularly information technology. Fifty years ago, companies suffered from the same bloat that government now does. Business has changed shape dramatically since then, slimming, focusing, and delayering. So can government. The state is still stuck in the era of vertical integration, when Henry Ford thought it made sense to own the sheep whose wool went into the seat covers of his cars. Government is lousy at spreading successful ideas. There is no good reason why California schools should be so much worse than Finnish or Singaporean ones, particularly given that California spends more per pupil. If all America's high schools were as good as those in Massachusetts, America would have finished fourth in the 2012 PISA rankings for reading and tenth for mathematics, rather than seventeenth and twenty-sixth. In Italy, Trento had one of the highest scores in the world for maths, but Calabria was two years behind. Government is also lousy at keeping itself under control: Think of the thousands of pages of the Dodd-Frank financial reforms. Or just look at the numbers. Britain's Office for National Statistics calculates that productivity in the private-service sector increased by 14 percent between 1999 and 2013. By contrast, productivity in the public sector fell by 1 percent between 1999 and 2010. Governments need to learn from best practice in much the same way that once-sprawling companies learned from the Toyota method of production in the 1980s.

Technology has even bigger potential than management. The Internet has revolutionized everything that it has touched, from the newspaper business to retail. It would be odd if it did not also revolutionize the state. The IT revolution is robbing the state of what was one of its great sources of power—the fact that it possessed so much more information than anybody else. The revolution is also part of a possible cure to "Baumol's cost disease." William Baumol, an American economist, argued that it was impossible to reduce the size of the state because it is concentrated in labor-intensive areas, such as health care and education, where spending will continue to rise faster than inflation. Productivity in the public sector has indeed been dire. But computers and the Internet are beginning to do for services what machines did for agriculture and industry. You can now watch the world's best lecturers for free on your iPad instead of having to pay good money to watch time-servers in smelly lecture halls.

Championing the cause of better management should be completely apolitical. Who doesn't believe in providing young children with a good start in life? Or old people with a decent retirement? It is unlikely to be that way, because the prime obstacles to modernization are often public-sector unions, be they America's teachers or France's railway workers, which are closely allied with parties of the Left. In fact, the Left has more to gain than the Right from improving the management of government for the simple reason that the Left invests more hope in the capacity of government to improve people's lives, especially the lives of the poor. It cannot make sense for people who believe in the benevolence of government to prevent government from hiring the best people (or firing the worst), or to allow the government machine to be run by vested interests. Consider a startling fact that emerged during America's fevered national discussion over the botched rollout of Obamacare: 94 percent of federal IT projects over the past ten years have failed—more than half were delayed or over budget and 41.4 percent failed completely. The Pentagon spent over $3 billion on two health-care systems that never worked properly. They failed partly because the government's rigid employment rules prevent it from hiring IT experts and partly because its even more rigid rules about contracting out mean that it is a captive of the few suppliers who have the resources to navigate the eighteen hundred pages of legalese in the Federal Acquisition Regulation. If the Left is serious about defending government, it needs to start by trying to make it as efficient as possible.

There is more to the future of government than just better management, however. At some point a bigger decision has to be made. No matter how well you make the existing state work, you are confronted with the question of whether that is the right sort of state to have. What is the state for? That question is at the heart of an old debate—a debate that disappeared during the "all you can eat" phase of modern democracy. For Hobbes, Leviathan existed to provide security. For Mill and the radical Thomas Paine, the answer was liberty. For the Fabians it was the welfare of mankind. But all these thinkers thought that you needed to address the big question before moving on to the practical details. Now these questions are discussed only in piecemeal form. Modern politicians are like architects arguing about the condition of individual rooms in a crumbling house, rushing to fix a window here or slap on a new coat of paint there, without ever considering the design of the whole building. We need to look at the design of the whole structure—and also to think hard about the proper role of the state in a fast-changing society, just as the Victorians did at the dawn of the modern democratic age.

In this great argument we should admit that we have a marked prejudice: We come from a newspaper rooted in classical liberalism, which generally places a high premium on the freedom of the individual (and which, incidentally, was founded at the time of that Victorian reinvention). In general we favor a smaller state. We think that part of understanding what's gone wrong is recognizing that government has to be kept in check; that it is often a blunt tool; that, left to its own devices, it will expand inexorably. But that is a prejudice to be tested against the facts, not an article of blind faith.

Thus we do not accept the libertarian idea that government is at best a necessary evil. Too little government is more dangerous than too much: You would have to be crazy to prefer to live in a failed state like the Congo, where the absence of Leviathan makes life truly "nasty, brutish, and short," than in a well-run big state like Denmark. By paying for public goods like education and health care, governments can improve efficiency as well as welfare. America's supposedly "private" health-care system costs its inhabitants more in taxes and delivers worse health than the Swedes' public one. One reason why Germany is so much more successful than Greece is that it has a successful state that is capable of gathering taxes, providing services, and commanding respect. The same could be said of Singapore versus Malaysia, China versus Russia, or Chile versus Argentina.

So government can be an instrument of civilization. But we don't accept the progressive idea that there is nothing wrong with the state that yet "more state" cannot solve. There may be a pragmatic case for using public spending in the short term to prevent an economy from sinking into recession. But there is no escaping the need to tame Leviathan in the medium term. The modern overloaded state is a threat to democracy: The more responsibilities Leviathan assumes, the worse it performs them and the angrier people get—which only makes them demand still more help. That is the vicious circle of progressive politics. More fundamentally, the modern state is also a threat to liberty: When the state takes half of everything that you produce, when it prevents people from earning a living braiding hair without an expensive license, when it dictates the race and gender of people whom you can employ, when it summons up draconian powers to fight "wars" on terror, speeding motorists, and marijuana, then it has begun to become a master rather than a servant. Leviathan has to be tamed. It has to be brought under control.

"We do not dance even yet to a new tune," John Maynard Keynes once said of another great shift. "But a change is in the air."[13] That is true today too. Western democracies stand the best chance of responding to change: Democracy provides governments with more flexibility, a way of listening to people. The change should be toward greater liberty, and democracy is also the freest form of government. But the West also runs the biggest risk: Listening to people is one reason why the West has become so overloaded, and politicians are tempted to burden the state with ever more obligations. At the moment democracy sometimes looks as if it were digging its own grave. Whether the West will now listen to its best or worst instincts is the question that will determine the Fourth Revolution's outcome.

PART ONE

THE THREE AND A HALF REVOLUTIONS

CHAPTER ONE

THOMAS HOBBES
AND THE RISE
OF THE NATION-STATE

WHY HAS THE WEST PULLED ahead of the rest of the world over the past three hundred years? And why has Western Europe, a mere proboscis of land on the far end of the Eurasian landmass, pioneered so much that is distinctive about the modern world? Historians have looked for the answer to this question in all sorts of places from Roman law, which entrenched property rights, to the Christian religion, which fostered moral universalism. But a large part of the answer lies in the machinery of government.

A comprehensive history of how the West established its lead in state making would be a monumental undertaking: Samuel Finer's great history of government, which he left unfinished when he died, runs to 1,701 pages.[1] Here we have decided to eschew any attempt to be comprehensive: We plan to focus on the three great reinventions that have redefined Western government and to view those reinventions through the prism of three great thinkers: Thomas Hobbes (an anatomist of the Nation-State who also paved the way for the Liberal

State), John Stuart Mill (the philosopher of the Liberal State, who also foreshadowed the Welfare State), and Beatrice Webb (the godmother of the Welfare State, who also personified its excesses). In chapter 7 we examine the half revolution against government through Milton Friedman, whose ideas had such an impact on Ronald Reagan and Margaret Thatcher. These thinkers occupied different positions in the spectrum from theory to practice. Hobbes wanted to produce a philosophy of politics. The Webbs wanted to change the world. Mill and Friedman occupied a position halfway between the two—they produced profound works of political economy but also played an active role in politics, Mill as a member of Parliament and Friedman as an adviser to presidents and prime ministers. But Hobbes's philosophical theory eventually had a profound impact on the nature of the state while the Webbs' relentless activism rested on firm philosophical foundations. And all four of them (or four and a half if we count Sidney as a half) gave strikingly different answers to the question at the heart of this book: What is the state for?

So we make no apology for the fact that we concentrate on people of ideas. We make a small apology for the fact that the first three of these thinkers are British and the fourth is closely identified with a British prime minister. Britain provides a spine for this part of our story, and it was a pioneer for many of the ideas, good and bad. No other country provides a better example of the gyrations of the Western state over the past four hundred years.

THE BIRTH OF "LEVIATHAN"

Dating the start of any great change is hard. Virginia Woolf made this point memorably in her essay on the advent of modernism:

On or about December 1910 human character changed. I am not saying that one went out, as one might into a garden, and there saw that a rose had flowered, or that a hen had laid an egg. The change was not sudden and definite like that. But a change there was, nevertheless; and, since one must be arbitrary, let us date it about the year 1910.[2]

By the same token, let us date May 1651 as the moment that political thought changed.[3] For it was then that Thomas Hobbes published his *Leviathan*—and it was with the publication of *Leviathan* that the modern concept of the nation-state was born.

Hobbes was not the first to base his political theory on a hardheaded view of human nature: That honor belongs to Niccolò Machiavelli. Nor was he the first to base his theory on deductive reasoning: Grant that to Thomas Aquinas. Nor was he the first to focus on the nation-state rather than the city-state or Christendom: That goes to Jean Bodin. But Hobbes was the first to bring all these three things together into a single volume. And he was the first to add the explosive idea of a social contract between ruler and ruled. If the modern state is one of the great products of human ingenuity, then it has an appropriate founding document in *Leviathan*.

The core idea in *Leviathan* is that the first duty of the state is to provide law and order. This is the ultimate public good—the one that rescues man from misery and makes human civilization possible. Hobbes reached his conclusion by remorseless logic. He deconstructed society into its component parts in much the same way that a mechanic might deconstruct a car in order to discover how it works. He did this by asking himself what life would be like in the "state of nature." Hobbes had no time for Aristotle's idea that man was by nature a social animal. On the contrary, he thought that man was by nature a little atom of ego, pushed this way by fear and that way by greed. Nor did he have any truck with the feudal notion that men were the inhabitants of preordained social roles, designed by nature to issue orders, if they were born lucky, or hew wood and draw water, if they were not. Men, he argued, are motivated to associate with one another neither by their affections nor by their class affiliations, only by their fear for their safety. In Hobbes's state of nature, men are constantly trying to get the better of one another, trapped in a "war of every man against every man" and condemned to a "nasty, brutish, and short" life. "This was not a portrait of man 'warts and all,'" George Will, a modern American conservative, once observed. "It was all wart."[4]

The only way to escape from perpetual civil war, Hobbes argued, is to give up your natural rights to do as you please and construct an artificial sovereign: a state whose function is to wield power, whose legitimacy lies in its effectiveness, whose opinions are truth, and whose orders are justice—Big Brother in philosopher's robes. There is no room for opposition to this "Leviathan": That would threaten to return man to the "miseries of life without government." The only right that the individual preserves is the right to save his life in extreme circumstances: Given that the state's purpose is to protect life, you cannot allow the state to snuff you out.

For all its logical rigor, Hobbes's argument was also emotional, shaped by his personal experiences. He had every reason to understand how easily an ordered life could dissolve into barbarism and chaos. Hobbes was born prematurely in 1588 when his mother was terrified out of her wits by the combination of a violent storm and a wild rumor that the Spanish Armada had landed. (Hobbes wrote in his autobiography that "at that point my mother was filled with such fear that she bore twins, me and together with me fear."[5]) His father was a poorly

educated clergyman who occupied one of the poorest livings in Wilt-
shire, spent more time in the local alehouse than in his church, and
was eventually obliged to "fly for it."[6] Elizabethan England was always
under threat: Witness Philip II's armada. And the paranoia, fanned by
religious conflict, continued under James I: Witness the Gunpowder
Plot in 1605. In 1640 the Stuarts' autocratic but cash-strapped regime
broke down. The resulting civil war between Charles I and his Puritan
foes in Parliament ended in regicide and dictatorship and claimed the
lives of a higher proportion of the British population than did the First
World War. Among the fallen was Sidney Godolphin, one of Hobbes's
closest friends and the brother of the man to whom he dedicated his
book.

Hobbes dealt with the uncertainties of his life by attaching himself
to powerful patrons. Shortly after he graduated from Oxford (where,
by his own account, he spent his time snaring jackdaws with pieces of
cheese rather than studying his books) he got a job as a private tutor
to the Cavendish family. This provided him with access to an aristocratic lifestyle: hawking and hunting and accompanying his pupil,
William Cavendish, on his grand tour. Indeed, it was while they were
abroad in 1628 that the forty-year-old Hobbes picked up a copy of
Euclid's *Geometry* (known today as *Elements*) and opened it on his forty-
seventh proposition, a geometric puzzle known as the Pythagorean
theorem, which remains much beloved by Freemasons. It shows three
squares with a triangle of blank space between them. "By God,"
Hobbes exclaimed. "This is impossible."[7] He was hooked. The direc-
tionless dilettante became a full-fledged philosopher. "The extreme
pleasure I take in study," he wrote, "overcomes in me all other appetites."[8]

Right from the beginning, Hobbes's ideas were controversial and
thus dangerous: He was a royalist with heretical ideas about the source

of monarchy's legitimacy and an absolutist with a taste for subversive ideas. In 1640, having already lived a decade longer than the average Englishman, Hobbes fled England for Paris and spent the next eleven years earning a living as a tutor for the royalist exiles, including the most royal of the lot, the future Charles II. Then, when he finally published Leviathan in 1651, he had to flee back to Oliver Cromwell's London because his obvious contempt for religion had alienated so many of the king's circle. Hobbes was safe only when Charles II reclaimed his throne in 1660—and made a pet of his old tutor, forgiving him for his Cromwellian dalliance and anticlerical barbs, providing him with a generous pension of one hundred pounds a year, and ordering that he be given "free access to his majesty."

At first glance much of Leviathan seems completely alien to our age—a book that appears to justify absolute power written by a fugitive at a time when life was savage and brief. But don't be fooled. The book's enduring relevance springs from the same source as its divisiveness. Leviathan was a thoroughly modern document.

Hobbes was the first political theorist to base his argument on the principle of a social contract. He had no time for the royalist argument that power was the product of divine right or dynastic succession: He argued that Leviathan could take the form of a parliament as much as a king and that the essence of Leviathan lay in the nation-state rather than in collections of family territories. The central actors in Hobbes's world are rational individuals trying to create a balance between their desire for freedom and their fear of destruction. And these individuals perform this feat through a social contract: They give up their lesser rights in order to secure the most important right, that of self-preservation. The state is ultimately made for the subjects, rather than the subjects for the king: The frontispiece of Leviathan shows a mighty king made up of thousands of tiny men.

Hobbes left room for a surprising amount of individual freedom.[9] The sovereign might have the right to legislate on whatever he chose. But a right did not imply a duty or a preference: Sensible sovereigns governed with a light touch and acted as if they were constrained by a liberal and constitutional order. Governments didn't need to tell people what work they could engage in. People would organize spontaneously in order to avoid starvation. Hobbes argued that the state needed to provide two kinds of assistance in a commercial society: laws in order to smooth business transactions and prevent fraud and a minimal welfare state to care for society's casualties.

For royalists Hobbes was also a dangerous egalitarian. The "state of nature" was like an acid applied to the social hierarchy: Some men might have fancier titles and nicer clothes than others, but in the state of nature they were all more or less equal. The smallest could kill the tallest through cunning. Hobbes was also a thoroughgoing materialist who rejected any religious justifications of the status quo. "The universe is corporeal," he wrote in *Leviathan*, "all that is real is material, and what is not material is not real." The state's legitimacy depended on its ability to advance man's material interests: All else was mere illusion.

Hobbes was a modern in his methods as well. Ever since that brush with Euclid he had tried to base his political theory on scientific reasoning—indeed, mathematical deduction—rather than on the casual empiricism of Machiavelli. "The skill of making and maintaining Commonwealths, consisteth in certain rules as doth Arithmetic and Geometry," he said, "not as in Tennis-play on practice only." The point of *Leviathan* was not to provide advice to courtiers as Machiavelli and his contemporary Castiglione had done. It was to provide a theory of politics in much the same way that the best scientists provided a theory of matter or motion. The result was deeply inconvenient. Hobbes's preference for law and order turned him into an enemy of the parliamentary forces, while his enthusiasm for the social contract and secularism turned him into an enemy of the royalist cause. Shortly after Hobbes's death, in his bed at the age of ninety-one, his old university condemned his writings as subversive and burned them in the quadrangle of the Bodleian Library. But today *Leviathan* is more likely to be condemned as a justification for oppression than as an exercise in subversion: The sculptor Anish Kapoor dedicated his giant PVC work, *Leviathan, Monumenta 2011*, to the Chinese dissident Ai Weiwei. In the 2012 American presidential campaign, the libertarian Ron Paul produced an advertisement lambasting *Leviathan*, complete with a shot of the famous frontispiece, and demanding to know what sort of "social contract" leads to one man ruling over all the others—a President Paul being presumably an exception to this reprehensible concept.

BUILDING LEVIATHAN

When Hobbes published *Leviathan*, Britain was not alone in suffering from civil wars. "These days are days of shaking," Jeremiah Whitaker, a British preacher, warned in 1643, "and this shaking is universal: the Palatinate, Bohemia, Germany, Catalonia, Portugal, Ireland . . ."[10] There was only a single year in the first half of the seventeenth century that was free from wars between European states (1610) and only two in the second half (1670 and 1682). During the brutal Thirty Years' War—a name worth contemplating in its own right—the German-speaking population fell by between 25 percent and 40 percent (the figure differs between urban and rural areas) or between six and eight million.

The most advanced civilizations were all in the East. Beijing was the largest city in the world, with more than a million inhabitants. Nanjing was a close second. Six more Chinese cities had 500,000 inhabitants or more and a score had 100,000 or more. India had three cities with 400,000 or more and nine with 100,000 or more. Istanbul had 800,000. Only three European cities—London, Naples, and Paris—had 300,000 and only ten had 100,000.[11] European visitors were overawed by the huge Ottoman Empire and its dazzling capital on the Bosphorus. Suleiman the Magnificent (who reigned from 1520 to 1566) was engaging in only a little poetic license when he added "Lord of Europe" to his ever-lengthening list of titles, which also included "Sovereign of Sovereigns, the distributor of crowns to the monarchs of the globe, the shadow of God upon Earth."[12] The Ottoman Empire was part of an arc of Islamic countries that extended from Turkey and the Arab world to the Balkans, Africa, India, Southeast Asia, and northwest China, dwarfing Christendom.[13] Imperial China was even more advanced. The Middle Kingdom was about the same size as Europe but was unified by a vast system of canals that connected the great rivers to various population centers. Its government seemed similarly constructed: A country that was at least as geographically diverse as Europe, with steppes and tropical jungles, terraced rice farms and Himalayan peaks, was ruled by a single ruler, the "son of heaven." Chinese maps of the world showed the Middle Kingdom surrounded by vassal states and then by barbarians whose countries did not even deserve the dignity of names.

"We thought learning had dwelled in our part of the world," Joseph Hall wrote in 1608 after a trip to China. "They laugh at us for it, and well may, avouching that they of all the earth are two-eyed men, the Egyptians the one-eyed, and all the world else, stark blind."[14] China operated on a grander scale than Europe. The Imperial Quarter of Beijing had a population of 300,000, consisting of the imperial family and its bureaucrats, eunuchs, guards, merchants, and other hangers-on. The Spanish Armada, which had so terrified Mrs. Hobbes, was nothing compared with the "treasure fleets" that Admiral Zheng He had taken to India, the Horn of Africa, and the Strait of Hormuz in the early fifteenth century.[15] And the attempts to systematize Western learning in the seventeenth century that so fascinated Hobbes paled against the "compendium of learning" set in motion by the Ming Emperor Yongle (1360–1424), which drew on the talents of more than two thousand scholars and filled more than eleven thousand volumes—and remained the largest encyclopedia in the world until Wikipedia surpassed it in 2007.

Yet during Hobbes's lifetime the balance of power changed dramatically. In 1683, four years after Hobbes died, the Turks were forced to raise their second siege of Vienna and contracted the infection that turned them into the sick man of Europe. The Asian powers seemed even more introverted. Japan had sealed itself off from the rest of the world and retreated into self-satisfied navel gazing. India's Mughal Empire had fallen into such profound decay that, in the century after Hobbes's death, a few thousand East India Company employees were able to conquer it. Zheng He's exploits marked the high point of China's premodern greatness: Starting in 1433, when the emperor banned further voyages overseas and ordered the destruction of all oceangoing ships and the records of the admiral's achievements, the world's most powerful country turned inward.

The new nation-states of Europe, by contrast, were surging overseas. European adventurers were everywhere: the British, French, and Dutch in North America and Spanish and Portuguese in South America. European scientists explored the heavens. European ships sailed the seas. European companies dominated India and the Far East. In 1500 only a madman would have bet that the future belonged to Europe. By 1700 only a madman would have bet that it belonged anywhere else.

Europe's secret was that its states were in a sweet spot: powerful enough to provide order but light enough to allow innovation. The continent's princes gradually subordinated rival centers of authority like the nobility and the church within their own realms. The degree of subordination varied from one country to another. The Protestant states transferred the halo of sanctity from the pope to the king. But a succession of Catholic monarchs, starting with Ferdinand and Isabella in Spain and Francis I in France, also succeeded in establishing quasinational churches. The French did more than any other nation to turn their aristocrats into the king's lapdogs. But there was a tendency everywhere for kings to promote powerful bureaucrats (Thomas Cromwell in England, Cardinal Richelieu in France, Count-Duke Olivares in Spain) who expanded the power of central government, established more efficient tax-gathering machines, and rationalized the higgledy-piggledy mass of local tolls, regulations, and restrictions that had characterized medieval Europe.

This allowed Europe to escape from the problem that doomed Indian civilization to impotence: a state that was so weak—or so "soft" in Gunnar Myrdal's phrase—that society constantly dissolved into petty principalities, principalities that inevitably fell prey to more powerful invaders, be they Muslims or Britons. At the same time even Europe's most powerful monarchs were far less powerful than the Chinese emperor, whose vast bureaucracy (staffed by the brightest people in the country chosen by rigorous examination) had no opposition from China's landed aristocracy or the urban middle classes.

In practice, Europe's princes had no choice but to share power with local worthies. So long as these worthies, be they cities or corporations or nobles, agreed not to challenge the monarch for ultimate power, they would be given a considerable degree of autonomy. Although the autocratic Louis XIV might have claimed that *"l'état, c'est moi,"* many other monarchs came to see themselves as servants of the state, rather as Hobbes had hinted. Frederick the Great, who once called a crown merely "a hat that lets the rain in," saw the ruler as "the first person" of the state: "He is paid well so that he can maintain the dignity of his office. But he is required in return to work effectively for the well-being of the state."[16] European governments embraced the idea of rule based on law rather than whim: *"non sub homine sed sub Deo et lege."* They also tolerated the existence of representative institutions such as estates and parliaments, institutions that were sorely tested at times, to be sure, as monarchs tried to accumulate more and more power, but that nevertheless survived and reemerged to assert their interests.

Europe's nation-states also succeeded in containing the problem that had threatened to tear them asunder during the first half of Hobbes's life: wars of religion. The Peace of Westphalia in 1648 not only put an end to the bloody Thirty Years' War. It also announced a radical new principle in European affairs: *cuius regio eius religio* (whose realm, his religion). Princes were sovereign when it came to religion within their own borders but had no right to interfere with the religious affairs of other kingdoms. This peace finally established the doctrine of raison d'état as the guiding principle of European diplomacy. Wars of religion rumbled on, of course: The English Civil War did not end until Charles II's return in 1660, and one legacy of that time, the dispute between Protestants and Catholics in Ireland, rumbles on even now. But sectarian conflict was no longer the centerpiece of European foreign policy. Rather than seeking to spread religious truth across borders, Europe's nation-states focused on competing with one another for secular supremacy.

Over the centuries European governments consolidated dramatically, slimming from perhaps four hundred sovereign bodies at the end of the Middle Ages to about twenty-five at the beginning of the First World War.[17] But no single state was powerful enough to establish hegemony over the entire region in the way that the Turks or the Chinese did; instead, Europe's rulers were constantly vying for supremacy. That led to an intense focus on both statecraft and economic development.

The search for security drove innovation. The Chinese might regard themselves as the Middle Kingdom; European monarchs were painfully aware that they were surrounded by enemies and potential enemies. They built up military machines, quickly adapting gunpowder for warfare while the Chinese kept it for entertainment. They turned sailing ships into "floating castles enveloped by all around batteries of quick firing guns" while the Chinese eventually abandoned warships altogether. If "war made the state and the state made war,"[18] as Charles Tilly argued, Europeans made war, and therefore the state, better than anybody else. Europeans also developed diplomatic machines that kept a constant watch on what was going on in other countries. Competition at home led to countries seeking to outdo one another not only in the small cockpit of Europe but also on the high seas. Europe's galleons conquered North and South America and created vast empires that extended from India to Southeast Asia.

Europe outtraded and outcompeted its rivals as well as outfought them. Governments needed money to pay for all those soldiers and sailors, and the supply of money ultimately depended on the health of the economy—or, as Sir Josiah Child, a seventeenth-century British merchant and politician, put it, "profit and power ought jointly to be considered."[19] Here Britain set the pace and the rest of Europe followed: British soldiers and sailors not only prevailed in most of their territorial conflicts but also provided support for Britain's merchants as they expanded farther and farther overseas. Britain set up most of the world's first limited-liability corporations (thanks to the Cavendish connection, Hobbes was a member of two of these, the Virginia Company and the Somer Islands Company).[20]

Such thinking sometimes promoted mercantilist policies: Even Britain, usually the freest trader among the great powers, provided the East India Company with a monopoly on East Indian trade and the full support of the British navy, because it believed that the company could promote national power. But European mercantilism was normally anchored in property rights, including patents, rather than driven by a sultan's favoritism or an emperor's whim. And in general commerce was far freer in Europe than in the Islamic or Asian empires.

China's emperors alternated between plucking the golden goose and killing it: One moment they were extracting huge rents from trade and the next they were banning it entirely as a threat to the social order. In 1661 the emperor Kangxi ordered everyone living along China's southern coast—then as now the most commercially active region of the country—to move seventeen miles inland.[21] The scholar-bureaucrats who ruled China for a thousand years believed in regulating the lesser beings who made their living by buying and selling. Étienne Balázs, the great Hungarian-German-French sinologist, argued that the "Moloch-State" and its obsession with pettifogging regulations killed any chance that China had in the long term of competing with Europe:

> There are clothing regulations, regulation of public and private construction (dimensions of houses); the colors one wears, the music one hears, the festivals—all are regulated. There are rules for birth and rules for death; the providential State watches minutely over every step of its subjects, from cradle to

grave. It is a regime of paper work and harassment, endless paper work and endless harassment.[22]

Pride in Chinese superiority inexorably ossified into lack of interest in the rest of the world. In September 1792 George III sent a trade delegation to China, under the command of Lord George Macartney, bearing numerous gifts including telescopes, clocks, barometers, a spring-suspension coach, and air guns. The Chinese emperor Qianlong first kept the delegates waiting for months and then, when he finally agreed to see them, sent a famously dismissive reply.

> We have never valued ingenious articles, nor do we have the slightest need of your country's manufactures. Therefore, O king, as regards your request to send someone to remain at the capital, while it is not in harmony with the regulations of the Celestial Empire, we also feel very much that it is of no advantage to your country.[23]

This was not just about a different attitude to "ingenious articles" but also about openness to ideas and enthusiasm for what would now be called product development. The Chinese produced an impressive succession of "firsts" (the first clocks and telescopes, as well as gunpowder) but repeatedly failed to harness their inventions. Indeed, the later emperors sank into an intellectual torpor so profound that visiting Jesuits had to construct telescopes and other "celestial instruments" for their Chinese hosts. At the same time the Islamic countries increasingly denounced science in the name of religion, encouraging clerics to burn books and schools to concentrate on forcing their students to learn the Koran. "In Islam, God is Caesar," Samuel Huntington once observed. "In China and Japan, Caesar is God; in Orthodoxy,

God is Caesar's junior partner. The separation and recurring clashes between church and state that typify Western civilization have existed in no other civilization."[24]

The second half of the seventeenth century saw an intellectual revolution in Europe, as the new philosophy put down roots, kings became patrons of ideas, and science turned itself into a profession, one able to question ever more principles.[25] Europe's rulers had grown exhausted with religious orthodoxies. They also realized that they could not survive the brutal competition with their neighbors if they lost the brain race. They began to compete to be patrons of ideas in much the same way they had once competed to be upholders of orthodoxy. Charles II's decision to give a charter to the Royal Society in 1660 quickly established a fashion across Europe.

The ferment of scientific ideas was matched by a ferment of political ideas. *Leviathan* was an early salvo in a heated political debate about the nature of power. John Locke (1632–1704), who embarked on his degree at Oxford a year after *Leviathan* was published, agreed with Hobbes that society was the result of a social contract but modified his chilling vision in various ways. Locke thought that the state of nature was harmonious rather than strife ridden. God had endowed humans with talents and skills and provided them with a world of resources on which to employ them. Locke pointed out that states were just as likely to be the cause of strife rather than the solution: The history of all hitherto existing societies was a history of wars and conflicts that had been generated by the ambition of rulers. Locke thought that people delegated power to a sovereign for reasons of convenience rather than just fear, so they should hand over far less. Why give the state a carte blanche to tax you or interfere with your belongings? ". . . for the preservation of property being the end of government" as Locke argued.[26]

Britain's Glorious Revolution of 1688 represented Europe's most successful attempt to curb the ambition of rulers. James II, a Catholic, tried to grab back some of the powers that the monarch had lost in the Civil War. He also tried to align Britain more closely with Europe's greatest Catholic power, France. The revolution resulted in James's being replaced by William of Orange, a Protestant who was conveniently married to James's own Protestant daughter, Mary, but on terms that limited the crown's powers. In February 1689 Parliament presented William with a Bill of Rights that listed the nation's "ancient rights and liberties" and reminded him that he needed Parliament's consent if he wanted to levy taxes, suspend laws, or create a standing army. The rights of property, and of a propertied elite, were beginning to trump those of the king. John Locke, who returned from exile with Mary in 1688, was a vigorous supporter of the new regime; he was also one of the investors in the new regime's most important achievement, the creation of the Bank of England in 1694, which prepared the way for Britain's emergence as the world's financial superpower.[27]

The Glorious Revolution was a turning point in the development of the modern liberal state: It put an end to any possibility that Britain would become an absolutist state on the French model while also giving radicals space to complain about the extravagance of British government.[28] A good measure for assessing a Briton's radicalism in the eighteenth century was how far he wanted to go in shrinking Leviathan. For some thinkers this was incidental: Adam Smith (1723–90) believed that the market was the real engine of progress, so the state was best kept out of it. His fellow Scot, David Hume (1711–76), focused on the division of power and the rule of law. A much more direct attack on the state came from Thomas Paine (1737–1809), who believed that people will naturally manage their affairs sensibly unless they are deceived by their priests or bullied by their rulers. In both *Common Sense* (published in America shortly before the American Revolution) and *The Rights of Man* (published in England shortly after the French Revolution) Paine dismissed the state as a parasite. "Society is produced by our wants, and government by our wickedness; the former promotes our happiness positively by uniting our affections, the latter negatively by restraining our vices," he wrote in one famous passage. "Society in every state is a blessing, but government even in its best state is but a necessary evil,"[29] he wrote in another. Paine dismissed the state as little more than an instrument for extracting taxes from the rest of society and using those taxes to support the extravagances of the rich and the fripperies of the court.

In much of the Continent the debate about the size of the state was a sideshow. The Dutch and Scandinavians shared Britain's worries. A few Continental liberals issued similar calls to arms. But for the most part the big guns focused on what they regarded as more profound issues. In *The Social Contract* (1762) Jean-Jacques Rousseau turned Hobbes on his head by arguing that "man is born free; and everywhere he is in chains." For him the proper aim of politics was not to constrain Leviathan but to make sure that it was controlled by the "general will." This made him a more democratic thinker than Locke. But it also blurred the line between liberation and totalitarianism, with disastrous consequences. Thomas Carlyle put it best: The second edition of *The Social Contract* was bound with the skins of those who had laughed at the first edition.[30]

These ideas were more than just idle speculation. Paine believed that "we have it in our power to begin the world over again,"[31] and for a couple of decades of the eighteenth century this seemed to be the case. In America the Founding Fathers turned to the English liberal tradition when they wanted a template for their new country. They accepted Hobbes's view that men were not angels but drew the opposite conclusion: Rather than gather power in the hands of a sovereign, you should divide power as much as possible, allowing factions to act as checks and balances on one another. They also accepted Locke's view that the most important purpose of government was to protect the rights of individuals to pursue their own purposes—particularly life, liberty, and happiness, all of which, of course, were bound up with the protection of property. The most distinctive part of the new American state was its division of sovereignty—dividing it between different branches and levels of government.

This was radical stuff. The American revolutionaries produced the most perfect embodiment of the liberal idea. America was "the land of the future, where, in the ages that lie before us, the burden of the World's History shall reveal itself," as G.W.F. Hegel later put it. But in the late eighteenth century America was a sparsely populated country on the periphery of the civilized world. The center of the civilized world was still Europe—and there the American revolt was overshadowed by a far bloodier event.

The French Revolution shook Europe to its foundations. It mounted a full frontal assault on the founding principles of old Europe—the rule of kings and nobles in earthly affairs and priests in spiritual ones. It proclaimed an entirely different set of principles: the idea that all men were created equal and all arguments should be subjected to the test of reason. And it embraced Jean-Jacques Rousseau as its reigning philosopher in much the same way the Russian Revolution embraced Marx: *The Declaration of the Rights of Man and the Citizen* in 1789 included passages that were lifted wholesale from Rousseau's great book, and a section of Paris was named "Contrat Social."

The revolution spread across Europe. But even as it spread, its founding principles were undermined from within: The rule of reason led to the rule of the guillotine and the rule of the people to the dictatorship of ideologues. The Terror of 1792–93, during which the revolution devoured its own children in the description of one of the revolutionaries, produced a search for a more sustainable order. Napoléon transformed himself into an emperor and distributed royal titles to his brothers and sisters. And the Bourbon Restoration in 1814 completed this return to the status quo. Unlike their American equivalents, the French revolutionaries never dealt with the question of limiting the power of the state. They simply decapitated the ancien régime and replaced kings and nobles with new functionaries.

So to understand the burgeoning liberal revolution we will bypass America and France and return to Great Britain: the heart of the world's mightiest empire and the vortex of the industrial revolution. The British philosophical radicals were in some ways just as extraordinary as the architects of the American Revolution: They took an ancient country, encrusted with historical traditions, and refashioned it according to the liberal principles of efficiency and open competition. The Victorian liberals swept away restraints on individual energy. They uprooted every anomaly that might place a check on individual liberty, especially economic freedom, and they thrust meritocracy into the heart of government. Here more than anywhere else, the Hobbesian state opened the door to its much more liberal successor, which in turn opened the door to the welfare state.

One Victorian embodied this.

CHAPTER TWO

JOHN STUART MILL
AND THE LIBERAL STATE

JOHN STUART MILL is a vivid example of European progress: Born in 1806, 127 years after Hobbes died, he belonged to a very different Britain, a Britain of improvement, reform, and optimism rather than dysfunction, patronage, and fear. Mill had no use for aristocratic patrons like the Cavendishes. His father, James, himself a notable thinker, raised his son to be a prodigy who could make his own way in the world. He pursued a relatively modern career—as a company man (for the East India Company), a member of parliament (representing Westminster), and a public intellectual (writing in most of the great journals of the day). Mill had no experience of civil war or exile: He began his autobiography by apologizing for telling the story of "so uneventful a life as mine."[1] The only battles Mill wrote about were the ones he fought to master Greek by the time he was three and Latin by eight. And the only revolution he saw was the peaceful transfer of power from a narrow landed aristocracy to a much broader educated elite that included the Mill family as well as the Cavendishes.

His thought reflected this. Mill's overriding political concern was not how to create order out of chaos but how to ensure that the beneficiaries of order could develop their abilities to the maximum and thereby achieve happiness. His focus was on removing barriers to self-fulfillment—and thereby increasing what Isaiah Berlin would later dub "negative liberty." But where did that leave Leviathan? To begin with, Mill thought the answer was easy: a minimal, noninterfering state—the "night-watchman state" (a phrase that he never used but that sums up his attitude). But as he grew older, he began to have second thoughts. Wasn't a state that denied a poor man a decent education also restraining his potential happiness and freedom? Mill epitomized a debate that was at the heart of Western liberalism: Raised as a pure small-government liberal, he gradually accepted the case for a bigger state.

Mill was the product of a group of Victorian intellectuals—the philosophical radicals—who devoted their lives to fashioning an alternative to Britain's ancien régime of landed aristocrats and Anglican clergymen. They included the most important influence on him by far, his father. James Mill (1773–1836) had been born in poverty in Scotland but had earned a plum job with the mighty East India Company by dint of talent and hard work, producing a classic study of Britain's involvement in India while also supporting his young family as a freelance journalist and training his eldest son, John Stuart, as an intellectual racehorse. James's great watchwords were "liberty," "reason," and "effort," and he believed that Britain's traditional overlords were threats to all three.[2] How could industry prosper when idle landlords lived off the fruit of other people's labor? How could scientific reason advance when ignorant clergymen told people what to think? John Stuart recalled that one of the most important lessons of his childhood was that the Reformation was "the great and decisive contest against priestly tyranny for liberty of thought."[3] He also recalled debates around the dinner table about universal suffrage, albeit confined to men over thirty years old.

James had a practical motive in subjecting his son to such an extraordinary educational regime: He wanted him to be a "reformer of the world,"[4] a supercharged missile aimed at the heart of the old regime. He introduced the young reformer to a veritable Tea Party of the small-government great and good. John Stuart's godfather, Jeremy Bentham, the inventor of utilitarianism, and by the boy's reckoning, the most "effectively benevolent man who had ever lived," taught him that the real test of institutions is not how durable they are but whether they provide the greatest happiness to the greatest number. David Ricardo, Britain's leading economist at the time, taught him that wealth was something that can be multiplied by human effort rather than something that is fixed in the form of land. Everyone the precocious young Mill bumped into agreed that the secret of success lay in releasing private enterprise from the dead hand of the state and making room for the happy play of free minds and free markets—for the freedom to think and speak, to inquire and invent, to buy cheap and sell dear.

The philosophical radicals were in the vanguard of a broader movement against what William Cobbett (1763–1835) dismissed as "Old Corruption." John Wade (1788–1875) compiled *The Extraordinary Black Book*, which appeared in numerous editions from 1816 onward, with hundreds of examples of places, pensions, sinecures, nepotisms, and pluralisms in the court, the church, government departments, colonial establishments, municipal corporations, guilds, fraternities, the judiciary, the military, and so on. In 1830 one radical publication pointed out that just two families, the Grenvilles and the Dundases, had "during the last forty years taken more money in sinecures alone than it had cost during the same time to maintain the whole of the civil government of the United States."[5] A popular verse began with the couplet:

> *What is a peer? A useless thing*
> *A costly toy, to please a king . . .*

It went on to describe the nobility as "a bauble," "a gaudy pageant," "an incubus," "a drone," and "a pauper on the public purse." Novelists also got in on the act. Charles Dickens caricatured the British legal system as a grotesque waste of time in *Bleak House* (1853) and created "the office of circumlocution," a division of government dedicated to obstructing progress, in *Little Dorrit* (1857).

Mill's life was bound up with the most important change in the nature of the British state since Hobbes's time: a silent revolution that replaced the ancien régime of privilege, patronage, and purchase with a capitalist state. In 1815–70 a succession of governments abolished a succession of affronts to the principle of free trade in goods, including the East India Company, the West Indian sugar preference, the Navigation Acts, and the Corn Laws. They also abolished a succession of affronts to meritocracy. In the past, powerful Britons had treated government offices as private property that they could buy and sell at will or use as instruments of patronage or simply enjoy without doing any work. In 1784 some busybody complained that one of the two solicitors on the staff of the treasury had not turned up for work since 1744.[6]

The Victorians demanded that officeholders be chosen on the basis of merit rather than family connections. More generally, they insisted that the state solve problems rather than simply collect rents. Growing cities were furnished with sewage systems and "bobbies" (as policemen were known after their inventor, Sir Robert Peel). Railways were built and roads repaved. Whitehall was tidied up. The franchise was expanded. When Mill was born, the franchise was limited to male property owners who were members of the Church of England (around one in seven men) and the country was littered with "rotten boroughs" (parliamentary constituencies that were controlled by powerful patrons). A succession of reform acts and emancipation laws extended the franchise, so that by 1884 the electorate included two in three men.

The Victorian reforms produced something extraordinary—the British state shrank in size even as it addressed the problems of a rapidly industrializing society. The early Victorians paved the way for this by disentangling themselves from foreign wars and making a provisional assault on "Old Corruption." Gross income from all forms of taxation fell from just under £80 million in 1816 to well under £60 million in 1846 despite a nearly 50 percent increase in the size of the population.[7] The mid-Victorians extended these gains by consolidating government power in the treasury and pursuing a policy of "peace and retrenchment." William Gladstone was at the heart of this second phase, first as chancellor of the exchequer from 1852 to 1855 and 1859 to 1866, and then as a four-time prime minister. A fervent believer in allowing money to "fructify in the pockets of the people," he cherished a dream of reducing the income tax to zero (though he failed to realize his dream, he nevertheless reduced taxes three years in a row in the 1860s from seven pence to four pence per pound). He also did what he could to free working people from the burdens of taxation by abolishing duties on essentials: He believed that the best response to the Chartist demand for "no taxation without representation" was not to increase representation but to reduce taxation.

Gladstone and other Victorian "economizers" forced central government to live on a diet of bread and water. They retrenched the basic functions of the state to the minimum and then economized as much as possible on those minimum functions. Gladstone prided himself on "saving candle-ends and cheese-parings in the cause of the country," as he put it. He fought a constant war on corruption and extravagance. He even told government departments to use cheaper writing paper. He used transparency—crystal clear accounting and brilliant exposition at the podium—as one of his most important weapons against waste: Whereas eighteenth-century finances had been basically incomprehensible, Gladstone and his contemporaries made sure that it was as easy as possible to see where the money was coming from and where it was going.[8] Transparency was a guardian of frugality, just as confusion had been a handmaiden of extravagance.

The economizers believed that "nothing should be done by the state which can be better or as well done by voluntary effort," as Gladstone wrote in one party manifesto. Voluntary hospitals should look after health care and trade unions' uenemployment assurance. They transferred as many responsibilities as possible to local government on the grounds that local government was more likely to spot waste and less likely to tolerate it. They also made extensive use of measurements and incentives to squeeze as much value as possible out of public spending. The government created a national curriculum that emphasized the importance of the three Rs—the Revised Code of 1862—and made sure that the curriculum was drummed into the heads of schoolchildren with a combination of national inspections of teachers and payment by results.

The mid-Victorians also redoubled the focus on meritocracy. In 1854 Sir Stafford Northcote and Sir Charles Trevelyan presented, in just twenty-three beautifully written pages, a far-reaching plan to reorganize the civil service on the basis of open competition.[9] "The great and increasing accumulation of public business" meant that Britain needed a new state for new times. The old system of patronage had allowed the aristocracy to use the public services as a dumping ground for their less talented members, for "the idle and useless, the fool of the family, the consumptive, the hypochondriac, those who have a tendency to insanity."[10] In well-run professions, argued Northcote and Trevelyan, "the able and energetic rise to the top and the dull and inefficient remain at the bottom. In the public establishments, on the contrary, the general rule is that all rise together."[11] Their solution was to recruit candidates on the basis of their performance in open examinations and then promote them on the basis of their achievement. The open examinations would test general intelligence rather than just the mere academic attainment of the candidates. Their message was one of moral reform as well as administrative efficiency. They wanted to promote the virtues of hard work and self-reliance and expunge the "moral diseases" of dependence and corruption. John Stuart Mill was a noted enthusiast for all this, looking forward to "the great and salutary moral revolution" where government bestowed "its gifts according to merit, and not to favor."[12] Many in the old order were less enthusiastic about meritocracy—conservatives managed to stop the Northcote-Trevelyan reforms being fully introduced into the home civil service until 1870. But by any measure Victorian government was a much leaner, more efficient beast than its predecessors.

The adamant commitment to keeping the state out of things made the Victorians seem simultaneously harsh and tolerant. On the one hand, the poor lost their liberty if they lost their jobs. You can hear the voice of James Mill (and for that matter Lee Kuan Yew) in their sermons on idleness. Losing your job reflected your moral failure, not the failure of the market. Paupers lost the right to vote and were consigned to semipenal workhouses in order to discourage idleness and provide incentives to work and save. On the other hand, the Victorians were more compassionate when it came to foreign asylum seekers—particularly after the failed European revolutions of 1848. The government gave up its old practice of opening people's mail after an outcry in 1844 over the government's decision to open letters from Giuseppe Mazzini, an Italian nationalist who was in exile in London. For the next three decades the state refrained completely from the surveillance of either its own citizens or visitors: this despite the fact that revolution was in the air on the Continent and that society was going through one of the most dramatic changes in history, as millions of people left the land for the city and thousands agitated for the extension of the franchise.[13] Peel insisted that his bobbies wear uniforms to distinguish them from the plainclothes spies who were so popular on the Continent.

The Victorians thought that lean-government liberalism represented the end of history. Harriet Martineau wrote a history of Britain arguing that practical Benthamism was the engine of progress. George Grote, another radical historian, argued that the ancient Greeks were philosophical radicals *avant la lettre*, exhibiting the virtues of a world of small states and liberal individualism. The Great Exhibition of 1851 was universally interpreted as a demonstration of the wonder-working power of free trade. So was the British Empire.

The liberal movements that flowered across Europe in the mid-nineteenth century embraced both small government and the Westminster model. The 1848 revolutions represented a howl of protest against aristocratic rule and its wasteful extravagance. For continental modernizers, the message was simple: If the world's most powerful country was run by people fixated on keeping government small, why should they put up with anything else? And Britain was not the only model. The United States acted as a liberal echo chamber across the Atlantic: Alexis de Tocqueville, who toured the United States in the

1830s, concluded that America's constitutional democracy was working so well that the country could get by without any government at all other than local town meetings. Andrew Jackson (1767–1845) regarded government as an "enemy" that devoted its energies to securing privileges and subsidies for the powerful.[14] The *Democratic Review* proclaimed in 1838 that "the best government is that which governs least"—and listed running the post office and lunatic asylums and inspecting bakeries among the functions that governments should never on any account attempt. "A strong and active democratic government, in the common sense of the term, is an evil," the *Review* continued, "differing only in degree and mode of operation, and not in nature, from a strong despotism. . . . Government should have as little as possible to do with the general business and interests of the people."[15]

Mill was at the heart of this global movement. He became such a prominent advocate of free trade, in his *Principles of Political Economy*, that one American critic dubbed him "his satanic free-trade majesty."[16] Mill's *On Liberty* (1859) remains the bible of small-government types even today. The only justification for interfering in other people's lives, he argued, was to prevent them from doing harm. Otherwise they should be left well alone. This radical view of freedom not only freed individuals to pursue their own interests in their own way but also allowed society as a whole to benefit from the energies of its component parts. Mill's greatest passion was for intellectual freedom. The unfettered clash of opinions, he believed, advances three great virtues at once: truth by weeding out bad ideas, good government by forcing rulers to defend their decisions, and self-development by encouraging people to take a more active role in running their collective affairs.

For a twenty-first-century radical looking for a way to reform an overmighty and underperforming state, nineteenth-century Britain is a good starting point. Victorian liberals produced cheaper, smaller, far better government. But before a Republican congressman starts trying to rename "JFK" airport "JSM," there is a catch: Liberalism did not remain a small-government creed. As the nineteenth century wore on, its aims broadened. And Mill himself, the apostle of liberty, was at the heart of that change.

THE BIG-GOVERNMENT LIBERAL?

There was also another side to Mill: activist, interventionist, even bossy. His small-government principles had always been qualified by a very British pragmatism, not to mention a degree of self-interest. Mill owed his comfortable life to the twin evils of patronage and monopoly. His father had gotten him his job in the East India Company as his immediate subordinate (and eventual successor).[17] And the company itself was a study in everything that was wrong with the old order—a monopoly that transferred a striking proportion of the world's wealth into the pockets of a handful of Britons, whose greed and ostentatiousness gave us the words "nabob" and "loot." Mill the free-trader always managed to make an exception for his employer. And Mill the liberal always had a kind word to say about imperialism: While Richard Cobden and John Bright dismissed empire as a system of outdoor relief for the upper classes, Mill defended it as part of the white man's civilizing mission.

Mill also embarked on an intellectual odyssey that many were to follow. He became increasingly critical of his father's laissez-faire certainties and increasingly drawn toward soft sociology. How could you judge each individual on his merits when dunces went to Eton and geniuses were sent up chimneys? How could individuals achieve their full potential unless society played a role in providing them with a good start in life? He questioned Bentham's belief that all societies can be judged by the same abstract standard of the greatest good for the greatest number. Surely what was good for the ancient Egyptians was not necessarily good for the modern British? And surely poetry was a great deal better for society than a popular game like push-pin? There was a role for the state in civilizing the masses.

This move leftwards toward a wider franchise and greater state intervention was not easy for Mill. Worried about democracy's becoming the tyranny of the uneducated rabble, he believed that university graduates should be given extra votes (and graduates of Oxford, Cambridge, and a few other British universities did indeed have two votes until 1950). But he kept on finding new things that he thought the state should do. Henry Sidgwick, one of his disciples, noted that Mill's *Political Economy*, the bible of Manchester liberalism, was transformed, in its third and fourth editions, into an apologia for collectivism. A. V. Dicey, one of the great defenders of classical liberalism, worried that Mill's utilitarianism was not just watered down but transformed in its later iterations: The idea that people should be willing to pursue their own interests (and thereby their own happiness) was transformed into the idea that people should be willing to sacrifice their own happiness in order to secure the happiness of others.[18]

In all this Mill was swimming with the tide of opinion. Free trade alone could not answer many of the practical problems that plagued a fast-industrializing society, such as controlling contagious diseases and providing schools. A growing number of people began to blame liberal individualism for the growing pains of a rapidly expanding civilization. Thomas Carlyle denounced laissez-faire as "mechanical" and dehumanizing. Elizabeth Gaskell provided a sympathetic portrait of striking workers in *Mary Barton* (1848). For a social reformer like

Dickens, utilitarianism was as much a target as "Old Corruption"; he turned it into a byword for heartless calculation in *Hard Times* (1854). Charles Kingsley equated government intervention with Christian morality in *Alton Locke* (1850), which was also sympathetic to the striking Chartists.

Education was one area where the old and the new versions of liberalism began to merge. The reformers began by focusing on open competition as a weapon against "Old Corruption." The Royal Commissions into Oxford and Cambridge, which were established in 1850, argued that the practice of restricting fellowships to candidates from particular districts, schools, and families had left Oxbridge populated with fools and sybarites who spent their time sitting over the port rather than teaching. "Men who are naturally well fitted to be country clergymen are bribed, because they are born in some parish in Rutland, to remain in Oxford as fellows until they are not only unfit for that, but for everything else," one of the commissioners, Frederick Temple, complained.[19] The only solution was to open academic jobs "to merit, and to merit only." Another commission into public (i.e., private) schools, which was established in 1861, was equally damning about the education they offered. Henry Sidgwick, then a young Cambridge philosopher, denounced Eton as an abomination: "a useless relic of past ages—a remnant of the monastic life; ideally, a life of self-denying and learned seclusion, actually so often a life of luxurious and unlearned sloth."[20] But as Britain's established institutions opened themselves to talent the reformers began to focus on broadening educational opportunity. Sidgwick championed education for the sisters of the new meritocrats, founding Newnham College in Cambridge. Matthew Arnold, William Foster, and Robert Lowe championed education for the masses. They wanted to build a system of elementary schools that would ensure that everybody had access to basic education; they also wanted to construct a ladder of opportunity that would take exceptional talent from the most humble schools to the most exalted professions. Lowe might have been a tax-cutting chancellor under Gladstone, but he also thought that the state had to spend more on "educating our masters."

In late-Victorian England, the lean, self-restrained state began to expand. Far from seeing its job as simply letting commerce free, it began to look for ways to civilize the dark, satanic mills.

LEFTWARD HO

By the time that Mill died in 1873, the high-Victorian liberalism of *On Liberty* was under fire from every direction—from politicians who worried about national greatness, churchmen who worried about compassion, philosophers who worried about justice, pragmatists who worried about the drains, and, of course, socialists who worried about capitalism.

There were still a few pure liberals left. Herbert Spencer (1820–1903) was arguably the most prominent public intellectual of the 1870s and 1880s, a regular contributor to leading periodicals (including *The Economist*, which provided him with a home for many years), and the author of best sellers such as *The Man Versus the State* (1884). Spencer was not just an uncompromising defender of the free market: He believed that any intervention in the market, even passing laws to prevent eight-year-olds from being sent up chimneys, would inevitably lead to socialism. He enlisted Charles Darwin in the free-market cause. He argued that the struggle for survival in nature (which he memorably described as being "red in tooth and claw") was analogous to the struggle for survival in the economy: Social reform would inevitably lead to national degeneration because it would punish the respectable classes while rewarding the profligate poor and their hordes of children.

Gladstone too stuck to the cause: "We live at a time when there is a disposition to think that Government should do this and that, and that Government ought to do everything," he warned in 1889.[21] "If the Government takes into its hands that which the man ought to do for himself, it will inflict upon him greater mischiefs than all the benefits he will have received." And that from one of Britain's great social reformers.

As the century drew to a close, the tide was flowing strongly against them, however. Gladstone died in 1898, revered but seen as a man of a different era. Spencer, who died five years later, was seen by then as a callous eccentric. A more interventionist state became more the norm, especially in Continental Europe, where the tradition of absolutism was much stronger and the tradition of classical liberalism correspondingly weaker. The French created a mandarin elite that ran the country in the name of social solidarity. In Germany, which was united by Bismarck in 1871, the Prussians created the mightiest state in Europe, with the best schools and universities, the most advanced pension system, the most orderly administration, and an army that could defeat the French with ease.

The rise of Germany transformed G.W.F. Hegel from a marginal figure—"a nauseating, illiterate, hypocritical, slope-headed scribbler" in Arthur Schopenhauer's famous put-down—into the prophet of a new era. Hegel (1770–1831) was a contemporary of James Mill who embraced everything that the great Scotsman despised—metaphysics rather than common sense and state worship rather than the play of the market. He regarded the state as nothing less than the embodiment of reason and progress—the "march of God on earth," as he put it—and bureaucrats (particularly of the Prussian variety) as a universal class whose job was to promote the general good over the selfishness of capitalists and workers. As the sun set on Victorian liberalism, Hegel found disciples in Britain as well as abroad. At Oxford T. H. Green mixed Hegelian metaphysics with Balliol high-mindedness and served the interventionist brew to a succession of bright young men such as Herbert Asquith, the future Liberal prime minister, and R. H. Tawney, one of the most influential intellectuals of the 1920s and 1930s. Suddenly the night-watchman state was the relic of an earlier age, and the Prussian *Reich* the measure of all things modern.

Historians like to explain this change primarily in terms of the rise of compassion: The British elite woke up to the "other Britain" of filthy slums and starving children and passed legislation to provide the poor with welfare and to keep children out of chimneys. Compassion helped. But there was also something more powerful at work: national greatness.

In the late nineteenth century a growing number of Britons began to ask uncomfortable questions. Could Britain remain top dog in a world in which new great powers—Germany in Europe and America across the Atlantic—were feeling their oats and Britain was losing its industrial edge? Between 1883 and 1913 Britain's share of world trade in manufactured goods dropped from 37 percent to 25 percent.[22] Britain's humiliation in the Boer War from 1899 to 1902 brought these anxieties to a head. If Britain could not crush a tiny nation of isolated Afrikaners, what would happen if it faced a bigger enemy? Politicians worried about the feeble quality of the British population. In Manchester, for example, eight thousand out of eleven thousand volunteers were turned away as unfit for military service—shortsighted, pigeon-chested, fallen-arched, rickets-ridden, diminutive, diseased, or otherwise substandard. The "outdated doctrine" of laissez-faire was condemning Britain to fall behind Germany, with its high tariffs, mighty companies, and budding welfare state. Lloyd George summed up the national mood when he worried that Britain could not run an "A1" empire equipped with a "C3" population.[23]

The earliest ventures in welfare provision were all designed to address this problem. The School Medical Service, the prototype of the National Health Service, was founded in 1907 to reverse the deterioration of the noble British race. The provision of free school milk and free school meals, the establishment of compulsory medical inspection, and the founding of maternity and child-welfare clinics were all inspired by a belief that "the nation marches forward on the feet of the little children."

Liberal Britain's embrace of state activism in the second half of the nineteenth century was repeated across the Atlantic. Abraham Lincoln lent the state's support to the expansion of the population westward (the 1862 Homestead Act) and to the creation of new technical and agricultural universities (the 1862 Morrill Act). "The legitimate object of government," he argued, "is to do for a community of people whatever they need to have done, but cannot do, at all, or cannot, so well do, for themselves, in their separate and individual capacities."[24] And his successors intensified state activism in the face of the rise of huge industrial conglomerates and the spread of labor unrest.

So from the 1870s onward Leviathan was swimming strongly to the left. The big question was just how far it would swim. The most powerful voice on the far Left was, of course, Karl Marx, a bearded beneficiary of those enlightened refugee laws who spent decades beavering away in the British Library. You might assume that Marx was a fan of big government, but in fact he had little interest in the size or scope of the state. As far as he was concerned, the engine of history lay in the forces of production rather than in epiphenomena such as ideas or constitutions. The conflict of interest between people who owned the means of production and those who sold their labor led to perpetual class struggle. The state was nothing more than an instrument of class rule: a committee to run the common affairs of whoever happened to be on top at the time—the bourgeoisie in Marx's time—and an instrument of oppression to keep down the workers. So once you got rid of classes, the state would "wither away." Rather than needing to govern (and oppress) people, its only role would be the mere "administration of things."

Marx's ideas were to prove enormously influential on the development of the very institution he decried. For decades half the world lived under a Marxist regime of one sort or another. Even today China's ruling Communist Party proclaims its fealty to Marxism as well as to the market. But in truth Marx's theory of the state was insubstantial—but insubstantial in an especially dangerous way.

It was not just that Marx had precious little to say about how you construct government. He was wrong to argue that political forms do not matter: There was a huge difference between a liberal London, where Marx could while away his time in libraries, and authoritarian Berlin, where he was a wanted man. Marx also ignored the fact that the state could be an interest group in its own right, as it was to become, in extreme form, in the countries that claimed his blessing. But his biggest failure lay in his refusal to come to terms with Hobbes's great insight that a state is necessary for the peaceable conduct of all human affairs.

Marx's naïve view of the state was strangely similar to the Tea Party's: Come the glorious revolution, nobody would need government, so the problem would disappear. That naïveté cost a lot of lives. In dismissing the state as nothing more than an instrument of class control he prepared the way for dictatorship. In a state devoted to the administration of things, people were treated as nothing more than things. If the German government had not put Lenin into a sealed train and dispatched him, like a deadly poison, to Finland Station in early 1917, Marx's theory of the state would be regarded as nothing more than an exercise in utopianism, a sorry contrast to his sometimes brilliant insights into capitalism; and now that the Soviet Union has collapsed and the Chinese have embraced state capitalism, it can be seen as what it was: a dead end.

Today only Pyongyang and Havana seriously claim to have Marxism as a guiding inspiration. By contrast Beatrice Webb sits at the heart of the modern debate about the size and scope of the state.

CHAPTER THREE

BEATRICE WEBB
AND THE WELFARE STATE

BEATRICE WEBB WAS THE GODMOTHER of the welfare state that most of us in the West now live under. She designed the blueprint for a new form of government that provided citizens with an "enforced minimum for a civilized life," thereby creating a ratchet toward ever-bigger government. And she trained a class of intellectuals and functionaries to spread the creed and staff the ever-expanding administrative machine. Her genius was to make the unthinkable seem thinkable and the revolutionary seem evolutionary—and to do it on a global scale.

Her own life, a little like Mill's, followed a leftward drift. Beatrice Potter was born in 1858 the daughter of high-Victorian privilege, or as she put it, "the cleverest member of one of the cleverest families in the cleverest class of the cleverest nation in the world."[1] Her father, Richard, made one fortune providing French troops with tents during the Crimean War and then another as a timber-and-railway tycoon. He ended up as chairman of the Great Western Railway with a country estate in Gloucestershire and a mansion in London. Her mother, Laurencina, was a brilliant intellectual in her own right, a loquacious disciple of laissez-faire economics. Herbert Spencer was a frequent visitor to the family's various houses and took a particular shine to the brilliant young Beatrice.

Yet as she grew older, Beatrice questioned many of the certainties of her youth, so much so that she was eventually sacked from her position as Spencer's literary executor. Why, she demanded to know, should the foolish offspring of privilege be sent to the best schools when the brilliant children of poverty were denied opportunities? Why should honest workers be thrown into destitution just because the market took a downturn? She fell in love with Joseph Chamberlain, a leading radical, and worked in the slums of London with another radical, her cousin Charles Booth. But her life was transformed when she met Sidney Webb in 1890. Sidney was as unprepossessing as Beatrice was beautiful—a huge head mounted on a tiny potbellied body that was invariably encased in an unfashionable shiny suit. But Beatrice admired his tireless mind and burning vision of the ever-expanding role of government: "collective ownership wherever practicable; collective regulation everywhere else; collective provision according to need for all the impotent and sufferers; and collective taxation in proportion to wealth, especially surplus wealth."[2] She shocked her class by marrying this industrious gargoyle in 1892 and amused knowing colleagues like H. G. Wells by sublimating her sexual appetites in the production of a succession of books on the minutiae of administration. "We saw that to the Government alone could be entrusted the provision for future generations," she wrote in an account of her life with Sidney.

Webb was not a political theorist in the mold of Hobbes and Mill: She spent her life worrying about administrative details rather than grappling with abstract concepts. Her most substantial book was a ten-volume study of local government, published periodically between 1906 and 1929. But her work was suffused with a philosophical vision—of the state as an embodiment of universal reason and British good sense. She provided pro-statists with the main components of their ideology—that the state stood for planning (as opposed to chaos), meritocracy (as opposed to inherited privilege), and science (as opposed to blind prejudice). And she grasped that intellectuals could have a huge influence on history provided that they organized themselves and kept preaching the same sermon—a tactic the Right would eventually copy. Gradual permeation was her method for bringing about change. Why risk the blood and tears of revolution when you could "impregnate all the existing forces of society" by publishing pamphlets and sitting on royal commissions? The Webbs founded the Fabian Society to provide a praetorian guard of socialist visionaries, established the London School of Economics to train a new breed of social engineers from around the world, and created the *New Statesman* to act as a cheerleader of their socialist revolution.

Beatrice also embodied the dark side of socialism. She and Sidney hailed Stalin as the architect of a new civilization, dismissing evidence that millions of people had died in famines in Ukraine (including proof provided by Malcolm Muggeridge, who was married to her niece) as counterrevolutionary propaganda. The Webbs had "little faith in the 'average sensual man'"; instead they trusted "the professional expert" to improve the lot of the common people.[3] She dismissed trade unionists as "nitwits and boozers" and was as enthusiastic about eugenic planning as about town planning: Given that people were building blocks of the mighty state, it made sense for Leviathan to manage people's breeding habits. Why should the unhealthy be allowed to breed if they were piling up problems for their fellow citizens? And why shouldn't the cleverest people be encouraged to produce more children if they were improving the overall quality of the state? This was a common view on the left: Her fellow Fabian, George

Bernard Shaw, believed that "the only fundamental and possible socialism is the socialization of the selective breeding of Man,"[4] while Harold Laski, a leading Labour intellectual and LSE professor (who, incidentally, included John F. Kennedy among his pupils), was a follower of Francis Galton, the founder of eugenics, and studied the subject under Karl Pearson, Galton's chief lieutenant.[5]

The Webbs' genius was to distill this mixture of anxiety and idealism into a coherent political movement. They courted all three political parties in Britain rather than simply throwing in their lot with the Labour Party they had helped create. They embraced every possible argument for "collectivism," from social justice to national efficiency to imperialism, rather than embracing any one political theory. They ended up converting most educated opinion to the view, inconceivable a generation earlier, that the state had to deliver "a national minimum" of welfare and education. Even Churchill, whom Beatrice dismissed as "egotistical, bumptious, shallow-minded and reactionary," embraced the idea of the national minimum and "the left-out millions."

Helping these left-out millions was the great domestic cause of the Liberal governments of 1905–15: a cause that led to free school meals for needy children (1906), old-age pensions (1908), a budget against poverty (1909), and national insurance for the sick and unemployed (1911), as well as less savory parts of the Webbs' agenda, such as legislation to sterilize the unfit (1913). Suddenly two things became normal that had never been so before: the taxation of the entire population to provide benefits for the unfortunate and the removal of the "Poor Law" stigma from social welfare. The poor were now victims, not layabouts.

The Webbs were at the heart of a wide-ranging philosophical revolution. The basic building blocks of the British political tradition—particularly the concepts of liberty and equality—were being rejiggered and reinterpreted. In the classical liberal tradition freedom meant freedom from external control. Equality meant equality before the law: Ending the legal privilege of the landed aristocracy had been the seminal battle of the eighteenth and nineteenth centuries. But now freedom was being reinterpreted as freedom from want, and equality as equality of opportunity (and to some extent as equality of respect). This entailed a much more activist view of government. Providing freedom from want meant social services. Providing equality of opportunity meant schools for everyone and university places for the talented poor: Education no longer simply marked people's social status but increasingly determined it. If the seminal political text of the high-Victorian era was Mill's *On Liberty*, the seminal text of the interwar years was *Equality* (1931) by R. H. Tawney, a protégé of the Webbs and a professor at the LSE.

Improving the welfare of the workers was the raison d'être of Tawney's Labour Party. More striking is the way that the Conservative and Conservative-led governments remained committed to the Webbs' concept of a national minimum even as they grappled with the Great Depression. The number of social-service employees doubled between 1914 and 1933 and quadrupled between 1933 and 1940. Harold Macmillan, the future Tory prime minister, was a fairly typical convert to big government in the 1930s: Patrician concern for the workingman (he had served as a Guards officer in the trenches), conservative pragmatism (the unfettered market seemed to have caused chaos), and a snooty dislike for financial "buccaneers" all convinced him that the state must intervene not only to look after the poor but also to direct the economy. National planning and state intervention were thoroughly "modern"—just the sorts of things that an ambitious politician wanted to be identified with.

The Great Depression also brought another British intellectual to the center of the global debate. John Maynard Keynes was a liberal rather than a socialist: He preferred sipping champagne with the Asquiths to drinking water with the Webbs and steadfastly refused to transfer his loyalty from the declining Liberals to the rising Labour Party. The Labour Party was too obsessed with class for his taste, and Keynes was "more than normally" partial to capitalistic speculation, as he put it, making a fortune for himself and another one for his Cambridge college, King's. He was also an unreconstructed elitist who wanted to preserve the high culture of the Victorian intelligentsia. But in *The General Theory of Employment, Interest and Money* (1936) he nevertheless produced the most devastating critique yet published of laissez-faire liberalism, particularly the central laissez-faire conceit that capitalism is a self-correcting mechanism.

Keynes's critique was far more devastating than Marx's because it was couched in the language of modern economics and because it was written—and very well written too—from a position of exasperated sympathy with the system rather than angry hostility. In essence Keynes presented a way of saving capitalism from itself by the careful use of government spending. The central observation in *The General Theory* is that there is no natural tendency to full employment as classical economics had argued. On the contrary, capitalist economies might be destroyed by high levels of unemployment, which reduced demand and threatened social unrest. In slack economic times the role of central government was to boost demand by spending money on public works and unemployment pay. Looked at closely, this came with plenty of caveats. Keynes argued that the state should never consume more than about a quarter of GDP.[6] He believed in organic social forces rather than abstract plans, and he was a pragmatist to his fingertips. "It is fatal for a capitalist government to have principles," he wrote. "It must be opportunistic in the best sense of the word, living by accommodation and good sense."[7] But he firmly believed that the hidden hand of the market needed the assistance of the visible hand of government, and as his insights hardened into a doctrine, people increasingly forgot the caveats: Keynesianism became the intellectual engine of big government.

The triumph of statist thinking in Britain was repeated around the world. In Russia and Germany the cult of big government came in the form of communism and fascism. There was more to totalitarianism than state worship. The Nazis and the Communists both fixated first on the party rather than the state—indeed, they used the party to capture and transform the state. For the Communists the proletariat rather than the state was the locomotive of history. For Hitler the state was "only the vessel and the race is what it contains." But Hitler and Stalin (and for that matter Mussolini, Franco, and Perón) all mixed a good deal of Hegelian state worship into their nightmares and brought the economy under state control. The longer communism lasted in the East the more it became an instrument of the bureaucracy, not the party. George Orwell was right to make Big Brother the government in *1984* (published in 1949).

Enthusiasm for big government took its most benevolent form in the United States. There were certainly some unabashed supporters of the Webbs. Herbert Croly, who argued that Americans should start thinking "first of the state" and second of themselves, turned himself into the Webbs' Yankee publicist and founded the *New Republic* in 1914 as a megaphone for their views. His magazine remained an ardent fan of the Soviet Union until the end of the Second World War. But the American version of big government was steered in a different direction, especially by the two Roosevelt presidents.

Teddy Roosevelt, who was president from 1901 to 1909, accepted the Webbs' view that the age of laissez-faire capitalism was over. The state needed to act as a lion tamer to the capitalist lion. Roosevelt established regulatory bodies, such as the Bureau of Corporations (the forerunner of the Securities and Exchange Commission) to break up monopolies and empower consumers. "The corporation is the creature of the people," he proclaimed, "and must not be allowed to become the ruler of the people." But he did not want to replace the Rockefellers and Carnegies of this world with local government officials. He saw capitalism as an unrivaled wealth-creating machine; he merely wanted to use the power of the state to make sure that capitalism worked better. He wanted to break up the giant trusts that threatened to crush competition. He recognized that it was competition rather than business per se that created mass prosperity. He wanted to protect consumers from rogue corporations with laws such as the Meat Inspection Act (1906) and the Pure Food and Drug Act (1906). He waged war on "crony capitalism"—or the unholy alliance between "corrupt politics" and "corrupt business" as he put it in the 1912 platform for his breakaway Progressive Party. He wanted to use the state to provide poor Americans with what he called a "square deal"—not an all-enveloping welfare state but a safety net in tough times—and to improve the quality of the country's human capital. If the Webbs used sensible causes, such as protecting consumers from degraded products, to advance the power of the state, Roosevelt used the power of the state to advance sensible causes.

This clever fusion of Republicanism and progressivism helped to protect the United States from the excesses of European-style statism. Even at the height of the New Deal championed by his distant Democratic cousin Franklin Delano Roosevelt, America refused to nationalize the commanding heights of the economy in the way the Fabians would have liked. FDR generally preferred tighter regulation to public ownership. He created a raft of commissions and boards, such as the Federal Communications Commission and the National Labor Relations Board, to help to regulate capitalism. The most important of these was the Securities and Exchange Commission, which he created in 1934 with one of America's leading speculators, Joseph Kennedy, as its first chairman (when critics complained about Kennedy's appointment FDR said that this was all the better because he knew all the tricks of the trade). He also created public corporations to make up for market failures: the Tennessee Valley Authority helped to bring electricity to the south and lay the foundations for the region's postwar growth. All the same, there was a clear move to the Left in America, as everywhere else in the 1930s. Even if he did not embrace the Fabians' belief in nationalizing companies FDR shared their enthusiasm for putting brainy experts in charge of everything. The Washington of the 1930s and 1940s was full of clever young Brain Trusters who busied themselves extending the power of government.

THE NEW JERUSALEM

The Second World War was the first great conflict of the era of big government. The war demonstrated the state's power to deploy resources on a scale not seen before. Virtually every industry was subordinated to the will of the state—and every aspect of society was subjected to detailed planning. In Communist Russia the state's control was so explicit, the sense of solidarity so engraved on the public imagination, that the regime would feed off it for decades to come. But in both Britain and America too the state was triumphant: This was the era of the ration book, of "digging together," of Rosie the Riveter striving in a Californian munitions factory, of common sacrifice for the collective good. It stimulated demand for a much fairer society. Common sacrifices demanded common protections.

The Second World War ensured the triumph of the big-state version of basic political ideas like "freedom" and "equality." It also meant a renewed emphasis on a more nebulous idea—"fraternity." In the nineteenth century "fraternity" had been the currency of workingmen's associations rather than philosophical salons: a feeling rather than an argument. But it found its philosopher in the person of T. H. Marshall, inevitably of the London School of Economics. Marshall argued that citizens had acquired new rights in three successive waves—civil rights in the eighteenth century, political rights in the nineteenth century, and social rights (such as the right to education and health care) in the twentieth century. These social rights rested on the fraternal belief that we share a common fate and common obligations, a belief that was reinforced by the war. But note the use of the word "rights": Benefits that had involved reciprocal obligations in the days of workingmen's clubs were being redefined as universal "rights" that people could demand from a powerful state.

In Britain, even by the time Beatrice Webb died in 1943, ideas were being developed for a still-larger welfare state. The 1942 Beveridge Report laid out plans for destroying "five giant evils"—Want, Disease, Ignorance, Squalor, and Idleness. The report's reception was nothing less than ecstatic. People queued up all night to buy the document. Crowds gathered to get a glimpse of "the People's William" (it was "like riding an elephant through a cheering mob," William Beveridge grumbled).[8] The report was translated into twenty-two languages, and British airmen dropped copies on occupied Europe. Two copies of the report, translated into German, were found in Hitler's bunker in Berlin.[9]

The 1944 Education Act raised the school-leaving age to fifteen and promised to educate every child according to his "age, ability and aptitude." The National Insurance Act of 1946 guaranteed a safety net for the unfortunate. And the National Health Service Act, which came into effect in 1948, meant that Britons no longer had to pay for health care (or rather that they paid for it out of their taxes rather than directly). "Homes, health, education and social security," Aneurin Bevan said in a phrase that summed up the mood of the times, "these are your birthright."

Bevan was a working-class firebrand—a coal miner's son who had risen to the deputy leadership of the Labour Party. But the real proof of the Webbs' powers of permeation lay once again in the welfare state's ability to leap across political divides. The three great pillars of postwar Britain—the Education Act, the National Insurance Act, and the National Health Service Act—bore the names of a Conservative (Butler), a Liberal (Beveridge), and a socialist (Bevan). When the Conservative Party returned to power in October 1951, it did nothing to roll back the welfare state, even though it was led by the supposedly reactionary Winston Churchill. *The Economist*'s Norman Macrae invented the word "Butskellism," from the names of R. A. Butler and Hugh Gaitskell, to describe the consensus policies of the next thirty years.

And so it was everywhere in Western Europe, as the idea of building a New Jerusalem blew across the channel. Between 1950 and 1973 government spending rose from 27.6 percent to 38.8 percent of GDP in France, from 30.4 percent to 42.0 percent in West Germany, from 26.8 percent to 45.0 percent in Britain, and from 34.2 percent to 41.5 percent in the Netherlands—all at a time when the domestic product was itself growing faster than ever before or since.[10] The state lubricated the wheels of European life in every way imaginable. It ran companies like

Électricité de France and IRI in Italy: companies that provided jobs for large numbers of workers, products for large numbers of consumers, slush funds for large numbers of politicians, and, of course, taxes for the state itself, in a merry-go-round of wealth creation. It ran universities and research institutes and libraries and broadcasting corporations. Graduates of the best universities—Oxbridge and the Webbs' LSE in Britain, the *grandes écoles* in France—increasingly sought jobs in the ever-expanding public sector rather than in the old professions or the private sector. The state even funded the young iconoclasts who spent their lives thumbing their noses at the establishment on TV and radio.

With so many members of the elites working together to build the New Jerusalem, it was not surprising that the consensus began to create international organizations. The closing days of the war saw the birth of the Bretton Woods twins, the International Monetary Fund and the World Bank (both partly under Keynes's influence) and the creation of the United Nations. The latter never quite became the "parliament of man" internationalists had hoped for: The cold war, with its competing ideologies, snuffed that dream out rapidly. But in Western Europe the social democratic consensus (and fear of Germany's potential to destabilize the continent, even after it had been split in two) led to deeper cooperation between governments, first in the European Coal and Steel Community, which was set up in 1951, and then, later, the European Economic Community and the European Atomic Energy Community, which were then all combined in 1967 into the ancestor of what is now the European Union. From the beginning two things stood out about the European dream. The first was its ambition: In 1952 the first bulletin of the new European Coal and Steel delegation to Washington was titled "Towards a Federal Government of Europe." The second was its technocratic bent. Europe's founders were deeply suspicious of the hot popular will, which led, in their experience, only to fascism or bolshevism. Far better for these new institutions to be steered by the cool wisdom of wise and dispassionate experts. More than any previous form of government, the new European one came into being with a bureaucratic heart.

America never adopted the European belief that the state should run the commanding heights of the economy and as a result had fewer nationalized industries. But postwar America was also entranced by big government. Dwight Eisenhower proclaimed that "gradually expanding federal government" was "the price of a rapidly expanding national growth" and occasionally referred to himself as a liberal in the American sense of the term. Lyndon Johnson called his welfare-state program "the Great Society" after the title of a book by Graham Wallas, a close friend of the Webbs. Richard Nixon proclaimed that "I am now a Keynesian" and even employed the young Donald Rumsfeld to impose price and income controls. America needed a big state to see off communism, to send a rocket to the moon, to police the world, to battle the scourge of poverty, and, in the words of LBJ's close ally, Senator Joseph Clark of Pennsylvania, to "rid our civilization of the ills that have plagued mankind from the beginning of time."[11]

A GLOBAL DREAM

Even in the West, statism also had a pronounced dark side. There was a very Beatrice-like bossiness about many of the leftish sorts who oversaw the state, often inspired by a dismissive view of the working class. In *The Socialist Case*, Douglas Jay, one of the Labour Party's leading luminaries, had argued that "in the case of nutrition and health, just as in the case of education, the gentleman in Whitehall really does know better what is good for people than the people know themselves." Beveridge had confided to Tawney, his brother-in-law, that he believed that "the well-to-do represent on the whole a higher level of character and ability than the working classes, because in the course of time the better stocks have come to the top. A good stock is not permanently kept down: it forces its way up in the course of generations of social change, and so the upper classes are on the whole the better class."

Many progressives continued to support "selective breeding" even after the horrors of the Holocaust were revealed. The Institute of Racial Biology at the University of Uppsala in Sweden remained in business until 1974. And social democratic governments continued to sanction sterilization for "hygienic purposes" into the age of ABBA: Between 1934 and 1976 some six thousand Danes, forty thousand Norwegians, and sixty thousand Swedes, 90 percent of them women, were subjected to compulsory sterilization.[12]

But for the time being the big state seemed to work—and rapid economic growth more than made up for a bit of bossy social engineering. For America the postwar era was one of unrivaled supremacy— of new freeways and schools, the GI Bill, and expanding opportunities. For the British it was an era when the ordinary people had never had it so good. The French had *les trente glorieuses.* The Germans basked in the *Wirtschaftswunder.* The state showed that it could be enlightened: In France and Germany many of the brightest minds went into government. It also showed that it could be flexible. In the 1960s, even as they hung on to the commanding heights of the economy and took away half of many people's income in taxes, politicians loosened their grip on people's private morals: Divorce, abortion, and homosexuality all became legal.

The 1960s saw the apogee of the Western state. The state had become the universal provider—a provider that gave without demanding much in return from many of its citizens and that responded to every complaint from its clients by offering yet more benefits. It also further redefined the concepts of equality and fraternity in a still more activist way.

With equality, the focus moved from opportunity to results. R. H. Tawney had dismissed the "romantic illusion that individuals do not differ in natural capacity."[13] He believed that equality of opportunity implied the opportunity to become unequal—indeed that the essence of human progress lay in stratifying societies on the basis of innate abilities rather than money or family connections. That concept of equality still cropped up in the 1960s, including in its most famous speech. When Martin Luther King Jr. argued that people should not be judged "by the color of their skin but by the content of their character," he was asking to be judged. But other progressives took a more utopian approach, demanding "equality of result."

This unleashed a huge amount of state activity. The British replaced grammar schools with comprehensives and decreased streaming by ability. The Americans introduced an increasingly aggressive form of affirmative action. Fighting discrimination no longer meant just getting rid of restrictions on people's ability to express their talents. It meant ensuring proportionality: Blacks and other ethnic minorities needed to be awarded places in universities and government contracts in line with their overall numbers. Meanwhile fraternity became ever more a concept for the giver, not the receiver. The man receiving the welfare check or the state pension was not grateful; it was a right—and he was entitled to it.

There were critics of all this, of course. Marxists complained that the Western state was just an instrument of class oppression. New leftists argued that it was not just a façade but a joyless façade. Some right-wingers even complained that the party would prove to be unaffordable: Barry Goldwater fought the 1964 election in America on a platform of cutting government and returning it to the night-watchman state of John Stuart Mill: "I have little interest in streamlining government or in making it more efficient, for I mean to reduce its size," the Arizonan proclaimed. "I do not undertake to promote welfare, for I propose to extend freedom."[14]

But the state won every argument hands down: Lyndon Johnson won that election by a landslide by saying exactly the opposite of what Barry Goldwater said—that the state was on the side of progress. One incident in the 1964 campaign epitomized this confidence in the state (and we apologize for using the same example that we used in a previous book, but we have yet to come across a more apposite one). It took place at a rally in Rhode Island. Tired and ragged, Johnson clambered onto the roof of a car in front of his cheering supporters and distilled his message down to a few words: "I just want to tell you this: We're in favor of a lot of things and we're against mighty few."[15]

CHAPTER FOUR

MILTON FRIEDMAN'S PARADISE LOST

IN 1981 ONE OF THE AUTHORS of this book visited the United States for his "gap year" (between high school and university).[1] He traveled around on a Greyhound bus with a friend, trying to convince American girls that he was charming and American barmen that he was twenty-one, as his amateurishly doctored British Rail student card indicated, all the time freeloading off indulgent Americans who had once met his parents. Of the numerous weird things that happened to him on this adventure none was as weird as a certain evening in San Francisco. The host was Antony Fisher, a patrician Briton who had made a fortune from chickens. Antony's friend Milton, who lived downstairs, joined them for a sauna—and together the two quizzed the young Britons about their new prime minister, Margaret Thatcher.[2] A few mumbled replies followed and then Antony and Milton launched into a wide-ranging conversation.

The conversation began relatively tamely—and rather boringly for an eighteen-year-old—with interest rates and the money supply. But as the two old men talked, especially the tiny Milton, it began to spiral into fantasy: British Leyland, British Rail, and British Telecom would be sold, taxes would be cut, parents would be given vouchers to "spend" on schools, the National Health Service would be broken up. Britain—cold, faraway, dysfunctional Britain, where his classes had to be taught by candlelight because the all-powerful miners' unions had turned off the electricity—would become a haven of free enterprise. It all seemed delightfully mad. To the author it was the political equivalent of the Grateful Dead concert he attended on the same trip, with Milton playing the role of Jerry Garcia.

Sir Antony Fisher, as he later became, was one of the godfathers of the libertarian Right: He helped set up the Institute of Economic Affairs in London, the Manhattan Institute in New York, and much else. But it was the other man in the sauna who played an even larger role in fomenting a revolution against the ever-growing Western state—a revolution that would "think the unthinkable" yet at best be only half successful.

Milton Friedman, even minimally dressed, was an extraordinary figure—just five feet tall but overflowing with intellectual energy. He ended up as the most influential economist of the second half of the twentieth century, a Nobel Prize winner and adviser to presidents and prime ministers. Yet his origins were humble. His parents were immigrants from Eastern Europe, and he grew up in Brooklyn. He also started life as a firm believer in big government. The young Friedman arrived at the University of Chicago in 1932 as a supporter of Norman Thomas, the socialist presidential candidate, got his first job as a New Deal apparatchik in Washington, D.C., and remained on the government payroll until 1943, even helping invent one of the most fiendish tools of big government, the payroll withholding tax. But by the time he moved back to Chicago, Friedman had begun to forge a different course. Three years later he announced his arrival with a furious attack on rent control, "Roofs or Ceilings" (1946), which immediately marked him out as part of the free-market resistance to Keynesianism.

For most of the previous two decades the resistance to big government had been headquartered in Europe rather than in America. The founding father of "the Austrian school" was Ludwig von Mises, who told government officials, "You are not the vicars of a god called 'the State.'"[3] During the Second World War, Karl Popper labored away on *The Open Society and Its Enemies* in far-off New Zealand, while in blitzed London his friend Friedrich Hayek, a pupil of von Mises, produced *The Road to Serfdom* in 1944, worrying that the book would sink without a trace because of paper shortages. In fact it was an instant best seller—and eventually converted millions to the idea that the overmighty state was an oppressor. Hayek was more than just a scribbler: Like the Webbs he had a talent for organization. He also believed that an elite of farsighted thinkers could change the entire climate of opinion through "permeation." The trick was to reeducate the broad intelligentsia—the people whom he memorably dubbed the "secondhand dealers" in ideas—and to build think tanks that could apply free-market principles to practical problems as they emerged: not just when the mood took them but day after day and decade after decade. In 1947 Hayek helped found the Mont Pelerin Society to bring the global vanguard together.

Mont Pelerin was in the Swiss Alps, but the future of the counterrevolution lay across the Atlantic. America had a much stronger tradition of individualism than Europe—and far more money for foundations and journals. *The Road to Serfdom* sold better in the United States than anywhere else—indeed, the *Reader's Digest* condensed and serialized it—and in 1950 Hayek moved from the London School of Economics to the University of Chicago. Oddly, he was employed there by an esoteric outfit called the Committee on Social Thought, but the real center of the counterrevolution against Keynesianism was the economics department. A stream of luminaries hacked away at the status quo: Frank Knight demonstrated that social reform was often counterproductive; Ronald Coase (another LSE import) and George Stigler argued that regulators were frequently captured by the people whom they regulated; Gary Becker invented the economics of human capital; James Buchanan and Gordon Tullock demonstrated that bureaucrats were motivated by the same profit-maximizing instincts as businesspeople.[4] But nobody wielded the ax more vigorously than Friedman.

Few academics have had Friedman's gift for evangelism. Looking back, what the young freeloader heard in the San Francisco sauna was a version of the "Road to Hell" lecture, which Friedman delivered at any university that would have him: a lecture in which he excoriated everything that the American Left—and indeed the American center—held dear and unveiled an entirely different future. Government-provided health care? A waste of money. Student grants? Compulsory transfers from the poor to the privileged. Foreign aid? A way of feathering the nests of third-world dictators. The ever-growing Western state was the favorite target of his one-liners: "If you put the federal government in charge of the Sahara Desert, in five years there'd be a shortage of sand." "Nothing is so permanent as a temporary government program."

All this was delivered with real passion. Friedman loathed the liberal conceit that government was the embodiment of reason and benevolence; he saw only muddle and selfishness. He believed that there was a direct correlation between government intervention and national decline: Just look at the history of the Greek and Roman and British empires. And he also loathed the idea that politicians and bureaucrats were somehow more enlightened and selfless than businesspeople: They simply chose to advance their personal interests in a different way. He even had doubts about whether there was any point in making government better, given that its main job was robbing the public: "Efficiency is a vice if it is devoted to doing the wrong thing. If the government were spending the forty per cent of our income that it now spends efficiently, we would long since have lost our freedoms."[5]

Nothing stirred Friedman more than the idea that big-government liberals were progressive, while small-government free marketers were reactionary. "Good God, don't call me that," he once said when he was asked if he was a conservative. "The conservatives are the New Dealers like [John Kenneth] Galbraith who want to keep things the way they are." He viewed himself as a "philosophical radical" in the same mold as John Stuart Mill and Jeremy Bentham. The same was true of Hayek, who often wrote an essay called "Why I Am Not a Conservative." When Russell Kirk, a Burkean conservative, visited the Mont Pelerin Society in the late 1940s, he complained that it might just as well have been called "the John Stuart Mill Club" or "the Jeremy Bentham Memorial Association."[6] Friedman once paid Margaret Thatcher the ultimate compliment in dubbing her a "nineteenth-century liberal." What Hayek and Friedman succeeded in doing was reinventing that old doctrine for a different age.

But if the cause was the same, Friedman and the Chicago boys were very different from Hayek and the Austrians. They were intellectually narrower—professional economists rather than universal intellectuals, products of the postwar American university, with its obsessive focus on disciplinary boundaries, rather than products of the Viennese intellectual hothouse. Yet they were also more self-confident. Hayek, discombobulated by the Great Depression and dazzled by Keynes's genius, was often on the defensive. He actually advanced a relatively subtle theory of the state, arguing that it had an important role in making markets work properly—in preventing monopolies from forming, supervising monetary policy, protecting the rule of law, and providing various public goods such as social services and even health care. (If "a list were made of all the forms of purposive direction which are blessed in the course of the book," *The Economist* observed in its review of *The Road to Serfdom*, "it would be seen that Professor Hayek does not want to go back, but quite a long way forward."[7]) By contrast, Friedman was aggressive to the point of oversimplification. He championed the legalization of marijuana and the abolition of the draft as well as the reduction of taxes. In his 1962 cri de coeur, *Capitalism and Freedom*, he proposed a program of government pruning that was astonishingly bold for the big-government Kennedy years: from the abolition of farm subsidies and the minimum wage to the elimination of border controls. The night-watchman state had been reinvented for the age of the Grateful Dead.

How did a man with such extreme views become such a hit? Partly because his economics was unimpeachable: He won a Nobel Prize in 1976, just seven years after the prize was first introduced, for his work on consumption and the history of monetary policy. Partly because he was an Olympic-class debater. The *Washington Post* conceded in 1963, "No other American economist of the first rank can match Freidman's forensic skills and persuasive powers."[8] Partly because he knew how to get his message out. He wrote a regular column in *Newsweek* and frequently contributed to newspapers. And partly because he was not scared of politics. He was a leading adviser to Barry Goldwater in 1964 and a close ally of Ronald Reagan thereafter: In 1973 he joined Reagan in giving a series of stump speeches in favor of California's Proposition 1 (which limited the size of the budget).[9] The bond was personal: Reagan "just could not resist Friedman's infectious enthusiasm."[10]

Confronted by this onslaught, even Friedman's sparring partner, Galbraith, admitted that "the age of Keynes" had given way to the "age of Friedman."[11] The most important reason for Friedman's success, though, was that history was increasingly on Friedman's side. He once defined "the role of thinkers" as primarily being "to keep options open, to have available alternatives, so when the brute force of events make a change inevitable, there is an alternative available to change it."[12] In the 1970s and 1980s "the brute force of events" transformed Friedman from a brilliant gadfly into a real force.

THE CRISIS OF THE WELFARE STATE

Put simply, big government overextended itself. Lyndon Johnson's faith in being "in favor of a lot of things" and "against mighty few" led to overload. The "basic minimum" now included fairness, equality, and happiness. By the end of the 1960s Leviathan was supposed to provide a university education for everyone, solve racism, and popularize opera. And why not? If the state was a good thing, then surely more of the state was an even better thing? It wasn't. By the 1970s the American government seemed to be failing at everything it touched—wars (Vietnam), the economy (stagflation), crime (the drug epidemic), social cohesion (the culture wars). Even Europe's love affair with the welfare state was beginning to sour. This was a time of strikes, energy crises, and riots. It was also a time when the modish ideas of the 1960s, such as comprehensive education in Britain or the "war on poverty" in America, got "mugged by reality," in Irving Kristol's classic phrase.

Worse, the welfare state was failing in its core functions—in the ideas that the Webbs and their disciples had trumpeted. R. H. Tawney had promised that, under the welfare state, Britain "would cease to be the rule for the rich to be rewarded, not only with riches, but with a preferential share of health and life, and for the penalty of the poor to be not merely poverty, but ignorance, sickness and premature death."[13] Yet in the 1970s the gap between Britain's upper and lower social classes in terms of age-adjusted mortality was more than twice as large as it had been in the 1930s.[14] The upper classes continued to be fitter and taller than the lower classes—3.2 centimeters taller, to be exact—as well as richer.[15] In America even the architects of the "war on poverty" admitted that "unprecedented generosity . . . had not made much of a dent in the poverty, dependency, delinquency, or despair against which the 1964 war had been declared."[16]

Many of the 1960s reforms aimed at producing equality of results, rather than just equality of opportunity, were producing very unegalitarian results, especially in education. Britain's decision to abolish the grammar schools reduced social mobility. America's enthusiasm for affirmative action increased the number of academic dropouts, as minority students who might have done perfectly well in less-demanding colleges struggled in elite institutions.[17] A. H. Halsey, one of the leaders of the educational Left, was forced to declare in 1972 that "the essential fact of twentieth century educational history is that egalitarian policies have failed."[18]

By the time Ronald Reagan and Margaret Thatcher came to power, Friedman's barbs about big government no longer seemed far-fetched. It was clear to middle-class taxpayers that Leviathan was spending a fortune and that much of that money, *their* hard-earned money, was being wasted. There was hypocrisy in this, because a lot of the extra cash went to the middle classes. In the suburbs nobody complained that Western universities were now packed with middle-class children. What they were cross about—and what rapidly became a rallying call for the Right across the West—was the idea of the state mollycoddling the poor and the delinquent. Racism and snobbery played a part in that. But so did the facts. Too much of the money that did reach the poor had proved counterproductive: For instance, welfare payments had created perverse incentives, undermining individual responsibility and trapping people in poverty. Across the West a hard core of people in even the richest societies dropped out of school, had illegitimate children, and lived as wards of the state. Friedman found unexpected allies. Few did more to push the breakdown of the black family to the center of political debate than a future Democratic senator from New York, Daniel Patrick Moynihan, and a group of left-wing social scientists who swung firmly to the right and became known as the neoconservatives.

Far from knowing best what the poor needed, bureaucrats and experts often got it spectacularly wrong. You could see this in any city in the West, thanks to the "New Brutalism" of urban planners.[19] In America they shoved poor blacks into "the projects," vertical ghettoes. Across Europe the planners tore down working-class neighborhoods (just as they did beautiful town centers and magnificent railway stations) and drove poor people, like cattle, into tower blocks that soon became bywords for crime and degradation.

The problem was one not just of inefficiency but also of bloat. In pre-Thatcher Britain nearly a third of the twenty-five million people in the labor force worked in the public sector. Nearly half the people in the manufacturing sector worked for nationalized industries—industries that produced less and less at the cost of bigger and bigger subsidies (in 1999 the coal industry produced a third less coal than in 1938 and the railways covered half as many miles of track).[20] Size bred complexity and unresponsiveness. There were hundreds of different types of benefits policed by hundreds of different departments: The British Department of Health and Social Security even produced a leaflet that listed all the other leaflets.

This inevitably imposed enormous burdens on the economy. In his master plan for the New Jerusalem, Beveridge had estimated that there would be no real increase in the cost of health services between 1945 and 1965: By producing a healthier population the welfare state would essentially pay for itself. In fact, spending rose astronomically. By the mid-1970s almost half of Britain's national income was devoted to public spending, much of it to welfare. In Sweden the proportion was even higher. With taxes rising to nonsensical levels—in Britain the rate on "unearned" investment income was above 90 percent, driving both Antony Fisher and Mick Jagger overseas—people began to reassess the relationship between public expenditure and economic growth.

Ever-bigger government meant ever-greater social dysfunction. Vested interests competed ever more viciously for their share of the pie. Government imposed ever-bigger burdens on the economy, and the productive economy stagnated or shrank. "Goodbye, Great Britain, It Was Nice Knowing You" was the title of one *Wall Street Journal* article in the Mid-1970s.[21] Britain was forced to take a begging bowl to the IMF in 1976: One of the leading architects of the Bretton Woods System became the first advanced country to need a bailout. Sweden, another champion of the Welfare State, was on its way from being the world's fourth-richest country in the 1970s to the fourteenth-richest in 1990.

The biggest disaster of all was unfolding to the east. It was now obvious to everyone that the new civilization that the Webbs had worshipped was in fact a new barbarism. In the 1950s the Soviet Union was at least growing quickly. By the 1970s it added slow growth to brutality and bossiness. There is a huge difference between a large welfare state and Soviet totalitarianism, of course. But for half a century supporters of big government in the West had drawn some succor from communism's triumphs—its defeat of Hitler, its ability to blast cosmonauts into space, its record-breaking production of pig iron. By the 1970s it was clear that even the economic progress of the 1930s had been brought at the cost of mass murder and ruthless repression. There was nothing noble, just something fake and cruel, like the doped athletes paraded at the Olympics.

THE BACKLASH

A few weeks after he won the Nobel Prize, Milton Friedman left the University of Chicago for the Hoover Institution at Stanford University, where he was to remain for the rest of his long life. Within two years of Friedman arriving in California, the first trumpet of the counterrevolution sounded.

In 1978, fed up with ever-rising property taxes and no apparent increase in the quality of services from local government, and furious with the bohemian antics of Governor Moonbeam (Jerry Brown, son of Pat), the sprawling suburbs of Southern California rose up in fury. Led by Howard Jarvis, an energetic antitax protester, Californians passed, with Friedman's enthusiastic support, Proposition 13. The referendum was a watershed: It not only halved and capped property-tax increases, forcing the California state government to bail out local government, but it also made it very difficult to raise taxes at all. It was followed by a string of other propositions trying to limit spending across the country. Suburban America had had enough.

This, though, was merely a revolt. The full revolution came in the shape of Margaret Thatcher, who arrived in Downing Street in Britain in 1979, and Ronald Reagan, who won the White House in 1980. Thatcher was the more strident: She spoke about "a world-wide revolt against big government, excessive taxation and bureaucracy"[22] and even quoted Herbert Spencer's favorite phrase, that there is no alternative. Reagan was more easygoing. He told jokes about the most terrifying words in the English language being "I'm from the government and I'm here to help." But they both translated inchoate rage into coherent policies. That required pragmatism. Thatcher chose when to battle the miners in the same way that Reagan chose when to battle the air-traffic controllers. But it also required conviction. They were far more ideologically "antigovernment" than anything conservatism had seen before. Reagan's heartland was the same Southern California that supported Proposition 13, and he drew many of the ideas for his first term from a huge briefing book produced by the Heritage Foundation: Thatcher had a similar relationship with the Institute of Economic Affairs, founded by Antony Fisher, and the Centre for Policy Studies, cofounded by her mentor, Sir Keith Joseph. You can still see Reagan's personally annotated copies of Hayek in the Reagan Library while Thatcher supposedly carried a copy of Hayek's *The Constitution of Liberty* in her handbag, together with a quotation widely (though erroneously) attributed to Abraham Lincoln: "You cannot bring about prosperity by discouraging thrift. You cannot strengthen the weak by weakening the strong. You cannot help the wage earner by pulling down the wage payer."[23]

Reagan has gone down in history as the man who defeated communism and reinvented American conservatism, but when it comes to reforming government, Thatcher's legacy was the more significant, not least because she had so much more government to reform. Until the 1970s, the prim, ambitious Thatcher subscribed to the postwar consensus. Edward Heath's government of 1970–74, in which she served as secretary of state for education, briefly tried to inject a mildly more free-market approach into economic management but chickened out when unemployment passed the one million mark, going on such a huge spending binge to bring unemployment down that inflation reached 25 percent.

It was then that Thatcher became a Thatcherite. This was not so much an intellectual conversion as a growing willingness to express her deepest convictions (Alfred Sherman, one of a handful of free-market intellectuals in 1970s Britain, rightly described her as a person of "beliefs, not of ideas").[24] As the daughter of a shopkeeper, she loathed debt, admired self-reliance, and lauded what Gladstone called "effort, honest manful effort."[25] She was hurt by Britain's relentless decline—during her lifetime Britain not only lost an empire but also saw its economy tumble behind France's and Germany's—and infuriated by sophisticated talk of "the management of decline." Her encounter with free-market ideas gave her hope. She listened attentively to Sir Keith Joseph, who played the role of the Right's "licensed thinker scouting ahead" and introduced her to a stream of radical thinkers, including Hayek and Friedman.[26]

Most of this radicalism was hidden from the British electorate that voted her into office in 1979, largely in frustration with the Labour government's ineptitude, especially its inability to control the trade unions during the "winter of discontent" of 1978–79, when strikers almost closed down the country, paralyzing the transport system, picketing hospitals and leaving the dead unburied. But once in power Thatcher revealed her true colors. She curbed government spending, controlled the money supply and abolished exchange controls, all decisive breaks with postwar orthodoxies. She sold off council houses, creating the basis for working-class Thatcherism. She cut industrial subsidies, sending many firms to the wall. Against the background of a world recession, the result was a sharp rise in unemployment. By

1981, when unemployment passed three million, police were openly battling Molotov cocktail–throwing protesters on many city streets in Britain, and the Tory wets were lined up against her. Rather than retreating in the same way that Heath did, she doubled down: "You turn if you want to, the lady's not for turning," she famously said at the Tory Party conference in 1981. She was, in retrospect, immensely lucky—lucky that the British Left fractured and insisted on choosing unelectable leaders and lucky that Argentina's General Galtieri decided to invade the Falkland Islands when he did, allowing her to wrest them back and then win an election in 1983. And economists still argue about whether the medicine was too strong: Across much of northern Britain manufacturing was obliterated. But her bitter medicine changed Britain. The inflation rate fell from a high of 27 percent in 1975 to 2.5 percent in 1986. The number of days lost to strikes fell from 29.5 million in 1979 to 1.9 million in 1986. The top rate of tax fell from 98 percent in 1979 to 40 percent in 1988.[27]

In 1984 there began the great round of privatizations, in which behemoths such as British Telecom, British Airways, and British Gas were sold off to the private sector. In all, Thatcher privatized three-quarters of Britain's state-owned companies, raising over £30 billion for the exchequer and shifting forty-six major businesses with 900,000 employees to the private sector.[28] She encouraged ordinary people to buy shares, thus creating the image, at least, of "popular capitalism." And she extended her crusade against Leviathan to the emerging sprawl in Brussels. "We have not successfully rolled back the frontiers of the state in Britain," she thundered in Bruges in 1988, "only to see them re-imposed at a European level."[29]

Thanks to Thatcher, the center of gravity of British politics moved dramatically to the right. The New Labourites of the 1990s concluded that they could rescue their party from ruin only by adopting the central tenets of Thatcherism. "The presumption should be that economic activity is best left to the private sector," declared Tony Blair. Blair abolished "Clause Four" (which had been put in place by the Webbs and pledged the party to nationalizing the commanding heights of industry), distanced himself from Keynesian orthodoxy, and repositioned the party to appeal to the newly affluent. Peter Mandelson, one of his closest advisers, declared himself to be "intensely relaxed" about people making a lot of money. What happened to Labour was a mirror image of what had happened to the Tories in the 1950s when they jettisoned their old free-market orthodoxies in favor of the welfare state.

Across the Atlantic Reagan had the same effect: He did not embrace privatization in the same enthusiastic way as Thatcher (Uncle Sam owned much less of the economy, so there was less to sell), but through a mixture of wit and idealism he made "more government" a very difficult answer for any American politician to propose to any question. Ever since then, being against "big government" has been a canon of the American Right even if it has not followed that doctrine in practice. On the left, the effect was even more dramatic. "Liberalism"—by which was meant a combination of faith in big government and progressive social attitudes—became something to be disowned by leading Democrats. In 1988, when Michael Dukakis, the governor of Massachusetts, was accused of being a liberal by George H. W. Bush's campaign, he complained of "mudslinging": The mud still stuck. Four years later Bill Clinton ran even further to the right, embracing the "third way" and taking on some of his party's more atavistic interest groups. He proclaimed that the "age of big government" was over and set about introducing some radical reforms of the state—he passed welfare reforms (with the prompting of the Republican Congress) and put Al Gore in charge of a reinventing government commission. In 2004, when the Democratic candidate, John Kerry, was asked whether he was a liberal, he replied, "I think it's the silliest thing I've ever heard."[30]

The Thatcher-Reagan revolution did not stop in the Anglo-Saxon world. The idea that government should focus on providing public goods like law and order, rather than interfering with the business world, spread widely. Governments looked to the Anglo-Saxon example as they grappled with bloated public sectors, waning productivity, and out-of-control inflation. And everywhere they withdrew from the commanding heights of the economy. Between 1985 and 2000 Western European governments sold off some $100 billion worth of state assets, including such well-known national champions as Lufthansa, Volkswagen, Renault, Elf, and ENI. "Industrial policy" was reduced to hanging on to a few golden shares in privatized companies. The post-communist countries embraced the Washington consensus especially heartily. Russia privatized thousands of industrial enterprises. Leszek Balcerowicz, Poland's finance minister after the fall of communism, declared that Thatcher was his "hero." In Brazil, Fernando Henrique Cardoso introduced a Thatcher-inspired privatization program that, measured by the value of the assets sold, was twice as big as Britain's. Even in India, the bastion of Fabianism, Manmohan Singh tried to tear up the License Raj to get "government off the backs of the people of India, particularly off the backs of India's entrepreneurs."[31] Palaniappan Chidambaram, who served as India's finance minister for a while during the 1990s, summed things up: "What happened under Mrs Thatcher was an eye-opener, a revelation. After all, we had gotten our Fabian socialism from Britain."[32]

It also became fashionable, especially in the Blairite and Clintonian 1990s, to see big government as incompatible with globalization: Leviathan would be leveled by the much mightier forces of international capitalism. This was a time when James Carville, Clinton's campaign manager, joked about wanting to be reincarnated as the bond markets, because they were so powerful; when Bill Gates seemed to grace more magazine covers than Bill Clinton; and when left-wingers claimed (inaccurately) that half the world's biggest economies were multinational firms. A special report on the state in *The Economist*, published in 1997, examined the then-fashionable idea that Leviathan was withering away.[33]

THE HALF-SUCCESSFUL REVOLUTION

So Reagan and Thatcher—and by extension Milton Friedman—won the argument. Ever since the 1980s, the debate about the state has changed. But they did not win the reality. Otherwise this book might well not exist.

Most obviously, Leviathan did not wither away. In her eleven momentous years in office Thatcher succeeded in reducing social expenditure from 22.9 percent of GDP in 1979 to 22.2 percent in 1990. Reagan failed to persuade his Democratic-controlled House of Representatives to enact the spending cuts that were supposed to accompany his tax cuts, producing an explosion in America's deficit. The state under Thatcher and Reagan—its supposed gravediggers—was much bigger than anything that Keynes or Beveridge had imagined. That was partly their own fault. Thatcher, for instance, was bad at reforming some bits of the public sector, notably the police. Her dislike of the left-wing councils that dominated many British cities was so great—and, it must be added, their sins were so egregious—that she did more than any other postwar prime minister to bind local governments into an ever-tighter net of restrictions and prescriptions.

As the new century began, Leviathan began to rise again. In America Bill Clinton's relatively frugal centrism gave way to George W. Bush's "compassionate conservatism," a license for government bloat. "Big governance"—the ever-expanding collection of rules and regulations that govern everybody's lives—expanded even faster than big government, prompted partly by the Left (diversity, health, and safety) but also partly by the Right (closed-circuit cameras, the war on drugs, and, after September 11, the war on terror). Some one thousand pages of federal regulations were added each year the younger Bush was in office. And when he left office in 2008, a big-government conservative was replaced by an even-bigger-government liberal.

Barack Obama has been keener on government activism and cooler toward the private sector than the New Democrats of the 1990s. It is very hard to imagine Clinton telling American entrepreneurs that their success was due to the state ("You didn't build that"). When Obama presented his life story to his party at its convention in Denver in 2008, it was a tale of redemption—a young sinner in the evil private sector (working for a company now owned by our employer, incidentally) escapes to the purer life of being a community organizer and discovers true love and a purpose. This is not to say that the real Mr. Obama has anything in common with the European socialist of conservative imagination. In general, his core economic policies have been thoroughly pragmatic: The nationalization of General Motors and Chrysler was a temporary solution to a pressing problem, and one that a Republican president might easily have adopted. But the general momentum has been toward slightly bigger government. His main domestic achievement—his health-care reforms—fit that pattern (even though they leave America's hopelessly muddled system very far from Sweden's).

Europe has followed much the same pattern over the past ten years.

In Britain New Labour became ever less prudent as it remained in office. Gordon Brown hugely expanded government spending on the mistaken grounds that he had abolished the boom-bust cycle. The state's share of GDP rose from under 37 percent in 2000 to 44 percent in 2007; with the British economy struggling, it then jumped to 51 percent in 2010.[34] But the part of the West where big government reappeared with the least introspection was in Continental Europe. In the early 1990s the EU was often an instrument of economic reform: It opened the single market in 1992 and its commission hounded states that supported their industries too crudely. Many southern European countries had to tighten their belts at least a little to get into the euro when it was set up in 1999. But once in the single currency, the southern Europeans discovered that they could borrow at the same rate as the Germans—and spent accordingly. Friedman had always warned against the single currency: Monetary unity, he argued in 1997, would lead to political disunity.[35] In 2004 he said he thought the euro could fall apart (alongside a jeremiad against big government across the Continent: "There is no doubt what the EU should do. Abolish your rules and regulations. Abolish your [high level of] spending.")[36] Nobody listened.

Greece was the most egregious offender: In the period from 2004 to 2009, when foreign capital flooded into the country, Greece's government, by its own numbers, managed to increase its tax revenues in nominal terms by 31 percent, but its primary expenditures increased by 87 percent. Its debts climbed and disaster eventually followed. But the truth is that from 2000 to 2012 public spending soared everywhere as a share of national income—from 51.6 percent to 55.9 percent in France, from 45.9 percent to 49 percent in Italy, from 41.6 percent to 46.9 percent in Portugal, and from 31.2 percent to 44.1 percent in Ireland. On average more than half this increase occurred before the financial crisis, with the euro encouraging countries to put their feet on the accelerator when they should have been applying the brake.[37] Meanwhile, the European Parliament, empowered to take decisions because of its theoretically democratic mandate, turned into a regulation machine.

Both Europe and the United States were able to escape from the consequences of their various contradictions for more than a decade. The markets were willing to extend credit to advanced economies for a remarkable period of time. But the economic crisis of 2007–8 has changed the tone of Western politics. There is now much less to give away (indeed, often nothing at all). In the euro area, prolonged dithering has turned a containable crisis into something that could shatter the world's biggest economic unit. In America almost every economist has been calling for a medium-term solution to the country's finances. So have at least two presidential commissions. But Congress and President Obama have proved unequal to the task. The Democrats refuse to countenance cuts in entitlements, the Republicans refuse to raise taxes, and America is caught in a fiscal trap, taxing itself like a small-government country, spending like a big-government one, and borrowing massively from private savers to make up the difference.

Where does this leave the state? In 2004, two years before his death, Friedman took a depressing view of his achievement: "After World War II, opinion was socialist while practice was free market; currently, opinion is free market while practice is heavily socialist. We have largely won the battle of ideas (though no such battle is ever won permanently). We have succeeded in stalling the progress of socialism, but we have not succeeded in reversing its course."[38] That verdict would arguably be even more depressing today, especially when you look not just at the size of government, but its power. The core of Friedman's message, like Mill's, was freedom. There are thirty-two closed-circuit television cameras near the flat where George Orwell wrote *1984*. The night watchman standing guard at the gate has become the nanny inside the home and the office, hanging over your shoulder in the kitchen, sitting room, boardroom, and even bedroom. But it is not a very good nanny. The state has accumulated ever more responsibilities and imposed ever more hidden costs on everybody else. But its ability to meet those responsibilities has declined. The only hope is that frustration is beginning to engender hope of change.

Nowhere illustrates this better than the state that Friedman ended up calling home.

PART TWO

FROM THE WEST TO THE EAST

CHAPTER FIVE

THE SEVEN DEADLY SINS—AND ONE GREAT VIRTUE—OF CALIFORNIA GOVERNMENT

THERE IS NO MORE VIVID EXAMPLE of the problems of Western government than the contrast between Sacramento and Palo Alto. The two cities are only ninety miles apart as the crow flies. But they live in different centuries. Sacramento is merely the capital of the state. Palo Alto is the capital of Silicon Valley, a city that is in the business of inventing the future, not just in cyberspace but also in manufacturing, robotics, and biology. Entrepreneurs have regarded it as a beacon ever since two Stanford students, Bill Hewlett and David Packard, set up a computer company in a garage there in 1938. Since then the Valley has spawned Apple, Oracle, Google—and almost every government in the world has tried to create its own version of this miracle machine.

Fifty years ago Sacramento was also a city on a hill. Students of government flocked there to study the California dream. How, marveled the visitors, had the Golden State provided its fast-growing population with water, freeways, and the world's best public university system? The great California governors of the time, Earl Warren and

Pat Brown, were only too happy to provide an answer: Even though the former was a Republican and the latter a Democrat, they shared a blueprint and a sense of mission. But for the past twenty years students from institutions like China's leadership college in Pudong have been more likely to come to Sacramento to study the crisis of Western government in its purest form. Famous for its budget wrangles, its extremes of partisanship, gerrymandering, and money politics, its pathetic levels of voter participation, its ruinous ballot initiatives, its absurdly complicated structure, and its crumbling infrastructure, California government has been big, broke, and inefficient.

The gap between Palo Alto and Sacramento is repeated all across the West: Wall Street operates in a different time zone from Washington, D.C.; Bavaria's *Mittelstanders*, Milan's fashion moguls, and Soho's multimedia entrepreneurs work to different rules (and hours and pay) from the politicians in Berlin, Rome, and Whitehall. But there is no political distemper that cannot be found in its most extreme form in California. It is hard to think of anywhere else where the rhetoric of small government and the reality of big government have collided so spectacularly—and where the failures of Milton Friedman's half revolution have been demonstrated so clearly. The state's obligations have continued to grow, even as taxpayers' disgust has robbed it of resources and legitimacy. Over the past few decades, Californians, usually among the most optimistic people on earth, have angrily resorted to every means at their disposal, from ballot initiatives to a superannuated cyborg, to sort out Sacramento. There is now a glimmer of hope that the state's restless writhing may finally be producing something useful—under, of all people, a reincarnated Jerry Brown. But for the period since one of us stepped into that surreal sauna in San Francisco, California has been an exemplar of everything that has gone wrong with the state in Europe and America.

What exactly are the symptoms? Seven things stand out: Call them the seven deadly sins of modern government.[1] And we will also add one great virtue. In all of these, California is, as usual, "like the West, only more so." It is as good a template as any to sum up what is going wrong.

1. FROM ANOTHER CENTURY

Look at an administrative map of California and you might conclude that a child had scrawled over the design, having previously experimented with Jerry Garcia's pill dispenser. It is a muddle of thousands of overlapping counties, cities, and districts. Beverly Hills and West Hollywood sit in the middle of Los Angeles but are separate cities. The LA school district has 687,000 pupils while twenty-three other school districts have twenty pupils or fewer. In Sacramento things are no clearer. California has more than three hundred unelected boards and commissions, ranging from the California Coastal Commission to the Speech-Language Pathology and Audiology and Hearing Aid Dispensers Board. It also has the world's third-longest constitution.[2] Three-quarters of the budget is outside the governor's control, thanks to a succession of ballot initiatives. The flow of money is clear as mud: Ever since Proposition 13 forced the state to bail out local government, Sacramento has been obliged to subsidize the cities while seeking subsidies itself from Washington, D.C. Cash for health, schools, welfare, and much else besides sloshes backward and forward among Sacramento, Washington, and various California cities, making it impossible to hold California politicians responsible for getting and spending.

The first sin of California government is that it is out of date. The last time it got a full makeover was in 1879, when the state's population was only 865,000 and most Californians worked on the land.

Today the population has swollen to thirty-seven million, and a single state Senate seat represents more people than the whole state Senate did back then. As the historian Kevin Starr observes, "it is not surprising that an organisation set up to look after fewer than a million people should have a collective political nervous breakdown when it governs something almost 40 times that size."[3]

In this California is merely an acid-laced version of Western government as a whole. Overlapping areas of responsibility are common throughout the West. In Australia the federal government runs primary health care but the states run hospitals. In most European countries taxes are raised centrally but tend to be spent by local or regional government. The European Union increasingly plays the same role in Europe that Washington does in America, adding another layer of rules and mandates. The American Constitution was designed for a country of thirteen states and four million people, when things like forming armed militias and preventing people from turning themselves into kings mattered a lot. The Founding Fathers had no plans to bring either North Dakota or California into their union, nor could they imagine the ramifications of those two states having the same number of votes in the Senate despite one state having fifty-seven times more people than the other. In Europe the state has been redesigned more recently, thanks to two world wars, but many ancient oddities, such as Britain's House of Lords, survive.

Too many parts of government function as if we were all still God-fearing yeoman farmers. American schoolchildren get three months off in the summer so they can help on the farm, as they did in the nineteenth century. The U.S. Department of Agriculture is one of the largest bureaucracies in Washington, despite the fact that agriculture now employs only 2 percent of the population. At a time when few businesses regard the Sabbath as sacred, the British National Health Service still honors the notion of a restful weekend: 129 of its 149 hospital trusts have higher death rates on weekends—27 percent higher in the case of one trust in Hillingdon—because fewer doctors work on Saturdays and Sundays.[4] In both Europe and America governments are trying to govern the world of Google and Facebook with a quill pen and an abacus.

There is no simple relationship between modernity and efficiency. Many ancient oddities work well in practice: Americans rightly revere their Constitution, because it gets far more right than wrong. Meanwhile, the West's most conspicuous attempt to build a new form of government, the European Union, is a mess of overlapping responsibilities. It is hard to answer even basic questions about the EU, such as "What is the European Parliament for?" The madness of setting up a single currency without a common system of financial regulation is now obvious; worse in some ways is the union's inability to fix these design faults, even with the help of a crisis.

So "new" is not always "better." But Europe and California are not that different. Both need to have a debate about exactly what sort of government they want. The problem in both places is to match structure to purpose—and that has been enormously complicated by the next two sins.

2. BAUMOL'S DISEASE

California has been useless at making its public sector more efficient. Our second and third sins, both named after famous economists, help explain why governments keep on costing more. Mancur Olson's law focuses on politics—and the power of interest groups. Before that, consider the second sin: Baumol's disease.

In a succession of classic papers from 1966 onward William Baumol argued that productivity increases much more slowly in labor-intensive industries than in industries where capital in the form of machinery can be substituted for labor.[5] Baumol used an example from classical music to demonstrate that there are certain human activities that are inherently labor intensive. The world has changed a lot since Beethoven wrote his string quartets, but you still can't perform one with any fewer than four musicians. Baumol's disease suggests that governments inevitably get bigger because they occupy labor-intensive areas of the economy. Manufacturing keeps on getting more efficient, but labor-intensive service sectors like education and health care (which tend to be provided either wholly or partly by the government) don't. The average college professor, Baumol argued, cannot give lectures any faster than he did a decade ago, nor can the average surgeon perform operations any more quickly.

There is another side to this. As people get richer, thanks to all those productivity improvements, they are willing to spend more of their money on their education and health, especially as the cost of regular commodities goes down. And the cost of many educational and health-care services goes up as science advances and standards rise. Larry Summers, Barack Obama's chief economic adviser until late 2010, points out that the average American salary has risen tenfold since the late 1970s, when measured against the cost of a television, but has fallen when measured against the cost of health care. The same is true for the average European salary.

Seen through this lens, much of the recent history of the state is a struggle against Baumol's disease, with the only variation being the method. California has cut some services and passed on the cost of others to consumers. Students in the state now pay around half the cost of their education compared with 12 percent in 1990.[6] But the main result has been a decline in quality rather than an improvement in productivity. Forty years ago California had the best public education system in the world. Today California vies with Mississippi in the illiteracy of its students and the amount spent per capita. More broadly, America's attempts to deal with ever-rising costs in higher education have created an epidemic of student debt, which is close to $1 trillion. In Europe universities have become near slums as administrators have skimped on facilities.

On both continents, people are furious that governments have failed to demonstrate the sort of productivity improvements that we expect in IT or manufacturing. If Baumol is correct, then there is very little that anyone can do to stop the state from getting bigger. This is a fundamental problem that we will return to in chapter 7. But the other rule suggests that politics is as much to blame as economics.

3. OLSON'S LAW

If William Baumol is one name that haunts government reformers, Mancur Olson is the other. In *The Logic of Collective Action* (1965) Olson pointed out that interest groups have a huge advantage in democracies. Getting organized is a pain, requiring lots of money, time, and energy, so narrow constituencies, pursuing goals that matter deeply to them, are much more likely to do the organizing than broad constituencies, pursuing general goals and plagued by free riders who want to enjoy the benefits of political action without incurring the costs. "The larger the group, the less it will further its common interests" was Olson's neat formulation of the problem.[7]

California has always had special interests, keen to grab scarce resources like water: Just watch *Chinatown*. In California's Central Valley you can see tax dollars evaporating before your eyes as farmers guzzle most of the state's precious resource, water, to cultivate crops that were never meant to grow in a desert. But something has changed. Fifty years ago California's business elite was far more public spirited: It may have consisted of male WASPs who wanted to keep their taxes down and their power intact, but they showed a broad interest in the well-being of the state. Nowadays the denizens of Hollywood, Silicon Valley, and other privileged enclaves show a profound contempt for their government. At the most extreme, the rich wall themselves off in gated communities, with their own security guards, health services, and schools. Their main relationship with the state, at least as they see it, is to write a check for their taxes—and their only interest in it is that the check be as small as possible. Meanwhile, the businesses they run and own have increasingly pursued narrow interests (for example, through targeted lobbying) rather than broader aims. That has made it harder to get businesspeople to support projects for the common good, such as transport in the Bay Area. It has also generated an increase in regulation as individual businesses have lobbied for rules that create barriers to entry for other firms. That is the heart of modern crony capitalism—it explains why so many subsidies go to so many people.

But Olson's law also applies to the public sector itself. Indeed, few Californians have exploited it better than a fedora-wearing conservative who began his career as a correctional officer at Folsom State Prison in the 1970s. Thirty years ago, when Don Novey became president of the California Correctional Peace Officers Association (CCPOA), only 2,600 members walked what he calls "the toughest beat in the state," and there were only 36,000 inmates in California's prisons. Today California has 130,000 prisoners, the CCPOA has 31,000 members, and the state spends roughly the same amount on prisons as it does on higher education—and that despite some recent cutbacks in the "prison-industrial complex"[8] that Novey built.

Novey shrewdly formed an "iron triangle" with Republican lawmakers and prison builders, and he gave it a cause: tougher sentencing for criminals. CCPOA sponsored the "three strikes" law, mandating life imprisonment for three serious felonies, and helped set up victims'-rights groups. California's gerrymandered electoral system, which made primary challengers the only threat for most Republicans, magnified Novey's power. Anyone who did not toe the line would find a lot of money going to their primary opponent, which meant that even fiscal conservatives signed up to the splurge. By the time Novey gave up the CCPOA's presidency in 2002, the state had built twenty-one new prisons, some guards were taking home more than $100,000 a year, with pensions of up to 90 percent of salary, and retirement starting as early as fifty.[9] In recent times, as these perks have been publicized, the "prison-industrial complex" has come under fire and the three-strikes law relaxed. But reformers have repeatedly run into Olson's law: A small determined lobby can fend off a wide public interest.

California's budget is patrolled by unions, with the teachers' unions keeping just as close an eye on schools (and Democratic lawmakers) as the CCPOA does on prisons and Republicans. The California Teachers Association spent more than $210 million between 2000 and 2010 on political campaigning—more than any other donor in the state and more than the pharmaceutical, oil, and tobacco industries combined.[10] There are now more union members in America's public sector than in its far-larger private sector, a trend that is copied across much of Europe. Public-sector unions have a great deal of leverage. They can shut things down, including vital services like underground trains, without suffering many consequences themselves. They enjoy close ties with left-of-center parties. Ed Miliband, the leader of Britain's Labour Party, owes his position to votes from public-sector unions. In America the biggest spender in federal elections between 1989 and 2004 was the American Federation of State, County and Municipal Employees.[11] And public-sector unions are also led by much savvier sorts than their private-sector equivalents. Officers of the British Medical Association (which represents doctors) and America's National Education Association (the biggest teachers' union) often appear on the news as experts on health and education rather than as representatives of interest groups.

This clout pays off in two big ways. One is that it is very hard to sack a public-sector worker. A minuscule 0.3 percent of California teachers are dismissed after three or more years on the job. The state's commission on professional competence balked at sacking a teacher who was found with pornography, marijuana, and vials containing cocaine residue in his desk.[12] The other payoff comes in benefits. Sometimes that is simply salary. In 2010 the residents of Bell, a poor Latino city of 38,000 people, were appalled to discover that their city manager earned $788,000 a year and their police chief $457,000. Two years later an investigation by Bloomberg revealed eye-popping salaries: A state psychiatrist was paid $822,000, a Highway Patrol officer received $484,000 in pay and benefits, and 17 prison officers and 900 prison employees were paid more than $200,000.[13] However, the main problem is not pay itself but the benefits.

Throughout the West politicians have repeatedly "back loaded" public-sector pay deals, keeping the pay increases modest but adding to holidays and especially pensions that are already generous. People were rightly shocked at how many Greek civil servants retired at fifty and how few of them had ever lost their jobs, but many American public-sector organizations have become virtuosos in the arts of "pension spiking," linking pensions to employees' earnings in their final year, rather than average earnings over a longer period, and encouraging soon-to-retire policemen and subway drivers to rack up heroic overtime. In 2012 California passed an antispiking law, but one California public-sector worker, ruthlessly exploiting every fringe benefit and overtime allowance imaginable, collected $609,000 on retirement, and seventeen public-sector employees collected more than $200,000 for unused holiday leave.[14]

In some countries, such as Italy, the elected politicians join in. Italian MPs have increased their salaries sixfold in real terms since 1948, and the country's Euro MPs are paid 150,000 euros a year—about twice as much as their British or German equivalents. Their perks are also better: Italy's president has nine hundred underlings at his disposal, eight times as many as the German president, while the state owns 574,215 official limousines for a governing class of 180,000 elected representatives.[15] But the main beneficiaries are usually unelected civil servants. William Voegeli, an academic at California's Claremont McKenna College, puts the point well: "This faction dominates because it's playing a much longer game than the politicians who come and go, not to mention the citizens who rarely read the enormous owner's manual for the Rube Goldberg machine they feed with their dollars. They rarely stay outraged long enough to make a difference."[16] And the big cost in all this is not just the people but all the rules that come with it.

4. THE OVERACTIVE STATE

There were few bigger believers in the power of government and the wisdom of experts than Sidney Webb, as we have seen. But as the son of a barber, even he might have been slightly surprised that, to become a hairdresser in California, you need to spend almost a year studying the art of cutting and blow-drying. For that we have to thank the California Board of Barbering and Cosmetology, whose Web site boasts a picture of the bald Governor Brown as well as dire warnings about "dangerous pedicures" and encouraging encomiums to "the safe sandal season." California is not alone: If you want to work in the wig trade in Texas, you need to take 300 hours of classes and pass an exam; Alabama obliges manicurists to sit through 750 hours of instruction; Florida will not let you work as an interior designer unless you complete a four-year university degree and a two-year apprenticeship and pass a two-day examination. Sidney and Beatrice might have written a ten-volume tome on local government, but even they never imagined Leviathan saving its subjects from clashing color schemes.

The fourth sin is the "overactive state"—the proliferation of rules that government produces and their complexity. Inevitably the overactivity that creates the most heartache comes in the form of taxation. California's state and local governments chew up 18.3 percent of their gross state product, against just 12.1 percent of GSP in Texas. Like everywhere else in the West, California is constantly inventing new ways of raising taxes (such as sin taxes) and then new ways of letting favored groups off those taxes. The dot-com boom made a messy system messier still by tempting politicians to rely on capital-gains taxes and then, as the bubble burst, snatching away many of those capital gains. The federal system is even worse. America's tax code has almost tripled in volume over the past decade—to four million words—and changes, on average, once a day. There are forty-two different definitions of a small business. The IRS publishes a ninety-page booklet to explain the fifteen different tax incentives for higher education. No wonder nine out of ten tax filers pay for help to complete their returns.

Tax is only one part of the regulatory burden.[17] It was not California's high taxes that drove Google to pilot its superfast fiber-optic Internet system in Kansas City and Austin, Texas; it was the prospect of grappling with the complexities of the California Environmental Quality Act. A 2013 survey of 1,142 large and small businesses found that more than six in ten businesspeople said it's still harder to do business in California than in other states.[18] Americans love to bash Europe for its addiction to red tape, but in some areas the problem is even worse in the land of the free. By law government departments have to publish new regulations in the Federal Register. In the 1950s the register expanded by an average of 11,000 pages a year. In the first decade of the twenty-first century it expanded by an average of 73,000 pages a year. From 2009 to 2011 the Obama administration produced 106 major regulations, with "major" defined as having an expected economic impact of at least $100 million a year, and thousands of minor regulations. The Obamacare health bill was over 2,000 pages long; the Dodd-Frank law on finance is 800 pages long and has 400 subsidiary regulations. The federal government requires hospitals to use 140,000 codes for the ailments they treat, including one for injuries from being hit by a turtle.[19]

Much of this is just Olson's law at work—industries lobby for exceptions or regulations that, once created, justify jobs. Take, for instance, all the "occupational legislation," like the law that would have frustrated Sidney Webb's barbering skills. In the 1950s fewer than 5 percent of American workers needed licenses. Today the figure is almost 30 percent. Add to that people who are preparing to obtain a license or whose jobs involve some form of certification and the share is 38 percent. The cost of all this pettifoggery is huge—unless, that is, you are a member of one of the cartels that pushes for pettifogging rules or an employee of one of the bureaucratic bodies charged with enforcing them. Morris Kleiner of the University of Minnesota calculates that licensing boosts the income of licensees by about 15 percent—about the same as membership in a trade union does. (Trade unionists who are also protected by licenses enjoy a 24 percent boost to their hourly wages.) Not surprisingly, jobs growth is higher in unregulated occupations than in regulated ones, and the rules stop people from crossing state lines to look for work.

Many of the new laws that have been passed in California (and indeed in both Europe and America) have admirable aims: better health care, cleaner air, less discrimination against minorities. But as Philip Howard of Common Good points out, they are both amazingly cumbersome and, once on the statute book, amazingly difficult, if not impossible, to remove. One solution is to follow Texas's example and let legislatures meet only occasionally. Another would be to introduce sunset clauses so that all regulations automatically expire after a while.

5. FUZZY MATH

On the face of it, Jerry Brown has done a heroic job in bringing California's budget under control, turning a $1.2 billion deficit into a $4.4 billion surplus. But a lot depends on what numbers you use. People rightly criticize the corporate world for poor accounting—for hiding things off balance sheet, for example. Enron was notorious for its addiction to off-balance-sheet accounting. But California's numbers are far dodgier.

It is not just that balancing the state's budget required all sorts of tricks, like raising taxes retrospectively and off-loading costs onto cities and counties; there is the huge buildup of unfunded liabilities— promises to state workers about health care and pensions that will be very hard to keep. The unfunded part of those liabilities in California is officially $128 billion, but if they were accounted for properly the hole would be $328 billion, according to the California Public Policy Center—around $8,600 for every person in the state. Brown, to be fair, has trimmed some of these, but they explain why California has the second-lowest credit rating among America's states, behind only Illinois, whose tactics have been even more Capone-like. Moody's, a credit rating agency, has thirty California cities under review largely for this reason.

Again California is typical of the nation. America's states admit that, as of 2013, their pension programs are only 73 percent funded. But that is based on a recklessly optimistic discount rate for those liabilities (so the liabilities seem smaller than they are likely to be). Apply the rate that a company would have to use and the true funding figure is 48 percent. This suggests a gap between income and obligations of $2.7 trillion, or 17 percent of GDP. Many individual states are carrying horrific liabilities: Illinois's pension shortfall is equivalent to 241 percent of its annual tax revenues. And that is before you include the cost of all the unfunded health-care benefits and additional pension promises that city governments have lavished on municipal workers. When Detroit went bankrupt in 2013, it had run up a tab of $5.7 billion for medical benefits and $3.5 billion for pensions. It is hard to imagine somebody on Wall Street getting away with that, let alone all the other dodges, such as promoting people just before retirement or giving workers overgenerous cost-of-living adjustments. More than twenty thousand retired public servants in California already receive pensions of over $100,000.

The federal government's numbers are little better. The Fourteenth Amendment to the Constitution declares that "the validity of the public debt of the United States . . . shall not be questioned." But what does "debt" mean? The declared national debt held by the public is around $13 trillion. Yet that excludes a lot of guarantees and commitments. James Hamilton, an economist at the University of California at San Diego, added the federal government's support for housing, loan guarantees, deposit insurance, debts built up by the Federal Reserve, and government trust funds and calculated that the federal government's off-balance-sheet commitments in 2012 came to $70 trillion, or six times the size of the reported on-balance-sheet debt. The two biggest holes were Medicare and Social Security, which he estimated at $27.6 trillion and $26.5 trillion respectively.[20] Others produce even bigger numbers by including things like defense commitments: Laurence J. Kotlikoff, who served on Ronald Reagan's Council of Economic Advisers, put the total fiscal gap between the American government's spending commitments and the taxes that it expected to collect at $211 trillion.[21]

Vagueness about numbers is a curse of the public sector. In the worst cases it borders on the criminal. Challenged to find one reliable number in the Argentine government's books, a group of the most respected economists in Buenos Aires went into a huddle and came back with the answer: "Maybe one of the trade ones, but we are not sure which."[22] And once countries slip into trouble the numbers go haywire. Greece responded to tougher times by using a secretive (though legal) system of swaps, masterminded by Goldman Sachs, to massage its debt-to-GDP ratio.

But even in well-run places it is hard to get reliable or consistent figures for the most basic things, such as GDP or the size of government. In one week in the summer of 2013 America's GDP rose by $560 billion, or 3.6 percent, mainly because it changed its system of measurement to the one used by Canada and Australia (but none of the other countries in the G20).[23] Bruce Bartlett, one of America's most prominent tax reformers, points out that one reason why Uncle Sam looks slim relative to his European peers is accounting. In Europe most health spending shows up directly as public spending. In America it is hidden as tax deductions. In 2012 the deduction for employer-provided health insurance cost some $434 billion, or roughly 3 percent of GDP. Include these "tax expenditures" in the budget and America's net social spending rose to 27.2 percent of GDP—putting it above Italy, Denmark, and the OECD (Organization for Economic Cooperation and Development) average. Tax breaks for education are a similar wheeze, hiding the state's commitment. Indeed, another critic, Suzanne Mettler, argues that when you factor in the full "submerged state," Uncle Sam is the same size as his European peers.

Obfuscation is even worse on the revenue side. The first thing most analysts look at when they assess a company is where it gets its money. With a few honorable exceptions, such as flat-tax Estonia, the revenue side of government is comically complicated—and as a result often unfair. Tax codes almost everywhere are riven with subsidies, exemptions, and complications that favor the rich. And they are seldom explained properly. One of the most distorting features of America's tax code—the fact that you can deduct the interest you are paying on your mortgage—is the accidental legacy of a 1913 income-tax law that spared interest of any kind.

Such obfuscation is mainly to the taxpayer's disadvantage. But dodgy numbers are increasingly to government's disadvantage as well.

How can you run a complicated organization when you can't trust the numbers? How can you plan for the future when you can't distinguish among different types of expenditures? Companies make a distinction between long-term debt to pay for investment and short-term working capital. Governments, perhaps even more than companies, have a reason to invest in long-term projects, especially infrastructure. Borrowing to build schools or bridges ought to be treated differently from borrowing to pay wages, unemployment benefits, or farm subsidies. But it isn't. When Britain's coalition government came to power, it cut infrastructure investment (which is generally regarded as a good way of generating economic growth) along with other kinds of spending.

6. TO THOSE WHO HAVE, MORE SHALL BE GIVEN

The sixth sin is the fact that government is no longer "progressive." Far from being focused on those who need it most, such as the poor and the young, government spending cascades toward the old and the relatively well off.

In California both the plutocrats and the poor do badly out of government. The former pay for a big chunk of it, especially through capital-gains taxes. The poor may not pay much income tax, but they don't attract much public spending either. That goes mainly to middle-income Californians. They attend better schools than poor Californians. Their streets often have more police (there are more volunteers to cruise around Beverly Hills than Compton). They are far more likely to go to a publicly financed university, to claim mortgage relief on their home, to own a farm that collects subsidies, or to attend a ballet supported by public funds. The only time when the federal government scatters its bounty to everyone in California is when they get old and those old reliables, Medicare and Social Security, kick in.

This again is typical. Despite a century of growth, big government is hardly progressive. In the 2012 election the Republicans made much of the fact that 47 percent of Americans (the "moochers") don't pay any income tax at all and that the richest 1 percent (the "makers") pay 40 percent of all income taxes. But the devil is in the details.[24] The poor pay payroll, state, and local taxes while richer Americans exploit all the deductions for things like health insurance, mortgage interest, and education. These "tax preferences" are now worth some $1.3 trillion, or 8 percent of GDP, and more than 60 percent of them go to the wealthiest 20 percent of Americans. Take all taxes into account and the share paid by the wealthiest 1 percent falls to 21.6 percent, close to their share of pretax income.

Turn to the spending side of the ledger and the poor do even worse. America is not generous when it comes to unemployment insurance and other cash transfers, and it does much less than other rich countries to help with preschool education, generally acknowledged as the best way to boost equality of opportunity. Stunningly, its budget for public housing is only a quarter of the amount that the richest 20 percent of Americans receive through the mortgage-interest deduction. Indeed, if you put spending and taxes together, including all the deductions, the government lavishes more dollars overall on the top fifth of the income distribution than the bottom fifth.

Europeans like to think of themselves as being "kinder" to the poor than Americans. Whether it is kind to give the poor as much as Europe does is a long argument: Handouts have a nasty habit of entrenching dependency. Britain, for instance, has a quarter of a million households in which no one has ever held a formal job. But European countries are less kind in other ways. They rely more on consumption taxes (which hit the poor disproportionately) than America does. They are also more inclined to subsidize the middle class through "universal" benefits, especially for the elderly: It cannot make sense to give free bus passes to Sir Mick Jagger and Sir Elton John.

The one thing that both continents have in common is that state spending favors the old over the young. America's Center on Budget and Policy Priorities calculates that over half of all entitlement spending flows to the elderly.[25] David Willetts, one of the most cerebral Tory MPs, thinks that Britain's baby boomers (those born between 1945 and 1965) will take out nearly 20 percent more from the system than they have put in.[26] The big losers from the generational struggle are the young. The burden of the 2007–8 economic crisis was borne disproportionately by young people, the group who, whatever their other failures, did the least to create it.[27] In Europe, especially, young people look like they are being left out.[28]

Again, this is partly Olson's law writ large. Most American politicians would rather appear naked in public than take on AARP, as the American Association of Retired Persons is now known. The West's population is aging rapidly—and older citizens are much more likely to vote than younger ones. This biases the system not only toward the old rather than the young but also toward the past rather than the future. Nicolas Berggruen and Nathan Gardels rightly worry that "democracy is a vote for the past because it is a vote for the vested interests of the present."[29]

7. POLITICAL PARALYSIS AND PARTISAN GRIDLOCK

Sixty years ago California's politics was rather cozy. In the early 1950s Pat Brown, Jerry's father, who was then the Democratic attorney general, used to share a car from Sacramento to San Francisco on Fridays with Earl Warren, the Republican governor. For most of the past thirty years it has been a story of unyielding partisanship, with California Republicans drifting to the right, Democrats to the left, and a vast no-man's-land opening up between them. Promoting his first budget proposal soon after taking office again as governor in 2011, Jerry Brown described politics as a primordial battle between "Modocians" and "Alamedans" (Modoc being a rural, conservative, Republican county and Alameda a liberal enclave east of San Francisco).

It is fashionable to blame this animosity on partisan media channels such as Fox News or on the blogosphere. But the problem is deeper than that. Californians are choosing to live in like-minded places. San Francisco is probably the most left-wing enclave in the country while the Central Valley is one of the most right-wing. A third of the U.S. Navy's Pacific Fleet is based in San Diego while San Francisco's residents have voted to prevent military recruiters from setting up shop in high schools. And this political version of "assortative mating" has been reinforced by gerrymandering, which produces a modern version of eighteenth-century rotten boroughs. The result is that politicians can get their party's votes only if they appeal to the extremes. The hedonistic Arnold Schwarzenegger became governor only because a recall petition allowed him to bypass the Republican primary process. Until Jerry Brown reappeared with a clearer Democratic majority, gridlock was the order of the day in Sacramento.

Washington seems even more paralyzed—unable to pass a budget, let alone deal with entitlements. In *It's Even Worse Than It Looks* Thomas Mann and Norman Ornstein, of the Brookings Institution and the American Enterprise Institute respectively, argue that American political parties are increasingly acting like parliamentary parties, fueled by ideology and loathing, but are stuck in a chamber where the majority party lacks the perks and bribes that majority parties use to impose their will in parliamentary systems. At a time when Americans are more pessimistic about their country's future prospects than at any point since Gallup first started asking them in 1959, Washington lives in a world of sequesters and shutdowns. In his 2013 State of the Union speech Barack Obama observed, "The greatest nation on earth cannot keep conducting its business by drifting from one manufactured crisis to the next. We can't do it." By October of that year the government had shut down.

The eurozone is in an even worse fix, lumbered with bigger economic problems and a more dysfunctional political system. Europe may lack the fierce ideological battles that divide Republicans and Democrats: Most politicians are pragmatic centrists who have little interest in American-style culture wars over abortion and gay marriage. But Europe is nevertheless paralyzed by a tug-of-war between powerful forces: for example between EU politicians who want to centralize decisions and national politicians (particularly in the north) who want to keep them local; and between Anglo-Saxon and Nordic countries that want to keep the state out of the private sector and the continental countries that think it belongs there. That has always made for slow decisions, even when they are in everybody's interest. It took a dozen years to produce a common patent, for instance: Even after all these years the single market only applies to around a quarter of Europe's goods and services. But the euro crisis has turned gridlock into an existential threat. Rather than forcing politicians into compromise, the gap between creditors and debtors, between northern Europeans fed up with bailing out shirkers and southern Europeans fed up with being bossed around, is becoming ever more poisonous. The result is that every rescue attempt is both half-baked and deeply resented.

Perhaps the most dangerous effect of all this gridlock, buffoonery, and bile is one few outsiders see: It is scaring talent away from a public sector that is already disfigured by low pay and rigid hierarchies. This is particularly true in the areas of the private sector that government most needs to understand if it is to move with the times. In California the real gap between Sacramento and Silicon Valley is in the quality of the recruits. The American election of 2012 returned only six engineers to the House of Representatives, along with one physicist, one chemist, and one microbiologist.[30] In Europe politics seems even further removed. The British general election of 2010 returned only three MPs to the Commons who described their professions as "science or research" (compared with thirty-eight barristers).[31]

MEET THE BIGGEST PROBLEM OF ALL: YOU

The most worrying thing about all seven deadly sins is that they are part of the human condition. It is always tempting to think of the problems of the state as the product of surrendering too much power to special interests or being visited by a plague of bureaucrats. But in the end it is the product of giving power to the people. Democracy is being disfigured by unrealistic expectations and contradictory demands.

California is the ultimate example of the perils of democracy because its system of ballot initiatives gives citizens a direct say in both taxing and spending. Californians have used that power in completely predictable ways—to vote themselves more entitlements and lower taxes. They have put limits on the amount of taxes that government can levy on, for example, property, while at the same time voting in favor of spending programs, both cuddly (the money for schools) and severe (the three-strikes law). All the other states have different versions of this. If the United States sinks into political paralysis, its epitaph could well be, "government of the people, by the people, for the people." If the eurozone collapses, its epitaph should be the words of Jean-Claude Juncker, the former prime minister of Luxembourg, in 2007: "We all know what to do, but we don't know how to get reelected once we have done it."[32]

Walter Bagehot liked to argue that the best safeguard against excessive taxation (and hence excessive government) is parliamentary sensitivity to public opinion. But he did not take into account the public's ability to want both low taxes and big government—and politicians' ability to provide them with what they wanted by hiding the bill or borrowing from future generations. Western voters were happy to embrace Milton Friedman's small-government revolution when it meant paying lower taxes and shredding red tape but not when it meant getting fewer services or unsafe meat (it is notable that Friedman spent his golden years living in liberal San Francisco rather than Friedmanite Laredo in Texas). Conviction politicians have disappeared not because backbones are in short supply but because voters no longer want them. "Berlusconi is us," as Luigi Zingales of the University of Chicago puts it.[33]

. . . AND THE ONE GREAT VIRTUE

It is not hard to get depressed about California. One hundred years ago Argentina seemed the future; now it is a basket case. Bankruptcy is now part of the California scene. When San Bernardino went bust, its city attorney advised residents to "lock their doors and load their guns" because the city could no longer afford enough police. Shortly after taking over the governorship, Jerry Brown complained that taking things away from people might easily lead to a Hobbesian war of "all against all."

But something has changed under Brown. The Greece of America is beginning to fix itself. It has taken the most important step for all substance abusers: admitting that it has a problem. Brown has managed to balance the budget (Darrell Steinberg, the leader of the California Senate, described the experience as "almost surreal"). The authorities now project budget surpluses some time into the future (so long as you ignore unfunded liabilities and the volatile nature of the tax base). And Brown repaired his fiscal house by forcing Democrats to accept deep spending cuts, as well as persuading voters to accept tax rises. More important, some of the design faults in California's structure have begun to be fixed, thanks to initiatives passed in Schwarzenegger's time. Budgets no longer need a two-thirds majority to pass the legislature. The state has forged ahead with both open primaries and redistricting, with some interesting results.

There is even something of a rebirth of centrist pragmatism. One trailblazer was Michael Milken, the former junk bond king, whose Santa Monica–based institute issues annual reports on the state of the state and produces a constant stream of ideas, many of them backed up by money, for fixing it. Another is Nicolas Berggruen's Think Long Committee, a technocratic group of Republican and Democratic grandees and business leaders, which is trying to narrow the gap between Silicon Valley and Sacramento. It has sponsored initiatives and worked closely with Brown. The governor himself reiterates that by denouncing both the Republicans' addiction to tax cutting and his own party's state-centric view of the world: "Welfare created dependency and builds the power of the state," he told *Bloomberg Businessweek*. "If everything is state-centric, it doesn't fit with the idea that we can do more on our own."[34]

That still leaves a lot to be fixed, including the pensions. The fiscal balance depends heavily on the rich: The top 1 percent pay half the state's income taxes. The finances of a lot of California cities still look precarious. But if even dysfunctional California can stir itself, surely there is hope for others? It is indeed possible to find a few flickers of hope: The region's ability to recover from misfortune and repair its mistakes is still its most admirable feature. The euro crisis is forcing some badly managed countries to change: Italy passed a pretty impressive piece of pensions reform, and Spain has begun to tidy up its skewed labor market. In America more is going on at the state level than in Washington. Kansas has created a post called "the Repealer" to get rid of red tape and pays a "bounty" to high schools for every vocational qualification their students earn in certain fields. Forty-five states are developing new curriculums, thirty-eight have introduced a performance element in teachers' pay, and forty-two allow charter schools. The list could go on.

Change is even coming to the country that was at the center of our three and a half revolutions. An old Etonian pragmatist, stuck in an unwieldy coalition, might seem an unlikely radical, but David Cameron is on course to reverse Gordon Brown's spending splurge by 2015, reducing public spending to below 40 percent of the GDP, roughly where Margaret Thatcher left it in 1990. Mr. Cameron has engendered far less opposition than Thatcher largely because most of the savings have been found in a nonideological way—through freezing pay, getting councils to share facilities, buying fewer police cars, and so on. Cameron could have slimmed the state much more dramatically if he had not "ring fenced" health spending (stunningly, spending on the

NHS in 2012–13, at around £120 billion, was double in real terms the amount in 1997–98, when Labour came to power). But Cameron has introduced braver reforms in education, where around half the state schools have now contracted out in one way or another so they can set their teachers' pay, and welfare, where payments are being simplified and capped. Localism has got a push forward, so police chiefs can be sacked by local elected commissioners, and at least some of Cameron's original attempt to create a "Big Society," with charities and volunteers doing more of the state's work, has survived.

Across the West a growing number of people are asking probing questions about the size and scope of the state, prodded by both the size of the current crisis and the inadequacy of the establishment's response. They are not only eyeing up some old sacred cows for slaughter. They are also producing blueprints for radical reform. Conservative think tanks, such as Sweden's Timbro, recognize that it is no longer enough just to preach deregulation. They are increasingly focused on redesigning the state. Left-wing think tanks, such as Britain's Policy Network, recognize that, if the Left is to have a future, it needs to conquer its addiction to the almighty state.

There have always been thinkers, such as America's Michael Porter (of the Harvard Business School) and Andrew Adonis (now at the Institute of Government in London), who have been interested in redesigning government. But it is noticeable how many have joined the fray in the past decade, including not just politicians and policy wonks but also businesspeople. Pete Peterson, the cofounder of the Blackstone Group, shares Berggruern's despair about the state of American government: He is spending hundreds of millions drawing people's attention to the size of the deficit. Old voices are talking with renewed urgency. Elaine Kamarck, who helped to create Al Gore's "reinventing government" initiative, has founded a center for effective government management at the Brookings Institution. Geoff Mulgan, a former head of Tony Blair's Policy Unit, is excited about the way that voluntary institutions can solve public problems. Steve Hilton, who did a similar job for David Cameron and who was the guru behind the Big Society, wants to redesign government for the age of Google. Peter Schuck of Yale University wonders "why government fails so often" while Philip Howard argues that part of the answer lies in the fact that "nobody is in charge." Management consultancies and other businesses recognize that fixing the state will be one of the major challenges (and business opportunities) of the next few years. McKinsey has established a center for government under Diana Farrell. IBM has a center for the business of government. The likes of Deloitte and Accenture have gigantic public-sector practices.

But for all this progress is slow, resistance is strong, and reversals are all too common. Politicians revert to their old ways. Voters continue their habit of promising to quit drinking and then sneak off to the toolshed for a sharpener. This slow progress would be dangerous enough if the West were still the only game in town. It is not. The East is not only advancing economically. It is also in the business of state building, trying to cram what took hundreds of years in the West into a few decades. In the world of economics "the periphery" (as it used to be called) is reemerging as the core. The great question is whether this will happen in the world of politics as well.

CHAPTER SIX

THE ASIAN ALTERNATIVE

ONE PILGRIMAGE IS OBLIGATORY for anyone who wants to look at the future of government—visiting one of the world's smallest countries to see an elderly Asian man who supposedly retired from politics many years ago. The lair of the "minister mentor" is a small suite of rooms located—by coincidence, of course—above the room where Singapore's cabinet meets. The minister mentor is a frail figure with stern eyes who quickly proceeds to tell his visitors where the world is headed and to explain why the Western model of government is out of date. His words are listened to. When one of us went to see him in 2011, the meeting was delayed because Xi Jinping, who had just been anointed as China's next leader, wanted to jump the queue to meet "the senior who has our respect."[1] Westerners too have waited in line. Margaret Thatcher declared that "he was never wrong." Henry Kissinger has said that none of the world's leaders he has met over the years has taught him more than Lee Kuan Yew.[2]

Lee is the founding father of what might be termed "the Asian alternative": George Washington, Thomas Jefferson, and James Madison rolled into one. Since the days of Thomas Hobbes, the West has been the only show in town when it comes to inventing political ideas.

Now it faces a rival—a different way of doing things that most Westerners associate with mighty China but that is to be found at its most advanced in tiny Singapore. Across Asia other countries are drawing on it as they develop their own states. This model has its faults and inconsistencies, most of which are on display in China. Put bluntly, we do not think that it is the ideal way forward. But the rest of the world can learn a lot from the Asian alternative. We live in an era when the West no longer has all the best policies.

WHEN HARRY MET HAYEK

Lee's life typifies this change. Fifty years ago, few Asians were more Western than "Harry" Lee: "the best bloody Englishman east of Suez," according to George Brown, a British foreign secretary. A star pupil in colonial Singapore, he drank deep of Fabianism at the London School of Economics and Cambridge University, where, like his wife, he got a first in law. He campaigned for the Labour Party. When he maneuvered his way to power in Singapore as the head of the People's Action Party after independence in 1959, it was as a disciple of Harold Laski and devotee of Beatrice Webb. Even now he is something of an Anglophile: As his wife lay dying, he comforted her by reading Lewis Carroll, Jane Austen, and Shakespeare's sonnets. But outside literature he has outgrown his youthful infatuations. Lee moved gradually to the right in the 1960s, setting up Singapore as a bulwark against communism and tightening his own grip on power. By the 1970s, as he explains in his memoirs, he had abandoned any illusion that socialism made sense: It was causing "the inevitable decline of the British economy."[3] By the 1990s he was reading Hayek's *The Fatal Conceit: Errors of Socialism* and pursuing an "open-door policy" to international business, with a well-educated labor force, the rule of law, and low taxes. He went on to create one of the smallest governments in the world.

It is easy to make fun of his creation. Singapore is Disneyland with the death penalty, paradise as designed by McKinsey, a supersized shopping mall where chewing gum is banned and litterbugs given a thrashing. For all his talk about "Asian values," Lee was a pragmatic opportunist with sharp elbows. Opponents have been sent to prison and citizens treated like children. And the great meritocrat has a weakness for family ties: Lee served as prime minister from 1959 to 1990 and his eldest son, Lee Hsien Loong, took the job in 2004.

Yet the simple fact is that the rise of Singapore is one of the miracles of the past seventy years: A country that was once an impoverished swamp is now a whirring hub of the global economy. Singaporeans enjoy higher living standards and better schools and hospitals than their former colonial masters in the United Kingdom—and all with a state that chews up a tiny proportion of GDP: 17 percent in 2012. Singapore is a model not just for China but for all the emerging Asian powers that are now building their welfare states.

Lee took the Western menu for a modern state—and tinkered with it: two parts Hobbes, one part Mill, with a dash of Asian values. It is the dash of Asian values that commands most of the attention, because Lee and his acolytes have advanced the idea that Asia is somehow culturally different: more focused on the family, more devoted to education and saving, more willing to put faith in a mandarin elite. But it is really a spicy flavoring, added later. The meat is more Hobbesian. Lee's starting point is that "human beings, regrettable though it may be, are inherently vicious and have to be restrained from their viciousness."[4] Singapore is more authoritarian, more interventionist, more bossy, especially when it comes to state-directed capitalism, than Western countries and unashamedly elitist, even a little royalist. The

Lees look like Leviathan personified. But there is some Mill too. Singapore is a tiny night-watchman state that provides people with the opportunities that they need to rise and then leaves them to sort out their own welfare: Provided that they do not challenge the social order, Singaporeans have enormous control over how they provide for their sickness and old age.

The Singaporean model of authoritarian modernization thus represents a direct challenge to the two basic tenets of the Western state: that government should be democratic and that it should be generous. Lee's model is elitist and stingy. Other Asian alternatives are less well constructed than Singapore's and take different paths, with a notably more brutal one in China. What they share with Lee is, first, a suspicion that the West does not have all the answers and, second, a sense that government is a vital part of the global race for success. In the West government is chaotic, casual, and unplanned. In Singapore it is thought out, serious, organized—and that is true across much of emerging Asia (with democratic India being the conspicuous exception).

This matters. The Asians are simply working harder at government than the West. In some cases, such as China, that is because they see themselves as being in competition with the West. But far more often it is because they are in competition with one another. Lee's friend Henry Kissinger points out that while Europe is in the process of rejecting the nation-state, or at any rate deciding how much of it to reject, Asia still operates in the Westphalian era, with increasingly nationalistic states butting up against one another. They are desperate for new ideas.

That does not mean that they will choose the right ones. There are, as we shall see, really big structural problems with the Asian model, especially when you begin to apply the model in a country as diverse as China. The Asian alternative could easily be destroyed by the very nationalism that propels it forward, just as the European model was almost destroyed by two world wars. It could also be undermined by the fact that the Asians are a lot less distinctive than Lee or the Chinese claim: They also want an all-you-can-eat buffet. What is clear is that some Asian countries are thinking about the state far more seriously than most Western countries—and that all that thinking is paying dividends. We will look first at Singapore, where the Asian alternative works best, and then at China, where its inconsistencies and faults become much more apparent.

AN ELITIST NANNY—BUT A SLIM ONE

The Singaporean state is something of a Mary Poppins—not just a wonderful nanny but a very bossy, perhaps slightly sinister one. "We decide what is right," Lee once observed. "Never mind what the people think."

Lee has always made it clear that Singapore is open for business: There are few places where it is easier for a big multinational to set up shop, where tariff barriers are lower, and where taxes are more manageable. But at the same time the state guides the economy. It chivies local businesses up the "value chain"—betting first on manufacturing, then on services, and now on the knowledge economy. It also owns shares in the island's biggest companies, such as Singapore Airlines and Singapore Telecommunications.

Lee's bossiness is even more noticeable in politics. To begin with, his authoritarianism was rather unsubtle: Suspected communists were locked up and elections rigged. In every election from 1968 to 1984 his People's Action Party won all the seats. Now the control is subtler:

There are curbs on the press, but all within the legal framework of parliamentary democracy. In 2011 the PAP put in its worst performance in a general election: just 60 percent of the vote and 93 percent of the seats! The Singaporean establishment argues that it has produced the perfect compromise between accountability and efficiency. Its politicians are regularly tested in elections and have to make themselves available to their constituents; but since the government knows it is going to win, it can take a long view. "Our strength is that we are able to think strategically and look ahead," the current prime minister, Lee's son, told us. "If the government changed every five years it would be harder."[5]

Obviously, this strength suits the Lees. But the old man's conviction that unfettered democracy does not work in developing countries plainly runs deeper than self-interest. "I do not believe that democracy necessarily leads to development," Lee rather impertinently told his hosts in the recently democratized Philippines in 1992. "The exuberance of democracy leads to undisciplined and disorderly conditions."[6] Elsewhere he has said that "what a country needs to develop is discipline more than democracy."[7] Having seen other countries in the neighborhood torn apart by ethnic strife, he has no qualms about forcing people to live in mixed neighborhoods in order to prevent ethnic polarization (more than 80 percent of Singaporeans still live in public housing).

Good government in turn relies on an educated elite of "good people" running the country.[8] To westerners, Singapore looks rather like Plato's *Republic*, with its caste of wise "guardians" presiding over the men of "silver" and "bronze." But the more direct influence is China's mandarin tradition, which selected the brightest people for government. No country works harder at perfecting its civil servants than Singapore, nor follows such an unabashedly elitist model: It spots talented youngsters early, luring them with scholarships, and then spends a fortune training them: Those who reach the top are richly rewarded, with pay packages of as much as $2 million a year, while those who falter along the way are thrown overboard. It is true that Western civil services often have very good people at the top—the British even call their highfliers "mandarins"—but in Singapore meritocracy reigns all the way down the system. Teachers need to have finished in the top third of their class (as they do in Finland and South Korea, which also shine in the education rankings). Headmasters are often appointed in their thirties and rewarded with merit pay if they do well but moved on quickly if their schools underperform. Testing is ubiquitous.

Singapore is producing a new type of elite—very different from either the capitalist elite of the West or the bureaucratic elite of the old state-dominated economies. The members of this elite are au fait with the latest management thinking and comfortable with importing private-sector methods into the public sector. But they are also happy devoting their talents to the state. Indeed, they spend their lives shuffling between the public sector and the private sector. Sitting around a table with a group of young Singaporean mandarins is more like meeting junior partners at Goldman Sachs or McKinsey than the cast of *Veep* or *The Thick of It*. The person on your left is on secondment at a big oil company; on your right sits a woman who between spells at the finance and defense ministries has picked up degrees from the London School of Economics, Cambridge, and Stanford. Highfliers pop in and out of the Civil Service College for more training: The prime minister has even written MBA-style case studies for them.

There are obvious holes in Lee's vision. Often it strays into the simple formula that if he says something, it is self-evidently right (if he had a motto, it would be Mary Poppins's: "I never explain anything"). In recent years ethnic tensions have begun to rise in Singapore. Plato said that the guardians should be brought up communally in order to break family ties. The Singaporean elite is cemented in place by family ties, and Lee has retained some of the Webbs' snooti- ness about clever people being more likely to breed clever people. And some of his ideas hark back to James Mill and his circle debating the merits of flexible franchises. He has talked about being keen on giving everybody over forty with two children two votes, to reflect their greater importance to the state, then restricting them to one vote again when they hit sixty.[9]

This points toward the other side of Singapore: the state as night watchman. Micromanager though he is, Lee, more than any other modern ruler, has concentrated on keeping the state small and on making people responsible for their own welfare. Singapore's world- class education system consumes only 3.3 percent of GDP. But the biggest savings come from restricting social transfers and refusing to indulge the middle class. Lee thinks the West's mistake has been to set up all-you-can-eat welfare states: Because everything at the buffet is free, everybody stuffs their faces. Singapore's approach, by contrast, is for the government to provide people with a good start in life—and then encourage them to cook for themselves.

Singaporeans pay a fifth of their salaries into the Central Provident Fund, with their employers contributing another 15.5 percent. That provides them with the wherewithal to pay for their housing, pensions, and health care and their children's tertiary education. In the West the welfare state is based on social assistance: Payments are based on your circumstances, so they increase the worse off you are. Singapore has a social insurance model: 90 percent of what you get from the Central Provident Fund is tied to what you put in, so hard work is rewarded. There is a small safety net to cover the very poor and the very sick. But people are expected to look after their parents and pay—or at least copay—for government services. Lee loathes free universal benefits. Once you have given a subsidy, he says, it is always hard to withdraw it. If you want to give people a helping hand, he argues, it is better to give them cash than to provide a service, whose value nobody understands. In his view, "westerners have abandoned an ethical basis for society. . . . In the East, we start with self reliance. In the West today, it is the opposite."[10] By allowing their people to blame everything on society, rather than accept that they are responsible, Western leaders have allowed charity to become an entitlement "and the stigma of living on charity disappeared."[11] Democracy is a big part of the West's problem: "When you have popular democracy, to win votes you have to give more. And to beat your opponent in the next election, you have to promise to give more away. So it is a never-ending process of auctions—and the cost, the debt being paid for by the next generation."[12]

With 5.2 million inhabitants, Singapore is very small by modern standards—though not much smaller than many of the premodern societies that shaped our current view of government. In different circumstances Lee might have been just another aged autocrat, grumbling about Western democracy and its degenerate ways: a neo-Victorian sideshow. But now his message carries further for two reasons.

The first is that Asia's newly competing states suddenly need a model, their craving fed not only by resurgent nationalism but also by demography. Across the continent countries are rushing to build welfare states. Indonesia started to roll out health insurance to all of its 240 million citizens on January 1, 2014. One government agency collects the premiums and foots the bills, in the biggest single-payer system in the world. China and the Philippines have massively expanded their health-insurance schemes too.[13] Asian countries are adding pensions, unemployment insurance, minimum wages, antipoverty programs, food credits, and so on. It took European countries about half a century to build their welfare states. Some Asian countries want to do it in a decade. And they are doing so on an epic scale: Introducing pensions across China or India is the same as providing them for the whole of the European Union and the United States combined.

Singapore is an obvious model for all this frantic building: The system works extremely well and chimes with many Asian countries' traditions of self-reliance. Overall social spending on the continent is only around 30 percent of rich-country levels and notably leaner than Latin America's notoriously convoluted systems.[14] So far Asia leans toward social-insurance schemes, like Singapore's, rather than the West's social-assistance ones. In South Korea, for instance, about 80 percent of what you get out of the system is tied to what you put in.[15] In Asia as a whole, public-health spending is still only 2.5 percent of GDP, compared with about 7 percent in the OECD group of rich nations.

The second reason is the crisis of the Western model of democracy and free-market capitalism. In the 1990s Lee's lectures on Asian values seemed somewhat eccentric, even to Asians. The Washington consensus was sweeping all before it. Francis Fukuyama talked about "the total exhaustion of viable systematic alternatives to Western liberalism."[16] Rather than associating Deng Xiaoping's China with economic greatness, Americans thought of the lone student walking toward the tanks in Tiananmen Square in 1989. Bill Clinton told China's president, Jiang Zemin, to his face that he was "on the wrong side of history."[17]

The Asian economic crisis in 1997 only reinforced the conceit of Western democracy, especially when the IMF had to launch a $40 billion program to help South Korea, Thailand, and Indonesia, which had all borrowed too much from foreign banks. Asian leaders, even those who did not need subsidies, still remember the omniscient bossiness of the men from the IMF, the World Bank, and the U.S. Treasury, who thought their wisdom stretched far beyond the three main countries affected. Greater democracy seemed the only way forward. In Indonesia the Suhartos, who had governed the country autocratically for thirty years, lost power. South Korea loosened up.

Today the picture looks very different. So far the twenty-first century has been a rotten one for the Western model. First America's war on terror, particularly its invasion of Iraq, did immense damage to democracy's image, then the credit crunch savaged the idea that liberal capitalism was the only answer, and finally the euro crisis and the shutdown of Washington in 2013 confirmed Asian suspicions that Western government is dysfunctional. To a growing number of people Lee's ideas provided precisely what Fukuyama had thought was impossible—"a viable systematic alternative."[18] Western intellectuals engaged in an agonized reconsideration of both democracy and capitalism. In *The Future of Freedom* Fareed Zakaria drew a distinction between liberal democracy, which puts checks on the power of governments, and illiberal democracy, which fails to do so. In *World on Fire* Amy Chua argued that democracy could encourage poor majorities to oppress rich minorities, such as the Indians in Uganda or the Chinese in Southeast Asia.

The 2000s saw both a "democratic recession" and an "antidemocratic renaissance."[19] Freedom House calculates that global freedom declined in every year from 2005 to 2010—the longest continuous decline in almost forty years.[20] The Bertelsmann Foundation calculated that the number of democracies that no longer really qualify as such (because of deficient elections and so on) roughly doubled between 2006 and 2009 to fifty-three.[21] In 2011 the overthrow of the Mubarak regime in Egypt and the arrival of the Arab Spring raised hopes for a new wave of democratization; with the overthrow of the Muslim Brotherhood's elected government in 2013, those hopes withered.

As a result, the Singapore model is attracting admirers far beyond Asia. Dubai is trying to produce a copy in the Arabian Desert, complete with a hypermodern financial district, ostentatious shopping malls, state-run companies, a Government Excellence Program, and "key performance indicators" borrowed from a Harvard Business School professor, Robert Kaplan. The tiny emirate "benchmarks" its performance against the world's best governments—Singapore, New Zealand, Australia, and Canada: Note the absence of America on the list.[22] Meanwhile, Rwanda is trying to become the Singapore of central Africa, with the same mixture of probusiness policies and authoritarian government.

Russia, seldom regarded as a paragon of good government, is fond of invoking Singapore's example. When one of us visited Skolkovo, one of the country's leading business schools, in 2010, it prominently displayed a large picture of Lee Kuan Yew next to a large picture of Arnold Schwarzenegger. Vladimir Putin cites Lee as an influence and in private can sound very similar to the minister mentor when he laments the constraints of democracy (or what passes for democracy in his Russia). Even a former KGB man, he jokes, often finds it hard to push through tough efficiency measures in the public sector if he wants to get elected: What a relief it would be to rule in Kazakhstan, whose ruler regularly gets above 90 percent of the vote! But like every other modern leader talking about efficiency in government, Putin also mentions another country even more enviously: China.

THE JOY OF GOOD SOCIAL ORDER

It is the rise of China, more than anything else, that has made the Asian alternative fashionable. It would obviously be wrong to claim that China is merely Singapore writ large. There is the small matter of Communist ideology: China's rulers continue to spout Marxist ideology (even as their children whiz past in Ferraris) and they will never fully embrace the idea of small government. China is also infinitely more brutal: The spoonful of medicine is sometimes applied this time by Rosa Klebb, not Mary Poppins. Above all, there is the size of the Middle Kingdom: Singapore would only just make it into a list of China's twenty biggest cities. With a fifth of humanity within its borders, China is sui generis. It represents a Chinese alternative, not the Asian one.

Yet in terms of direction—and direction matters enormously in China—Singapore plays an outsized role. Deng Xiaoping discovered the Singapore model in the 1980s as he tried to rebuild China after the disaster of Mao's final years. "There is good social order in Singapore," he observed in 1992. "We should draw from their experience, and do even better than them."[23] And ever since then China's leaders have made pilgrimages to Singapore to visit Lee while their underlings, from places like CELAP, have been sent to study in Singapore. China is too proud to describe anything as Asian, but Xi Jinping's "Chinese Dream" makes a nod toward Asian values, just as the regime's previous slogan, "the harmonious society," did. Above all, China's current leadership shares three of Lee's convictions: that Western democracy is no longer efficient; that both capitalism and society need to be directed; and that getting government right is the key to their regime's success and survival.

The success so far is what makes westerners swoon. The one thing that the world's tycoons agree upon when they meet at the World Economic Forum in Davos is that the Chinese state is a paragon of efficiency—especially compared with the fevered gridlock of Washington or the panicky incompetence of Brussels. "Beijing really gets things done," sighs one American chief executive. "Their government people are so much smarter: it's terrifying,"[24] enthuses one of the world's richest men. The Swiss chalets resound with stories of contracts rapidly signed in China, roads speedily built, and young engineers designing brilliant cars and revolutionary software programs.

There is a lot of truth in this. China's rise to greatness is the most remarkable geopolitical story of the past thirty years. It is now the world's second-largest economy, the largest energy consumer, the largest merchandise exporter, the largest foreign holder of American government debt, the largest repository of millionaires and billionaires. It has also achieved the biggest reduction in poverty in history. Government has played a large role in this. The Chinese state (or the Chinese Communist Party: they are basically the same thing) can be ruthlessly impressive when it wants to be. It has presided over breathtaking social transformation without unleashing anarchy. It has even so far done a better job of handling the "capitalist crisis" than most capitalist countries have. Authoritarian China is the only country in which a majority of the citizens approved of their government's response to the financial crisis.[25]

The size of that achievement becomes even more obvious—and difficult for democrats—when you compare it with India. The latter has been a democracy since its foundation in 1947 (indeed, half the people in the world who live in a democracy live in India). It has a vigorous free press and independent judges and auditors. And yet India is still lagging behind China in all sorts of ways, from its rate of growth to the quality of its infrastructure. Having opened up its economy in the 1990s, India has stalled while China has kept on reforming. India's state is simultaneously too big and too weak: too big because it smothers everything in red tape; too weak because it fails to perform its core functions adequately—or indeed at all. Lant Pritchett, of Harvard's Kennedy School of Government, calls it a "flailing state."[26] The quickest way to discover what does not work in India is simply to drink a glass of its tap water. A more cerebral (and safer) one is to look at its higher-education system. In 2000 Indian universities enrolled 10 percent of young Indians, compared with China's 8 percent. Seven years later Chinese universities enrolled 23 percent and Indian universities enrolled 13 percent. In the QS World University Rankings for 2013, not a single Indian university—not even one of the famed Institutes of Technology—made it into the top two hundred.

China's comparative performance, against not just India but also the United States, accounts for its arrogance. Yet there is also fear. Chinese officials know that their country is still much further behind America than people think: If its overall economy may soon be as big as America's, it lags far behind in terms of income per head; if its workers labor for long hours for modest pay, they are still only a twelfth as productive as their American equivalents; if its defense budget is growing fast, it is still a fraction of America's (the Chinese are still rather frightened of Japan's navy); if its soft power is growing in Asia, it lacks America's global web of alliances. For all his dismissal of the West's weaknesses and his belief in Asian superiority, Lee Kuan Yew has no doubt who is in front: He sees China's catch-up as a thirty- to fifty-year task, though he warns that it if it tries to become a liberal democracy "it would collapse."[27]

Perhaps more fundamentally, the Chinese leadership knows that the Chinese state is not all that it is cracked up to be, especially at the local level. This is a country where in the run-up to the Chinese New Year supermarkets sell briefcases with two bottles of whiskey pre-packed inside as a necessary "thank you" to local officials: One Western retailer was furious when sales fell by a fifth in 2013 because Xi Jinping had thundered against bribery.[28] China finishes eightieth in Transparency International's 2012 Corruption Perceptions Index, seventy-five places below Singapore. Indeed, if you look at any of the global measures of comparative effectiveness, the vaunted mandarin state that so impresses Davos man is full of holes: It finished only thirtieth in the World Economic Forum's own Global Competitiveness Report in 2013–14, with lousy marks for bureaucracy as well as graft.

The further you go down the Chinese system, the less impressive it appears. Most Chinese cities make ends meet through landgrabs. They buy property on the edge of town, using compulsory-purchase orders that seldom pay the landowners properly, and then sell it on to developers, who in turn sell on the houses they build to the richer urban middle classes. In 2012 revenue from land-rights sales made up more than half of local-government tax revenue.[29] And public services, such as education, are especially patchy. Yes, the universities are better than India's, but many Chinese complain that they are middle-class bastions, where few poor youngsters get a look-in. Yes, Shanghai hurtled to the top of the OECD's Programme for International Student Assessment (PISA), beating sixty other countries, but most Chinese schools belong to a different world. Investment remains low, even by developing-country standards. *China Youth Daily*, an organ of the Communist Youth League, has observed that China spends five times more on wining and dining local-government officials than it does on educating children up to sixteen.[30] The schools in the countryside can be dismal. They are better in the cities but it still often takes a bribe to get a child

The CELAP cadre-training school in Pudong with its bright red desk. | *Imaginechina*

A Chinese Mandarin—a representative of the first professional civil service.
| *Heritage Image Partnership Ltd/Alamy*

Thomas Hobbes, the intellectual father of the modern Western state. | *Mary Evans Picture Library*

"His satanic free-trade majesty": John Stuart Mill. | *Mary Evans Picture Library/Alamy*

The frontispiece of *Leviathan*, with the king's body composed of his subjects. | *Image Asset Management Ltd/SuperStock*

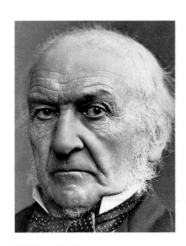

William Gladstone, a small-government liberal, "saving candle ends and cheese paring in the cause of the country." | *Pictorial Press Ltd/ Alamy*

Would Teddy Roosevelt tolerate crony capitalism in today's Washington? | *The Granger Collection, New York*

Beatrice and Sidney Webb, godparents of the welfare state. | *The Granger Collection, New York*

Friedrich Hayek, a stop sign on the Road to Serfdom. | *Hulton Archive/ Getty Images*

Government* spending
% of GDP

	1870	1913	1920	1937	1960	1980	1990	2000	2011
Austria	10.5	17.0	14.7	20.6	35.7	48.1	38.6	52.1	50.7
Belgium	na	13.8	22.1	21.8	30.3	58.6	54.8	49.1	53.3
Britain	9.4	12.7	26.2	30.0	32.2	43.0	39.9	36.6	48.2
Canada	na	na	16.7	25.0	28.6	38.8	46.0	40.6	41.9
France	12.6	17.0	27.6	29.0	34.6	46.1	49.8	51.6	55.9
Germany	10.0	14.8	25.0	34.1	32.4	47.9	45.1	45.1	45.2
Italy	13.7	17.1	30.1	31.1	30.1	42.1	53.4	46.2	49.8
Japan	8.8	8.3	14.8	25.4	17.5	32.0	31.3	37.3	42.0
Netherlands	9.1	9.0	13.5	19.0	33.7	55.8	54.1	44.2	49.9
Spain	na	11.0	8.3	13.2	18.8	32.2	42.0	39.1	45.7
Sweden	5.7	10.4	10.9	16.5	31.0	60.1	59.1	52.7	51.5
Switzerland	16.5	14.0	17.0	24.1	17.2	32.8	33.5	33.7	33.9
United States	7.3	7.5	12.1	19.7	27.0	31.4	33.3	32.8	41.4

Sources: Vito Tanzi and Ludger Schuknecht; IMF; OECD   *1870-1937 central government, 1960-2011 general government

Heading ever upward? | *Courtesy of* The Economist

Milton Friedman meets the Gipper.
| *Courtesy Ronald Reagan Library*

Margaret Thatcher selling off council houses. | *Keystone/Hulton Archive/Getty Images*

Jerry Brown, with Linda Ronstadt and assorted Eagles, in his first term as California's governor.
| © *Chuck Pulin*/Splash News/*Corbis*

An older, wiser Governor Brown watches basketball with Xi Jinping. | © Splash News/*Corbis*

State capitalism in action in Beijing.

| *Imaginechina*

Lee Kwan Yew, the Asian alternative.

| *Mohd Fyrol/AFP/Getty Images*

Mothers in South Korea pray for their children's success in exams. | © *Ahn Young-joon/AP/PA Images*

Sloan's General Motors. | *The Granger Collection, New York*

The Googleplex. | © *Peter DaSilva*/The New York
Times/*Redux/Eyevine*

Devi Shetty, health care's Henry Ford.
| *Manjunath Kiran/AFP/Getty Images*

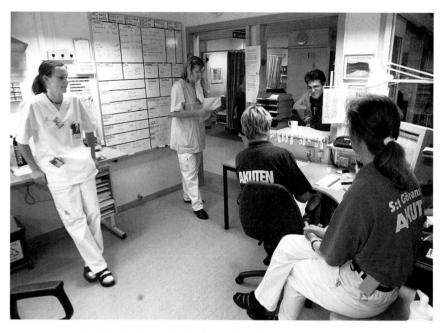

St. Göran's Hospital, bringing total quality management to
public health care | © *Guardian News & Media Ltd 2001*

In France people want pensions to start at
age fifty-five. | © *Michel Euler/AP/PA
Images*

The Tea Party versus big government.
| © *Paul Beaty/AP/PA Images*

Congress has its critics. | New York
Daily News *via Getty Images*

Protesters against government
corruption in Brazil. | © *Andre
Penner/AP/PA Images*

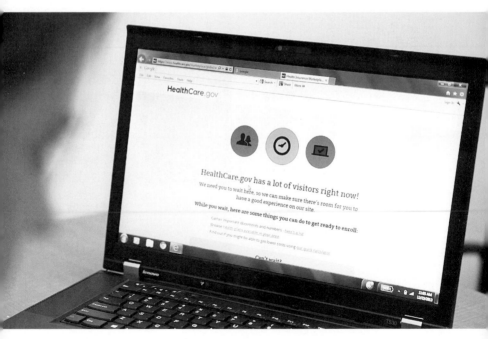

Obamacare: why Leviathan and technology do not always mix. | *Joe Raedle/Getty Images*

into a good school—and a whole class of migrant workers are excluded because the *hukou* system of benefits ties them to their place of birth.

Government in China often seems to operate in two centuries simultaneously. Visitors are awed by the twenty-first-century China of Beijing and Shanghai with their postmodern skyscrapers. But China can also feel like early-nineteenth-century Britain. There is "Old Corruption." The Chinese elite is still trying to restrict the "political nation" to people who have a "stake in society," denouncing reform movements as "hooligans" and using the *hukou* system a bit like the Poor Laws—as an incentive to work harder. There is the Dickensian smog. And there is the massive movement of people from the land to the cities: Close to thirty-five million Chinese made that migration in the first five years of this century (by way of comparison, only thirty million people crossed the Atlantic to America in the century before 1920).

So China is not the paragon some claim. Far from supplying a new model, China's Leviathan is grappling, often in an ad hoc and piecemeal fashion, with this transition. It is at best a clumsy work in process, with highly uneven results. But what matters again is the direction. Rather than trying to solve the whole puzzle, we will look at the two parts of the Asian alternative where China has most obviously tried to follow Singapore, but on a far grander scale: state capitalism and its reliance on a cadre of meritocratic planners rather than democratically elected politicians.

LEVIATHAN AS CAPITALIST IN CHIEF

The headquarters of China Central Television looks like a monstrous space invader striding through the Beijing smog. The headquarters of the China National Offshore Oil Corporation resembles an oil tanker emerging from a shimmering sea and sits directly opposite China's ministry of foreign affairs. All over Beijing state companies are erecting giant monuments to their new power.

The idea of Leviathan guiding business is hardly new. In 1791 America's first treasury secretary, Alexander Hamilton, presented Congress with a "Report on Manufactures," his plan to kick-start the young country's economy. Hamilton had no time for Adam Smith's ideas about the hidden hand. America needed to protect its infant industries with tariffs if it wanted to see them grow up. For better or worse, pretty much every rising economic power has relied on the state to ignite growth. From the East India Company to the Korean *chaebol*, countries have taken what might be described as a team mentality to business. Yet the Chinese have taken it a lot further.

The Chinese state no longer tries to run the entire economy, as it did under unreconstructed communism. It has also deliberately eschewed nationalized industries like the ones that were common in the West before Margaret Thatcher. Instead it controls the "commanding heights" by directing capitalism. The private sector is often not as private as it seems. Some companies, such as Lenovo in computers and Geely in cars, have been given state money. More generally, the party makes sure its voice is represented. The party has cells in most big companies—private as well as state-owned—complete with their own offices and files on employees. (Geely's owner is reportedly the secretary of his own company's party branch.)[31] The party holds meetings that shadow formal board meetings and often trump their decisions, particularly on staff appointments. A newspaper published by the Central Party School expressed the situation pithily in an article about establishing party branches in companies operating abroad: "Where there are people, there are Party organizations and Party activities."[32]

But the main instrument of state direction is the 120 or so state-owned companies that dominate strategic industries. These are nominally separate companies with stakes owned by the state. They have become wealthier and more powerful even as the overall state sector has shrunk: China Mobile has more than 700 million customers.[33] They are overseen by two institutions. One is the State-Owned Assets Supervision and Administration Commission, which holds shares in the biggest companies, making it the world's largest controlling shareholder. SASAC has been spearheading the creation of national champions by pruning its portfolio, reducing it by around a third in the past decade. Yet many state-owned enterprises (SOEs) pay as much respect to SASAC as the provinces pay to the central government, especially when it comes to paying it dividends. By contrast the other control center, the Communist Party's Organization Department, has sharp teeth. Created in the 1920s with Mao Zedong at its head, it is now the world's mightiest human-resources department. It holds files on every cadre in the country, monitoring the careers of highfliers in detail, and appoints all the senior figures in corporate China, routinely moving them with minimal explanation. In 2004 it rotated the heads of the three biggest telecom companies, in 2009 it did the same for the three biggest airlines, and in 2010 it was the three biggest oil companies. In *The Party* Richard McGregor points out that the bosses of China's fifty-odd leading companies all have a "red machine" sitting next to their Bloomberg terminals and family photographs that provides an instant (and encrypted) link to the party's high command.[34]

All the same, the party gives a lot of freedom to the SOEs. They are expected to behave like private companies, competing abroad and using modern management techniques. "Sometimes we find companies doing things inconsistent with China's policies and interests," Ye Lucheng, an assistant foreign minister, has said laconically. "We tell them to stop, but they don't stop."[35] Indeed, the relationship can be the other way around. SOEs can manipulate their political masters. China's oil giants, for instance, have far more influence over energy policy than their American peers. Again, this is the idea: The bureaucrats and managers work toward common strategic goals (normally dominating a particular industry) while leaving the day-to-day operational decisions to the managers.

State capitalism, argue the Chinese, is a learning device. National champions have provided a way for China to pick up skills in different industries, such as cars or electronics. Another big gain, insist the Chinese, comes in talent management. Just as Singapore sends its civil servants into the private sector, the bureaucrats who return from the SOEs know how to run things better. If state capitalism allows politicians to shape companies, it also allows companies to shape politicians. It is "joined-up capitalism," to coin a phrase, unlike its messy Western peer.

China's version of state capitalism has gone global. That is partly because China's companies are going abroad. Across Africa China is in hot pursuit of oil, timber, diamonds, copper, and iron ore while Chinese merchants have been building malls and infrastructure. It has also cut energy deals with Iran and Russia. State capitalism has been at the heart of all this foreign activity. State companies have funded four-fifths of the foreign direct investment. State banks have woven a web of soft loans. And the beauty of state capitalism from the Chinese point of view is that diplomacy and commerce advance together. Now that Gazprom and PetroChina are entwined in various convoluted ways, China has found it much easier to get along with Russia. It is also rebuilding the old Silk Road to the Middle East, becoming both the biggest single importer of oil from the region and the biggest single exporter of manufactured goods to the region.

China is doing more than promoting a web of connections: It is deliberately promoting a model. When foreign officials come to China for training programs, their tutors at places like CELAP now emphasize the virtues of the Chinese model—the way the state can focus on national champions or attract foreign investment into special economic zones or ensure that entrepreneurs join the Communist Party and thereby contribute to political stability as well as economic dynamism. They also compare China's sleek government with America's gridlock and India's chaos. The government has seeded Confucius Institutes in universities across the world and is trying to use the Boao Forum for Asia as an ideological counterweight to Davos. *China Daily*, CCTV, Xinhua, and the rest of the Chinese media follow suit.[36] China even provided the African Union with its new headquarters in Ethiopia.

This soft power is having an effect: State capitalism is back in vogue. For Vladimir Putin and his KGB, this is an easy doctrine to absorb. Two state-controlled companies, Sberbank and Gazprom, account for more than half of the turnover of the Russian stock exchange. In Brazil Dilma Rousseff's government has poured resources into a handful of state champions and produced a new model of industrial policy, often acquiring small stakes in companies. (Sergio Lazzarini and Aldo Musacchio, two academics, have nicely dubbed this model "Leviathan as a minority shareholder."[37]) South Africa has also edged toward interventionism. And even in Europe, there are attempts to reforge industrial policy, with François Hollande and Ed Miliband both prepared to boss around companies and, in the latter case, set prices.

The original version of state capitalism, with its huge nationalized industries, collapsed because it did not work. Will this one do any better? China's new model of state-directed capitalism certainly looks more refined and robust, but it also comes with some serious weaknesses.

The most obvious is the scope for corruption. In September 2013 it was announced that the head of SASAC, Jiang Jiemin, was being investigated for a "serious discipline violation," code for graft. Jiang had previously had a long career at the China National Petroleum Corporation. This may have been politically inspired: He was an ally of Bo Xilai, the deposed mayor of Chongqing. But there are also deeper worries about how well SASAC does its job. In other countries, notably Russia, state capitalism has given way to kleptocracy. The Peterson Institute for International Economics, a think tank, believes that graft and inefficiency cost Gazprom a massive $40 billion in 2011.

Investors have soured on state capitalism. Its high point may have been in 2007 when PetroChina was listed on the Shanghai market—and briefly became the only firm in history to have been worth over $1 trillion. In 2009 six of the ten biggest companies in the world by market capitalization were state owned. Yet by 2013 only one of the top ten was an SOE: PetroChina, which was now worth only a quarter of its peak value. In industry after industry, investors don't trust SOEs. Gazprom is valued at three times earnings, compared with eleven times for Exxon. China's banks and telecom companies are also less prized than their private-sector equivalents, because investors fear that they are being forced by the state to do things, such as build networks or go on lending sprees, that are not in their shareholders' interests.

Even if some Chinese SOEs do well, most of the economic growth in their country is being driven elsewhere. The Beijing-based Unirule Institute of Economics argues that, when you allow for all the hidden subsidies such as free land, the average real return on equity for state-owned companies between 2001 and 2009 was –1.47 percent. Older studies suggest that productivity decreases with every step away from 100 percent private ownership toward 100 percent state-owned.[38] SOEs suck up scarce capital that could have gone to real pioneers like Alibaba, and the state-capitalist system as a whole suppresses innovation. You need intellectual freedom to come up with breakthrough ideas and broader cultural freedom to have vibrant cultural industries. "We have gongfu [martial arts] and we have pandas," says one Chinese commentator woefully, "but we could not make a film like *Kung-fu Panda*."[39] PetroChina was the only SOE to make it into Booz & Company's listing of the world's one hundred most innovative companies.[40]

A fair judgment is that state capitalism's record is patchy. It seems to work better in some industries, like infrastructure building, than others, such as software. Similarly, timing matters. State capitalism can boost a country's growth at one stage of development and impede it at another. It can be a good way for a young economy to bring in knowledge fast, but it is less successful when it comes to getting the most out of limited resources or generating new ideas (which is one reason why China is so bent on cyberespionage). Some of the most far-seeing Chinese bureaucrats argue that SOEs will die a natural death as the Chinese economy matures: They should be understood as staging points on the road to full-blooded capitalism rather than ends in their own right.[41]

The reckoning in the rest of the world is even worse. Authoritarian modernization may have a successful record in Singapore and South Korea. But look at the Arab world: Egypt's state capitalism was an excuse for rent seeking and incompetence (not least on the part of the dozens of companies, accounting for 10 percent of the economy, run by the military). Or look at sub-Saharan Africa: Crony capitalism is lowering growth and increasing inequality. For the state to direct capitalism, you need a strong and competent state—and sadly, most countries that are attracted to it have weak and incompetent ones.

But the Chinese will stick with it. There are state-capitalist banks, billionaires, bureaucrats, and paid-up ideologues. One Chinese analyst, having listed all of the system's manifold inefficiencies, says that its days are clearly numbered: He gives it "no more than 50 years."[42]

FROM MAOISM TO MERITOCRACY

The second prong in the Chinese assault on the Western model is support for meritocracy as an alternative to democracy. Over the past three decades the Chinese Communist Party has gradually replaced its faith in revolution with a new faith, or perhaps a new version of an ancient faith, in an educated mandarinate. The current Chinese elite shares Lee Kuan Yew's feeling that meritocracy can provide the benefits of democracy, such as a regular change of guard at the top, without democracy's vices, such as short-termism and potential social breakdown. Its leaders can think in terms of decades rather than the next election cycle while also preventing the country from disintegrating under the pressure of seismic social change. Chinese history is littered with death and destruction on a massive scale, from the thirteenth-century Mongolian invasion, which took the lives of a third of the population, to Mao's Cultural Revolution. A permanent meritocracy has allowed China to take up challenges democracies shy away from, such as rapidly extending pensions and health care.[43] A few years ago about 80 percent of people in rural China had no health insurance. Now virtually everyone does.

The party's case is that it works hard on making sure that the top jobs go to people of merit. The road to the summit is long and hard: You need to shine at the Central Party School and CELAP, prove your administrative mettle running a province (which might be the size of several European countries), and, increasingly, prove your business acumen by running a state-owned enterprise. The party monitors your performance at every step: Provincial governors are evaluated on their success on a number of measures, such as promoting economic growth and eradicating poverty, and are rapidly downgraded if they fail to hit their targets.[44] The pitch is that this is performance-related government on a continental scale.

To find the Platonic guardians of the future, the party works hard to replenish its lower ranks. These days it is universities rather than factories that are the main recruiting ground for new members. Richard McGregor recalls talking with three students at Tsinghua University, China's equivalent of MIT, in 2009. They reported that "to be a party member is a symbol of excellence" and that "if you are a party member, you will get more opportunities with government jobs." At both the high-school and university levels, positions in the party were offered as a prize for the best students.[45] Daniel Bell, who has been teaching at Tsinghua for almost a decade, notes that 28 percent of undergraduates, 43 percent of graduating seniors, and 55 percent of graduates were party members in 2010.[46] The party has also worked hard to build a bridge to business and now counts a third of the country's entrepreneurs as members. A better name for the Chinese Communist Party would be the National Development Party.

The regime's enthusiasm for meritocracy has deep roots: Chinese parents have been telling their children for more than a thousand years that "those who work with strength are ruled. Those who work with their minds manage others. Those who excel in scholarship become officials." Polling indicates that most Chinese like the idea of being ruled by a wise guardian class.[47] The worship of intellectual prowess helps. This is a country where infant formulas are routinely packaged to tiger moms as "brainpower boosters" and McDonald's Web site features a Professor Ronald who offers Happy Courses for multiplication and language learning.[48]

It is not hard to find examples of the way that bright young people, carefully selected and promoted, are tackling big problems. In Shenzhen a young civil servant called Ma Hong is doing what David Cameron tried to do in Britain: build a "big society" by getting nongovernmental organizations to deliver public services, mainly care for the elderly. She has dismantled most of the controls on local NGOs, so all they need to do is register with her. By mid-2012 she had brought in more than five thousand "social groups" and paid out several hundred million yuan to them to perform social work.[49] All the groups are evaluated by third parties on things like corporate governance: The higher their rating, the more money she trusts them with. By 2012 she had closed down twenty-six NGOs and warned seventy others that their internal standards were not up to par. Already her model is being copied around the country.

Ma epitomizes the businesslike way in which China's best civil servants are trying to tackle social problems. Her starting point is to look around the world at what works. She studied in Hong Kong in 2005 and noted that some 90 percent of social work was done by NGOs, paid for by the state. She is also an admirer of Singapore and has borrowed its balance between easy registration for NGOs and stern punishment for underperformance. She wants her social groups to become the engines of Chinese society, "just as private companies are in the economy."[50] Indeed, she thinks that the public sector needs to be changed in the same way as the private sector, with the state creating the right environment for companies and charities to do more of its work. "We are in a transition from a big state to a small state," she says, "and from a small society to a big society."

All this won Ma her country's most prestigious award for public-sector innovation—and she is typical of a slice of the mandarinate:

global, well informed, and with a long-term plan. But China is a big place. How well does the system work in practice?

The Chinese system can claim two victories: the circulation of elites and a long-term approach. The top three officials—the general secretary, president, and prime minster—now serve a maximum of two terms in office, or ten years. In recent times that changeover has been completely peaceful. The party has put safeguards in place to prevent the reemergence of a Mao-style personality cult. The incoming leader is chosen not by the outgoing leader but by the collective wishes of the senior leaders. Davos man is also right: The top level of the Chinese civil service is at least as efficient as its Western peers.

And just like Singapore's, the leadership does genuinely take a long-term outlook—especially compared with its Western rivals. Not many people in Washington are thinking beyond the 2016 presidential election. It is sometimes argued that an American administration operates strategically for only about six months, at the beginning of its second year—after it has gotten its staff confirmed by the Senate and before the midterms campaign begins. There are plenty of people across Asia who are planning for the long term. Nicolas Berggruen, a philanthropist who has sponsored reform efforts in California, argues that Chinese-style meritocracy is good at focusing on long-term problems and bringing in independent experts. He would like to set up a Western version of this, even if the people concerned are not elected.

But elitism without democracy comes with a lot of problems: problems that are beginning to show up strongly in China today, particularly at the local level. For instance, just around the corner from Ma Hong, Yang Jianchang is having a harder time. He is a deputy in Shenzhen's Municipal People's Congress and the head of the Luohu District Office of Market Supervision (Industrial and Commercial

Bureau), which deals with counterfeiting. He also has a reputation as China's most accountable representative. In 2005 he took the unusual step of opening an office to deal with complaints. People and mail came flooding in, mostly complaining about the government. By 2012 he had taken up three thousand cases on behalf of some twenty thousand people and been threatened, bamboozled, and roughed up for his pains. A particular cause has been migrants, who make up more than ten million of Shenzhen's fourteen million people and find it hard to transfer their *hukou* registrations to the city. Some of the villains and bureaucrats whom he has pursued—for instance, for selling unsafe food—have gone to prison. Many more have not, thanks to the intervention of what people in Shenzhen describe as "powerful interests."[51]

Like Ma, Yang is a proud party person: His office is adorned with pictures of him in his uniform and with citations from various Communist dignitaries. You might imagine that a meritocratic regime on an anticorruption drive would embrace this example of accountable government. Instead, it has banned deputies like Yang from setting up personal offices. (Yang continues his campaign and mail continues to flood in, most of it by registered mail, so people know he has gotten it and will send it on to the right bureaucrat.) This underlines the cloth-eared unresponsiveness of much of China's government to reform. It might be easy for the boss of a large Western multinational to see a senior state official, but for an ordinary Chinese citizen, merely getting a few minutes with a lowly bureaucrat is an ordeal: You need to fight your way past aggressive guards and obstructive assistants whose main function in life is to keep you out. And people are getting angry. Sometimes it boils over—in 2011 in Wukan, another town in Guangdong Province, the citizens even managed to kick out their local government over a disputed land deal. But most of the anger and frustration is less explosive—more similar to the sort of complaints that Yang deals with. And with Weibo, China's equivalent of Twitter, a disgruntled populace has found the perfect forum: It is a stream of moans about public-sector inefficiency, poor schools, untidy hospitals, incompetent officialdom.

Xi Jinping is trying to impose discipline in the provinces, sending out many more people from Beijing. Half of the country's twenty-two governors—most of whom were elected during the 18th Party Congress leadership reshuffle in 2012, which coincided with Xi's coming to power—now have central-government backgrounds.[52] Five years earlier, only two governors had been directly installed by Beijing. A fiscal crackdown is also likely: While the central government's debt is only 22 percent of GDP, the provinces may have debts of at least that amount. But it will be hard to rein them in. In Shenzhen, when departments have been amalgamated, the principal bureaucrats have all kept their jobs, leading to an abundance of deputy directors, all battling for influence. The central government has the clout to compel bureaucrats to act quickly on issues of national importance, such as foreign investment or the SARS epidemic; but on plenty of other issues the local government ignores them. The mountains are high and the emperor is far away, as the old saying goes.

The emperor's court is not quite as meritocratic as the Chinese claim. Many members of the party elite, including Xi Jinping, are "red princelings." And all China's leaders, whether they are princes or commoners, systematically use their power to accumulate wealth and privilege. The *Hurun Report*, a Shanghai-based wealth monitor, estimated in 2012 that the eighty-three richest delegates to the National People's Congress and the Chinese People's Political Consultative Conference, an advisory group, had a net worth of over $250 billion.[53] And that is just the published net worth. In 2012 David Barboza of the *New York Times* demonstrated that close relations of the then prime minister, Wen Jiabao, controlled $2.7 billion in assets.[54]

The perks of privilege cement the entire system together. *Xinmin Weekly* magazine reported in 2012 that China has more than 3.5 million government cars costing about $50 billion and that the government spends about $300 billion annually on overseas travel, cars, and receptions.[55] A popular Internet posting sums up a common perception of the elite: "They drive top-brand cars. They go to exclusive night bars. They sleep on the softest beds in the best hotels. Their furniture is all of the best red wood. Their houses overlook the best landscapes, in the quietest locations. They play golf, travel at the public expense, and enjoy a life of luxury."[56] The children of the party's leaders all seem to find their way to the best schools, both at home and abroad, and thence to the best universities in America and Britain. Bo Xilai's son was educated at Harrow and Balliol College, Oxford. He was even awarded a place at Harvard's Kennedy School despite the fact that his tutors at Balliol refused to provide him with a reference: He spent his time at Oxford socializing and playing politics in the undergraduate Conservative Association.[57]

It would nevertheless be a mistake to dismiss entirely China's claims to be a meritocracy. The system's faults are not unique to China. If Hillary Clinton wins the presidency in 2016, the list of American presidents since 1989 will read Bush, Clinton, Bush, Obama, Clinton. Ivy League universities are dominated by the children of the rich and well connected. Democratic India suffers from similar problems of nepotism. The Congress Party has been a Nehru-Gandhi family firm since independence. In 2009 almost a third of India's parliamentarians had a family connection to politics—and dynasticism is more marked among the younger generation than the older one. All the MPs under thirty had "inherited" their seats and two-thirds under forty had inherited them.[58]

So the verdict on China's meritocracy is the same as on state capitalism: They are both good in parts. They have allowed China to take a long-term view in a way that very few Western governments do. Both run the risk of corruption—more than their Western equivalents do. And what is relatively easy to discipline in Singapore becomes unwieldy in such a large country. Four of China's provinces would be among the world's twenty most populous countries.

RECKONING WITH THE BEIJING CONSENSUS

What does this amount to? The Asian alternative is undoubtedly the most substantial challenge that the Western model has ever faced: far more substantial than the old Soviet Union (or Maoist China, for that matter). In China authoritarian modernization has guided the country through an astonishing period of material progress. And in the process it has succeeded in legitimizing itself in the eyes of the average Chinese. The Pew Global Attitudes Project 2013 Survey showed that 85 percent of Chinese were satisfied with the country's direction. This was the highest level of satisfaction of the countries surveyed: By comparison America scored 31 percent.

China's success has produced a widespread reassessment of the relative merits of the Beijing and Washington consensuses. Thomas Friedman, the West's best-known writer on globalization, has revised his catechism: "One-party autocracy certainly has its drawbacks. But when it is led by a reasonably enlightened group of people, as China is today, it can also have great advantages."[59] Martin Jacques has asked what things will be like *When China Rules the World*.[60] Even John Williamson, the man who coined the term "Washington Consensus," admitted that the Beijing consensus was rapidly gaining ground on his brainchild. In the wake of the financial crisis it is the Chinese who are doing the lecturing about government, not the Americans. "When other countries want to learn from China they should first of all adopt a similar form of government," advised Wang Jisi.[61] Another Chinese intellectual, Zhang Weiwei of Fudan University, has turned the tables on America and argued that its political system is dooming it to decline. The electoral system is throwing up second-rate presidents like George W. Bush. The welfare system is imposing unsustainable burdens on the economy. There was a time when people who lost the election simply accepted defeat. But now polarization is so advanced that they devote themselves to undermining their opponents. According to Zhang, the world is seeing a competition between two different political models—one based on meritocratic leadership and the other on popular election—and "the Chinese model may win."[62]

But China's next phase of development will be much more difficult than the last. The growth rate is slowing as China becomes richer: The leadership's Great Firewall shows how nervous it is about public opinion.[63] The regime is also painfully aware that its legitimacy is performance related. It needs to keep the economy growing, to be sure. But it also desperately needs to deliver better health care and education. The China dream put forward by Xi Jinping includes an implicit promise that the state will help look after its people better than it has done—just at a time when China is starting to age. China already has only five workers for every old person, and by 2035 the ratio will have fallen to two. An ever-increasing demand for services, lousy demography, and an inefficient state: China's future may be more Western than it imagines.

The same probably goes for the Asian alternative more generally.

Even if they admire the Singaporean model and start with relatively restrained welfare states, all the other Asian governments are likely to come under pressure to expand their services, not least from aging populations. By 2030 Asia, excluding Japan, will account for over half of the world's elderly and about half of the global burden of noncommunicable diseases, like cancer and diabetes. And as they get richer, Asians are showing disturbingly Western signs of wanting a more generous safety net. Across much of Asia, welfare promises win votes, and temporary programs, like Thailand's scheme in 2009 to help poorer workers deal with the credit crunch, have tended to become permanent. As one of our colleagues has noted: Asia's "tigerish economies are turning marsupial, carrying their dependents along with them as they prowl."[64]

The chances are that many Asian countries will thus become more Western. Lee Kuan Yew's vision of small-state authoritarianism will become less clearly defined. But Asia will still be notably different for three reasons. First, most of the region's governments have seen what has happened to the West: Indeed, that is the bit of Lee's "Asian values" lectures that other Asian leaders pick up on most. And second, because the Asians are starting afresh, technology does give them opportunities to leapfrog to better social systems: It is much easier to build a smart card–based system of benefits from scratch than if you have countless software systems already. There are some promising signs that Asia is being inventive—and we will look at many of them in the rest of this book.

That points to the third reason why Asia still feels like an alternative: It is trying. Even if Lee's Asian-values lectures turn out to be bunk and Xi's China dream becomes a nightmare, there is patently far more thinking going on about how to improve government in Singapore and Beijing than there is in Rome or Washington. The lesson of history is that when countries compete to produce better government, they tend to raise standards. If you want to look at the future of higher education, can you learn more from the United States and France, where 40 percent and 25 percent of the students drop out,[65] or from South Korea, which beats the world in college enrollment? If you want to set up a pension system, would you look at America's Social Security system or Singapore's Central Provident Fund?

These are not hard questions to answer—and they do not reflect well on the West. But there is one big exception to the idea that the West is the past—one even Asians bring up. Dominique Moïsi, a French writer and intellectual, has a nice story about visiting Oslo in 2010 (the same year the Norwegians gave the Nobel Peace Prize to a prominent Chinese dissident, Liu Xiaobo). At every ministry and think tank he visited he found the same group of Chinese bureaucrats, scribbling furiously. Eventually it was politely explained to him: "Norway is the future of China."[66] That might be pushing it. But the Chinese are right to be looking to the Nordic world as well as Singapore for enlightenment.

PART THREE

THE WINDS
OF CHANGE

CHAPTER SEVEN

THE PLACE
WHERE THE FUTURE
HAPPENED FIRST

FOR MOST OF THE TWENTIETH CENTURY Sweden was the closest thing to a socialist paradise: the Fabian dream in Nordic dress. Enlightened bureaucrats built the *folkhemmet,* or "people's home," where the state looked after everybody's needs and blond bureaucrats organized everything along rational lines, right down to the correct design for your kitchen. Meanwhile socially responsible companies like Volvo and Ericsson generated wealth. This was "the middle way" between capitalism and communism, celebrated by Marquis Childs in his 1936 book of that name. Sweden even had its own version of the Webbs in Gunnar and Alva Myrdal, who championed economic planning, eugenic breeding, and men sharing the housework.

But in the 1960s, as the concept of equality broadened, Sweden veered even further left than the rest of Europe. It abolished selective education in the name of "child-centered learning" (i.e., letting teenagers run riot) and advocated the equalization of incomes in the name of social solidarity. The answer to every problem was always the same: more government. Public spending as a share of GDP nearly doubled from 1960 to 1980 and peaked at 67 percent in 1993. The public sector added more than a million new workers between 1950 and 1990 at a time when the private sector added no new net jobs whatsoever. And the answer to the question of how you paid for all this government was equally unvarying: higher taxes. In 1976 Astrid Lindgren, the creator of Pippi Longstocking, received a tax bill for 102 percent of her income and produced a fairy tale about a writer, Pomperipossa, who gave up producing books for a carefree life on the dole, providing economists with a new phrase, the Pomperipossa effect.

The Social Democratic Party, which ruled the place for forty-four uninterrupted years from 1932 to 1976, kept squeezing business with higher taxes and more regulations. "The era of neo-capitalism is drawing to an end," said Olof Palme, the party's leader, in 1974. "It is some kind of socialism that is the key to the future." That was also the year that Gunnar Myrdal was given a Nobel Prize in economics, sharing it, in a bizarre twist of fate, with Friedrich Hayek. Eight years later Alva won the Nobel Peace Prize for her work on disarmament. By 1990 it would be hard to think of anywhere that more perfectly illustrated Lee Kuan Yew's dismissive "all you can eat" state.

Yet look around now. Sweden has reduced public spending as a proportion of GDP from 67 percent in 1993 to 49 percent today. It has also cut the top marginal tax rate by 27 percentage points since 1983, to 57 percent, and scrapped a mare's nest of taxes on property, gifts, wealth, and inheritance. With the rest of Europe sunk in debt it shines as a beacon of fiscal rectitude: Its government has bound itself in a financial straitjacket where it must produce a fiscal surplus over the economic cycle. Its public debt fell from 70 percent of GDP in 1993 to 37 percent in 2010, and its budget moved from an 11 percent deficit to a surplus of 0.3 percent over the same period. This allowed a country with a small, open economy to recover quickly from the financial storm of 2007–8. Its budget deficit has climbed to 2 percent of GDP, but its public debt is still below 40 percent.

The change in thinking is even greater. The streets of Stockholm are awash with the blood of sacred cows. The local think tanks are overflowing with fresh ideas about "welfare entrepreneurs" and "lean management." Indeed, Sweden has done most of the things that politicians know they ought to do but seldom have the courage to attempt. It has put its pension system on a sound foundation, replacing a defined-benefit system with a defined-contribution one and making automatic adjustments for longer life expectancy. It has reinvented its state as well as reducing its size. The Swedes have done more than anyone else in the world—certainly more than the cautious Americans—to embrace Milton Friedman's idea of educational vouchers, allowing parents to send their children to whatever school they choose and inviting private companies or voluntary groups to establish "free" schools, that is, schools that are paid for but not run by the state. In Stockholm half the schoolchildren go to independent schools. In the country as a whole almost half have opted out of their local schools (so they go either to another one, farther away, or to an independent school). More than 60 percent of independent schools are organized as profit-making institutions: Most are small businesses of one to four schools, but a few belong to big chains such as the International English School.

St. Göran's hospital in Stockholm provides an excellent example of Sweden's willingness to apply new thinking to the most sacred part of the welfare state, health care. From the patient's point of view, St. Göran's is no different from any other public hospital. Treatment is free, apart from a nominal charge, which is standard throughout Sweden, to stop people from abusing the system. But St. Göran's has been run since 1999 by a private company, Capio, which is now owned by a consortium of private-equity funds, including Nordic Capital and Apax Partners. The doctors and nurses are Capio employees, answerable to a boss and a board. And behind the scenes the atmosphere is very different too. Doctors talk enthusiastically about borrowing "the Toyota model of production" and improving "flow" and "quality." Doctors and nurses used to keep a professional distance from one another: Now they work (and sit) together in teams, just like the Japanese car firm's employees. Everybody looks for methods of improvement. One is a series of magnetic dots to keep track of each patient's progress and which beds are free. Another is discharging patients throughout the day rather than in one batch, so that they can easily find a taxi. For all the talk about Toyota, St. Göran's feels most like the medical equivalent of a budget airline. There are four to six patients to a room, and the decor is spartan. But the focus is on reducing waiting times and increasing "throughput," which also has the added advantage of reducing the number of diseases that are picked up in hospital.

All these numbers, like the success rates of operations, are public data, so they can be checked by both patients and taxpayers. Sweden has been a pioneer in health registries, which provide statistics on the performance of individual hospitals. Fear of coming out badly in a national league table is a powerful incentive to try harder. A study by the Boston Consulting Group found that Sweden's National Cataract Register not only reduced the severity of astigmatism resulting from eye surgery but also narrowed the variance between the best and worst hospitals by half. St. Göran's has done well. Stockholm County Council, which had been thinking of closing the hospital in 1999, recently extended Capio's contract until 2021.

St. Göran's is at the front of a broader revolution. Its chief executive, Britta Wallgren, an anesthesiologist by training, likens her hospital to a hare that sets the pace of a greyhound race. Swedish health care is now arguably the most efficient in the rich world. The average length of a hospital stay in Sweden is 4.5 days, compared with 5.2 days in France and 7.5 days in Germany. Its efficiency also means that it needs fewer hospitals. It has 2.8 hospital beds per thousand citizens. France has 6.6, Germany 8.2. Yet by virtually any measure of health, the Swedes do well: They live longer lives than most people in the developed world. And their economic health has soared too. In 1993 the Swedes were poorer than the average Briton or Italian. After two decades when growth and productivity have surged ahead of their European competitors, they are ahead again.

The other Nordic countries have been in the same health spa, albeit working out less vigorously. All four Nordic countries have AAA credit ratings and debt loads significantly below the eurozone average. Denmark has ushered in a series of reforms, raising its pension age from sixty-five to sixty-seven and pioneered a system of "flexicurity": Companies can sack employees with almost American ease but the government helps displaced workers get new jobs. It also has added a useful twist to education reform, allowing parents to "top up" public vouchers with (limited) cash of their own. This is creating a flourishing market, particularly in Copenhagen, ranging from academic schools for traditionalists to religious ones for Muslims to experimental ones for children of aging hippies. And it has also become a leader in what some call the intelligent state. The Danes are ahead in the transition to both e-government and the cashless economy. Locals boast that they pay their taxes by SMS. Instead of ordering wheelchairs from the same old provider, Denmark is now asking companies to come up with broader "mobility solutions" in the hope that this will spawn a new industry. Not all these innovations work: A fat tax, which was supposed to "nudge" people into leading healthier lives, had to be withdrawn. But like the Swedes (and the Singaporeans), the Danes are experimenting—attempting to preserve what is best about their welfare state while trying new ways of delivering services.

So far the experiment seems to be working remarkably well. The Nordics dominate indices of social inclusion as well as competitiveness and well-being. They have exceptionally high rates of female labor-force participation and the world's highest rates of social mobility.[1] They continue to pride themselves on the generosity of their welfare states. About 30 percent of their labor force works in the public sector, twice the average in the OECD. They continue to believe in combining open economies with public investment in human capital. But the new Nordic model begins with serving the individual rather than expanding the state. It begins with fiscal responsibility rather than pump priming. It begins with choice and competition rather than paternalism and planning: Both Denmark and Finland are now ahead of the United States in the economic-freedom index run by the Fraser Institute, a Canadian think tank, and Sweden has been catching up. The old ratchet has been reversed: Rather than extending the state into the market, the Nordics are extending the market into the state.

I HAVE SEEN THE FUTURE AND IT IS BLOND

The Nordics are important for three reasons. First, they are the part of the West that has hit the future first: They ran out of cash before everybody else did. Second, they settle one of the central debates about Leviathan: whether it can be brought under control at all. For the past century, there has seemed no escape from Baumol's disease and the demographic burden of an aging society. The Nordics show what can be done. Third, they have only just started to exploit the powers of technology: There is, we think, much more to come. One of Bismarck's favorite phrases was that politics was "the art of the possible." The Nordics are a good starting point for revising the view of what is possible.

The Nordics reached the future first. They were forced to change because their old model went bust, and they kept on changing once they discovered that they could produce a better state. Looking back, Sweden's revolution had several stages. The 1970s and 1980s were marked by growing frustration. The more Swedes got used to exercising choice in IKEA and H&M, the more frustrated they became at having to queue up for the government's one-size-fits-all offerings. Free-market ideas also began to creep into the country, through think tanks such as Timbro and business organizations like the Employers' Federation. In 1983 the Left overreached itself in a particularly foolhardy way. The Social Democrats considered nationalizing the commanding heights of the economy by using trade-union funds to purchase shares in Sweden's biggest companies. This was too much even for Palme and prompted a huge march of about 100,000 businesspeople on parliament, known as the "march of the executives."

So there were cracks in Sweden's model well before the 1990s. But the main reason why it changed was collapse. In 1991 Sweden was plunged into what was known locally as the "black-of-night crisis": The Swedish banking system seized up, foreign investors lost confidence in the third way, and mortgage rates briefly rose to 500 percent. Carl Bildt's conservative government seized on the crisis to put through a succession of radical reforms, including sharp cuts in public spending and radical changes in the way public services were delivered. In retrospect, Sweden was fortunate that it was cutting when other economies were doing well and external demand was high. But it was all done in a very Swedish way, with the government trying hard to generate consent. A commission of wise men was asked to produce a blueprint of change and came up with 110 policy proposals for freeing the economy and reforming the political system.

The other Nordics were also forced to change by similar upsets. Denmark faced a "potato crisis" in the early 1980s, so called because people thought that they might be reduced to living off potatoes. Norway and Finland endured bone-jarring financial crises in the early 1990s along with Sweden. Finland's crisis was particularly serious because the collapse of Soviet communism killed its most reliable market (the free market for two left shoes is limited). But the crisis was more than just a cash crunch. The old Nordic model depended on the ability of a cadre of big companies to generate enough money to support the state; by the 1990s the likes of Ericsson and Volvo faced global competition. The old model also depended on people's willingness to accept direction from above, but Nordic populations had become more demanding. A paternalist welfare state cannot survive in a postpaternalist society. The Nordics had overloaded their state.

Around the world, plenty of other governments now face the same problem the Nordics did in the 1990s. The Western state has made promises it cannot hope to keep. More interesting, though, is the reason why the Nordics kept on going: Once they started redesigning their government, they found that it worked.

Many of the reforms have produced not just cheaper government but better government. Denmark's system of "flexicurity" has helped preserve a skilled workforce while ensuring that Denmark escapes from one of continental Europe's biggest problems: a dual labor market divided between heavily protected insiders and casual outsiders. Vouchers in Sweden have produced not just cheaper schools but better ones. Anders Böhlmark and Mikael Lindahl examined data for all Swedish schoolchildren between 1988 and 2009 and found that increasing the share of "free" schools in a particular district leads to better performance on a variety of measures, from school grades to university attendance.[2] The biggest gains are recorded in the regular public schools rather than in the "free" schools.

That should give us some hope as we review the Western state. Albert Jay Nock concluded his 1935 book, *Our Enemy, the State*, by insisting that "simply nothing" can be done to stop the growth of government. And as we have seen, supporters of small government have had a bad 150 years. Politicians have repeatedly tried to reverse the growth of government. They have sometimes even succeeded for a while. But even small cuts require heroic efforts: Witness the Sturm und Drang of the Thatcher and Reagan era. And after brief periods of retrenchment the bloat resumes: Witness George W. Bush's splurge. It has been hard not to believe that the iron law of modern politics is that government will go on getting bigger.

Elephantiasis has been complemented by lousy productivity. For years consultants have been touting the virtues of management efficiency and computerization, but so far they have not had much impact. Reorganization has produced demoralization and new computers have become white elephants. Britain's Office for National Statistics calculates that productivity in the private-service sector increased by 14 percent between 1999 and 2013. By contrast, productivity in the public sector fell by 1 percent between 1999 and 2010. Alan Downey, the head of KPMG's public-sector practice, points out that if public-sector productivity had increased at the same pace as private-sector productivity, the British government could have provided the same services for £60 billion a year less—a sum almost exactly equivalent to the structural deficit.[3]

The Nordic countries provide strong evidence to the contrary: that it is possible to contain government while improving its performance. St. Göran's is a model in improving service and productivity. The question is: How far can you take that? Pessimists come up with all sorts of objections. Surely the Nordics are too small—a collective population of only twenty-six million? Surely they just started with a huge state sector, so there were plenty of easy savings to make? In the end, they argue, there is no way round Baumol's disease and the rapid aging of society.

Our argument is precisely the opposite: that the Nordics are just the beginning. In the twentieth century technology tended to focus power and supersize administration. In the twenty-first century it will increasingly push in the opposite direction. Technology will not only shrink government but make it better too. In the twentieth century good government reforms were repeatedly undone by the special interests. In the twenty-first century it is getting easier for good-government types to harness the common interest. That does not mean that the state is bound to slim. But the main claim of this chapter is that it is at least possible.

BAUMOL REVERSED?

William Baumol's central argument was that the mechanisms that boost productivity in the manufacturing sector do not extend to the service sector. Thankfully, there is mounting evidence that what he regarded as a "disease" is in fact a case of technological lag. The digital revolution has already transformed large sections of the service sector, such as retailing, and the intellectual sector, such as journalism and book publishing. It will soon transform education and medicine by applying similar labor-saving techniques.

Baumol's favorite example of a string quartet in fact increasingly proves the opposite: that the price of first-rate services is falling dramatically. It may still take four people to produce a live performance of a Beethoven string quartet. But the gap in sound quality between a live performance and a recording is shrinking. And access to first-rate recordings is getting much cheaper. With an MP3 player and ten-dollar-a-month subscription to Spotify you can not only listen to a string quartet without any of the coughing and spluttering of a concert hall, but you can listen to any Beethoven recording that you want when you want and where you want, not to mention pretty much every recording ever made.

What is true about music is also true about government. There are now opportunities to reverse the Baumol effect. Take the example of the star college lecturer. Hitherto, productivity in education has indeed been limited by how many people you can get into a room. Technology is now changing that. Why pay thousands of dollars a year to go to a college to listen to second-rate lectures when you can watch a video of a global superstar for nothing? In America a tenth of university students now study exclusively online and a quarter do so some of the time. Harvard University has seen students spontaneously organizing study groups in which they watch TED Talks and discuss them among themselves. Leading universities such as MIT, Stanford, and the University of California at Berkeley are already putting their lectures and course materials online. The University of the People offers free higher education (not counting the few hundred dollars it costs to process applications and mark exams). Measurement Incorporated has developed technology that enables a computer to grade student written papers, including essays.[4]

People have often exaggerated technology's ability to transform education. Thomas Edison forecast that motion pictures would replace college lecturers. There was a time when correspondence courses were seen as the future: By 1919 around seventy American universities were sufficiently worried about it that they set up their own versions. There have been successes, like Britain's television-based Open University, but they have not changed the nature of education. However, there are signs that education is now going interactive. This revolution is not limited to advanced education.

New technology encourages more efficient teaching methods. Schoolteachers can "flip the classroom": record their bread-and-butter lessons so that students can watch them at home and then use the classroom for personal instruction. It even provides personal tutoring for nothing. In 2004 Salman Khan made a series of videos and posted them on YouTube to help tutor his extended family. The videos soon acquired millions of fans (including Bill and Melinda Gates, who used them to tutor their own children): Khan is an excellent tutor and you can stop and rewind the videos if you want to go over the material again. The Khan Academy now serves more than four million students a month, ranging from the children of billionaires to the children of day laborers, and provides more than three thousand lessons ranging from simple arithmetic to calculus and finance.

Look around the public sector and there are similar opportunities beginning to open up everywhere thanks to technology. In nearly every case it comes down to the same things. It can make workers more productive; it can spread information, so that people can see how good their school or hospital is; and it can put more power in the hands of ordinary citizens. Technology is making it easier for ordinary people to come together to solve collective problems, often bypassing government in the process. Ride sharing is a way to reduce pressure on public transport. Road pricing makes it easier to price a public good. Indeed there are opportunities right across the public sector.

Very quietly, the delivery of services in the public sector has gotten a lot more efficient in what was its original core area. The main reason for the existence of the state, according to Hobbes, was to provide law and order. Even the toughest philosophical radicals thought that the state should protect people from crime. What else is a night watchman for? Doing that job has traditionally been one of the state's most labor-intensive activities. It has also been an activity that conservatives have exempted from their demand for a lean state. On the contrary: Conservatives have been in the forefront of pointing to the dangers posed by superpredators and feral criminals and of demanding more bobbies on the beat. Even Margaret Thatcher quailed before the police unions. This is the field that Don Novey exploited brilliantly in California.

Yet in the developed world the crime rate has fallen dramatically since about the mid-1990s (the starting point of the trend varies from country to country). In England and Wales 86,000 cars were stolen in 2012. The figure in 1997 was 400,000. There were 69 robberies of banks, building societies, and post offices in 2012. In the 1990s the average was 500 a year. The number of violent crimes in America has fallen by 32 percent in the country as a whole and by 64 percent in the big cities.[5]

The reason for this? Many on the right would claim tougher sentences. That does not really stand up: The crime rate has fallen just as quickly in places that no longer throw as many people in prison. A more solid reason is decline in the supply of criminals: Most crime is committed by young men, and the number of young men is going down. The main reason, however, seems to be an improvement in our ability to prevent crime. This has very little to do with bobbies on the beat and a great deal to do with smarter technology.

Some of this technology is being used by the police. They can use computers to discover crime "hot spots" and distribute their forces accordingly: In some parts of Manhattan this has helped reduce the robbery rate by over 95 percent.[6] They are using CCTV cameras (which are ubiquitous in Britain and spreading elsewhere) to keep an electronic eye on the public and mobile-phone location to track down miscreants. They are also using DNA databases (which can easily be searched by computers) to identify criminals. But the biggest reason is that technology is putting more crime-fighting power in the hands of ordinary people. Intelligent devices are getting cheaper. Even small shops invest in CCTV and electronic tags. Alarms are ubiquitous. Cars are harder to steal because of central locking and car immobilizers. Banks are harder to rob because of bulletproof screens and marked money.

It is possible that technology may even substitute for human labor in Hobbes's other great state function, fighting wars. Armed drones can kill high-value targets. Armed robots can fight on the battlefield alongside regular soldiers—or perhaps take their place completely. Microdrones can detect intelligence through video surveillance or by sniffing out chemical and biological weapons. Unmanned ground vehicles can detect explosives. Robots not only save people from danger. They can also do things that people find impossible, such as lifting tanks, surviving explosions, and surviving for days on end without food or water. The U.S. Army has no fewer than twelve thousand robots serving in its ranks, including tiny "insects" that perform reconnaissance missions and giant "dogs" to terrify foes. The Pentagon is also working on the Energetically Autonomous Tactical Robot (EATR), which fuels itself by eating whatever biomass it finds around it. Robots will increasingly invade other areas of the public sector—offering the chance to radically reduce costs while improving efficiency.

THE FUTURE IS GRAY, NOT RED

But won't any gains from treating Baumol's disease be wiped out by demography? By 2030, 22 percent of people in the OECD club of rich countries will be sixty-five or older, nearly double the share in 1990. China will catch up just six years later. An aging society is going to bury the state in two ways: First, entitlement costs for pensions will rise hugely; and the spread of chronic diseases will put an ever-greater burden on the least efficient part of the public sector, health care. The Nordics show that this need not be the disaster that it appears.

It would be unrealistic not to expect health-care costs to come under pressure from an aging society. It may also be the hardest part of the economy in which to reverse the effects of Baumol's disease. But that does not mean it is impossible. We will look at the possible gains to be had from introducing technology to health care in the next chapter: We think a revolution could be under way where ever more health care is done by nondoctors—nurses, patients, and even machines. But as St. Göran's shows, it is quite possible to provide health care more efficiently without all those new additions. The Swedes are far ahead in two areas. One is their use of hospital registries, showing how well each part of their system treats different ailments. The other is the small fee every hospital charges each time you visit it: A small fee helps stop the buffet welfare state that Lee Kuan Yew identified.

For some purists on the Left, that is a denial of the great promise of institutions like the National Health Service: that they would always be free at the point of delivery. The Swedes are far more practical. Those promises were made when health care was far more basic. It is not in society's interest that hospitals be overused. By changing the benefit slightly, they can keep it more open to all.

The Nordics have taken the same attitude to entitlements. In 1998 the Swedes introduced a radical new approach to pension financing in order to keep the pension system from going bankrupt and avoid severe tax rises. They changed the system to make it less of a defined-benefit system and more of a defined-contribution system. They introduced an element of privatization by allowing Swedes to put some of their pension money into a private system. Today more than half of the population has, at some point, actively chosen to participate in the private market (the money for those who choose not to participate goes automatically into a state-run investment fund). And the Swedes raised the retirement age to sixty-seven and introduced an automatic mechanism that raises retirement age along with life expectancy. They installed a circuit breaker that kicks in when the economy is in recession: Pensions go down if the economy can't afford them.

This was all done on the basis of a cross-party consensus: The Swedes recognize that the "people's home" can only survive if it manages its household finances responsibly. They also continue to worry away at the problem. The government has appointed a "Commission on the Future" that is trying to grapple with the implications of an aging society. At the very moment that François Hollande, in one of the most irresponsible exercises in pandering in recent years, restored France's retirement age to sixty, Fredrik Reinfeldt, Sweden's prime minister, suggested that the Swedes will need to work until they are seventy-five.

Other sensible countries are doing likewise: Britain has raised its retirement age to sixty-eight, and America is raising its to sixty-seven, with various provisos. Delaying retirement has a triple benefit: It reduces outgoings by saving government money on pensions, increases incomings by getting workers to pay in for longer, and boosts the overall productive power of the economy. The biggest reason for retire-

ment was that human bodies got worn out by hewing wood and drawing water. But people are living longer and healthier lives. The Urban
Institute, a think tank, calculates that 46 percent of jobs in America
make almost no physical demands on their workers whatsoever.[7] And
there is ever more evidence that older workers can be useful, with
studies showing entrepreneneurial activity peaking between the ages
of fifty-five to sixty-four.[8] Ray Kroc was in his fifties when he began
building the McDonald's franchise system while Colonel Harland
Sanders was in his sixties when he started the Kentucky Fried Chicken
chain. Forty years ago it was assumed that rockers would fade away
before they got old. Despite a lifetime of gloomy prognostication and
complaints about "aching in the places where he used to play," Leon-
ard Cohen spent his seventy-fifth birthday onstage in Barcelona.

HAVING YOUR CAKE AND EATING IT

More than most big issues these days the debate about the state assumes a zero-sum world: The Left invariably argues that "cutting"
government will hurt the poor while the Right argues that expanding
welfare services will damage the economy. But there are in fact lots of
cost-free ways to improve the state. Getting rid of agricultural subsidies is one simple way: Abolishing the modern equivalent of the Corn
Laws would produce an immediate gain by reducing public spending
while raising the economy's growth potential. The Victorian liberals
made a particular target of "Old Corruption." Today it is another example of how government can be cut without damaging basic services.
A surprising amount has already been achieved. In the early 1990s
graft was treated as a fact of life, an inevitable cost of doing business
in some countries. There were no international laws devoted to getting

rid of it and no civil-society organizations dedicated to fighting it. Germany even allowed its corporations to deduct their foreign bribes from their taxes, and France and Great Britain did the same thing a little more subtly. Since then the laws have tightened significantly, with a growing number of bribery acts. Thirty-eight countries have now signed up to the OECD's 1997 anticorruption convention, and a host of big companies have been prosecuted, including Germany's Siemens and Britain's BAE Systems. And technology has made it much easier for organizations like Transparency International to draw attention to graft.

Nobody would claim that corruption has been defeated. Indeed, in Russia and China there has been what Moisés Naím has called a "corruption eruption" as they have joined the global capitalist economy. But the simple fact is that in many Western countries bribery is no longer tolerated in the way that it once was. The example of corruption is powerful evidence against the idea that the only way to balance the books is on the backs of the poor. It is possible to change.

That also is the broader lesson from Sweden. The Nordic model is no more perfect than the Singaporean one. In 2010 Sweden was seized by a scandal about an old people's home run by a private-equity company. The press filled with stories about how old people were being consigned to a "house of death" while private-equity executives hid their ill-gotten gains in the Channel Islands. There is still a strong undercurrent of nostalgia for the old world of social solidarity and proud egalitarianism. Perhaps more rules will be introduced. But ordinary Swedes will not go back to a system in which the state told them where to send their children to school. And the Swedish government will not deprive itself of the money and expertise of the private sector.

For all its faults the new Swedish system is in fact a highly successful update of the old middle way. Sweden continues to act like a "socialist" country in that it provides public goods such as health and education free at the point of delivery. But it uses "capitalist" methods of competition to ensure that those public goods are delivered as successfully as possible.

Both Sweden and Singapore demonstrate something beyond doubt: Government can be made slimmer and better. The dire warnings of William Baumol and other economists are misplaced: There is no reason to assume that government reform is a doomed enterprise. It is not a zero-sum game. But how should reformers go forward? There are two answers to that question. The first is practical: Everybody, whether from Left or Right, could make their governments work better. The second is ideological: It requires people to ask just what they want government to do. Our next two chapters look at how this revolution will proceed on those two fronts.

CHAPTER EIGHT

FIXING LEVIATHAN

IN 1930 GENERAL MOTORS WAS the most admired company in the world: a masterpiece of centralized decentralization. Alfred Sloan, the company's boss, sat at the apex of a pyramid of managers who oversaw everything from the purchase of the raw materials to the administration of car loans. But at the same time he gave lots of operational freedom to the company's various divisions in their quest to produce cars for "every purse and purpose": Cadillac for the rich, Oldsmobile for the comfortable but discreet, Buick for the striving, and so on. Silent Sloan, as he was known, understood far better than his noisier rival, Henry Ford, that the source of competitive advantage was changing: from selling people their first car to selling them a replacement and from one big revolutionary idea, streamlining production, to another, relentlessly improving the whole process. He liked to boast that his profession was management.

Today there is plenty of competition for the title of the world's most admired company, but Google would appear on any list. To Sloan, Google's headquarters in Mountain View, California, would look more like a kindergarten than an office, with its primary colors, Ping-Pong tables, and pods for napping. But there is nothing kindergartenish about the company's success: Google has grown from an inspired hunch of two Stanford students in 1998 to a veritable Googlezilla that controls 80 percent of all searches online, dominates online advertising, and is even promising to revolutionize Sloan's old business with the driverless car. Only 1 percent of applicants to the company are given a job. They work much longer hours than the GMers of old (who, to Sloan's disapproval, were not averse to three-martini lunches and leisurely golf games), and to keep them at work, Google provides them with everything they need, from dry cleaners and masseurs to Wi-Fi–equipped company buses.

Since Sloan's day, companies have rethought almost all the great man's assumptions about management. They have replaced steep hierarchies with fluid networks. They have taken to contracting out all but their core functions. Sprawling conglomerates are out and focused specialists in. And they collaborate on even core functions like innovation: Procter & Gamble, once as self-contained as GM, now gets more than half of its ideas from outsiders. But above all companies are constantly on the move—rethinking what they do and then rethinking the rethinking. It is not so long since Nokia and AOL were the companies of the future and people talked about taking pictures with a Kodak. Ten years ago Facebook did not exist and Skype was an Estonian start-up. In Sloan's day, jobs were for life and age brought seniority. He ran GM for two decades. The tenure of the average American CEO has halved over the past two decades to around five years. Lower down the chain, people move on even more quickly: The average length of job tenure in the American retail sector, which now employs far more people than manufacturing, is closer to three years.[1] The new high-tech firms usually employ a slither of their industrial predecessors. Some 145,000 people worked for Eastman Kodak in its heyday. When Facebook paid $1 billion for Instagram in April 2012, a few months after Kodak filed for bankruptcy, the photo-sharing firm was only eighteen months old and employed just 13 people.[2]

Three forces have turned the corporate world upside down. The first is embodied by Google itself: technology. It took telephones seventy-one years to penetrate half of American homes, electricity fifty-two years, and television three decades. The Internet reached more than half the population in a mere decade.[3] Now Google is experimenting with super-high-speed connections that operate more than a hundred times faster than regular broadband.[4] The second force is globalization. Sloan's GM was upended by the Japanese, not Ford or Chrysler. Fast-growing emerging markets are throwing up global companies, such as China's Huawei in telecoms. Even Africa is leapfrogging ahead of the West, as Kenya is doing with "mobile money" (using cell phones to make payments). The third force is consumer choice. Henry Ford's world, in which you could have a car in any color so long as it was black, has been replaced by a rainbow of choice. Cable-TV companies offer hundreds of channels. Amazon offers you a selection of a million or more books and can deliver the next day. "One size fits all" is giving way to the "market of multitudes," as Chris Anderson puts it.[5] The customer is not so much a king as a tyrant.

All this has made the art of management even more important. For all their faddishness, management techniques make a significant contribution to productivity. Nothing illustrates this better than General Motors: Detroit stumbled in the 1970s because Japanese car companies like Toyota adopted an American management idea, lean production, and the Americans only revived when they learned lean production from their Japanese rivals. Even now when companies watch one another like hawks management can make a big difference: Two economists, Nick Bloom of Stanford and John Van Reenen of the London School of Economics, have demonstrated that companies that use the most widely accepted management techniques, of the sort that are taught in business schools, outperform their peers.[6]

THE FOUR TERRIBLE ASSUMPTIONS

Government's problem is that it is stuck in the age of Sloan's GM. Even people inside the belly of the beast know it. "We live and do business in the Information Age," Barack Obama once complained, "but the last major reorganization of the government happened in the age of black-and-white TV."[7] The core problem is not a lack of computers or money but a complete inability to catch up. The public sector has not budged thanks to four assumptions, all of which would have made sense to Sloan's GM but make no sense in the age of Google.

The first is that organizations should do as much as possible in-house, just as carmakers once smelted their own steel. At its most extreme, that means the state having a monopoly over everything that might conceivably touch on the public interest. That was the version that triumphed in the Soviet bloc and largely perished there too. But the softer version—that the state should do as much in-house as possible—is still with us. This imposes enormous costs: It has institutionalized powerful producer lobbies such as the teachers' unions at the heart of the welfare state and crowded out private and voluntary organizations from the public sector.

The second assumption—that decision making should be centralized—also dates back to the midtwentieth century, when central governments drew up blueprints for the welfare state. In the United States the New Deal and the Great Society increased Washington's power over the states so radically that Everett Dirksen, a senator from Illinois, quipped that soon "the only people interested in state boundaries will be Rand-McNally."[8] There are times when the state's ability to centralize power is crucial: when a country is attacked by an enemy or convulsed by a huge crisis. But the logic that helped FDR breathe life into the American economy or enabled France to rebuild after the Second World War does not seem to work quite so well when it comes to running universities or providing welfare.

The third assumption is that public institutions should be as uniform as possible. Bureaucrats have a professional penchant for uniformity: Exceptions mean anomalies and anomalies mean confusion. For much of the twentieth century this seemed in tune with the times. The success of mass production convinced people as different as Beatrice Webb and Dwight Eisenhower that the secret to efficiency in government lay in transforming everything into cogs in a great machine. And the cult of equality suggested that the state's duty was to make sure that nobody was given less than their fair share thanks to ill luck or class prejudice. But today this emphasis on uniformity seems out of date in a world of flexible production and consumer choice.

Few things are more uniform about the public sector than its workforce. It is certainly diverse when it comes to race and gender, usually because of laws it has itself set. But it is depressingly uniform when it comes to attitude and experience. The public sector is dominated by people who believe that they have a job for life and that they are scandalously underpaid (both sometimes true). Promotion is linked to age. Fast-tracking is the exception rather than the rule. The private sector is now global: A third of British companies are run by foreigners and it is more than a decade since the English premiership was won by an English football manager. But national civil services have remained national.

In some countries, the uniformity extends to the whole ruling class. In theory France is very good at shuffling people between the private and the public sector; but, as in China, it is the same clique of people, notably the elite set of *énarques* from the École Nationale d'Administration, who do the shuffling. There is a wonderful picture of the "Voltaire year," the 1980 graduating class of ENA, that includes four of the people who ran for president in 2012, including the eventual winner, François Hollande, as well as his former partner, Ségolène Royal, who was the Socialists' defeated candidate in 2007, and the bosses of the financial-markets regulator, the huge AXA insurance empire, and the Paris Métro.[9] Of six hundred-odd French senior bosses, 46 percent come from one of three *grandes écoles*, including ENA, according to research by two academics.[10]

The final assumption is that change is always for the worse. If the public sector has a motto, it is "Never do anything for the first time." You get ahead by following the rules, keeping your head down, and keeping the show on the road. In the public sector innovation is what gets you into trouble—often the only thing that will get you the boot. Trying to change the system can lead to congressional inquiries and tabloid witch hunts. The greatest comedy about the public sector, *Yes, Minister*, is about resisting change: Sir Humphrey, the civil servant at the heart of the show, sees his job as preventing his bumptious boss from implementing any of his harebrained schemes: "Yes" is always a prelude to "no." Tony Blair complained that public-sector workers "are more rooted in the concept that 'if it's always done this way, it must always be done this way' than any group of people I've come across."

This helps explain the huge variance in performance. In the private sector in the Google age, a new technology or idea is copied in months. In the public sector there are startling differences among the performances of different systems. McKinsey has calculated that some

Western countries spend 30 percent more than average on a student getting a college degree without any gain in quality while others spend 70 percent below it without any loss. The variance is not just among countries but within them. McKinsey estimates that the achievement gap in education between America's low-performing states and the rest costs the country up to $700 billion a year or 5 percent of GDP.[11] Sir John Oldham, an expert in health productivity, points to two similar adjacent areas in southern England where "unscheduled admissions" to hospitals (i.e., the expensive sort) vary by a factor of eight. He also points out that there is a thirteenfold difference in the number of hospital referrals from similar doctors' practices. Merely bringing the costs of the most spendthrift hospitals down to the mean level of the entire NHS would save somewhere close to the £15 billion that the coalition government asked the health service to save over five years.

Far from closing these gaps, there is some evidence that governments are getting even more sluggish. It took America four years to build the Golden Gate Bridge, starting in 1933, and fifteen years to build the bulk of the Interstate Highway System, starting in 1956. As Philip Howard points out, a project to build a wind farm near Cape Cod has already been under scrutiny for a decade while seventeen agencies studied it, and it could well be under scrutiny for another decade, while eighteen lawsuits wind their way through the courts.[12] Governments are devoting ever more resources to fulfilling inherited obligations rather than investing in the future. The Steuerle-Roeper index of fiscal democracy in America measures the percentage of revenues that are available for discretionary spending (i.e., that are not already allocated to mandatory programs such as Social Security and Medicare). The percentage has fallen from almost 70 percent in 1962 to about 10 percent in 2012—and the line is headed yet further down.

IT IS ACTUALLY RATHER DIFFICULT

Put in these terms it can sound as if making government more effi-cient were simply a matter of will: Bring in some decent managers from Google and things will be fine. But there is one final reason why government has remained half a century behind the private sector: It is actually extremely difficult to reform—indeed usually more diffi-cult than private business.

The record of businesspeople in government is pretty lousy. That is sometimes because the people themselves are egotists bent on only protecting their own business interests. Italians have repeatedly voted for Silvio Berlusconi in the hope that he could use his skills as a busi-nessman to revive a sclerotic economy. Well, *si monumentum requiris, circumspice.* Berlusconi was prime minister of Italy for eight of the ten years between 2001 and 2011. During that time Italy's GDP per head fell by 4 percent,[13] the worst growth record in the world apart from Haiti and Zimbabwe, and both its debt and its taxes rose as a propor-tion of the economy. On the other hand, the greedy old lecher did— just—manage to stay out of jail.

Another media mogul, Michael Bloomberg, by contrast made a proper go of government. He was reelected twice as mayor of New York and enjoyed astonishingly high levels of popularity. But he says that he had not realized how different running a city would be from running a company:

> People are motivated by different things and you face a much more intrusive press. You cannot pay good staff a lot of money. . . . In business you experiment and you back the proj-ects that win. The healthy bits get the money, and the un-

healthy bits wither. In government the unhealthy bits get all the attention because they have the fiercest defenders.

Almost everything is harder in government. As a media tycoon Bloomberg could measure how many terminals a salesman in Japan had sold. But how do you measure what a teacher does in the classroom? In particular, how do you measure the spark of genius that makes Mr. Chips truly exceptional? Many of us can remember teachers who made a profound impression on us. Many of us can also remember teachers who were dull and lazy. But how do you develop a system of measurement that punishes the latter without crimping the former? Exceptional teachers often break all the rules to make their points, so any system that confines them to following a set formula is likely to be self-defeating. This is not an excuse for giving up on measurement: There are plenty of areas in the private sector where productivity is hard to measure, including journalism. But we need to recognize that fuzziness is a significant problem in much of the public sector.

There are also big philosophical reasons why governments are less efficient. Governments are very different entities from private companies—and citizens are very different creatures from customers. Governments cannot get rid of difficult citizens in the way that companies can get rid of difficult customers. They have to stop us from doing things we might want to do, like building a skyscraper in our back gardens, because they have to balance our desires against those of our fellow citizens. They also have to force us to do things we do not want to do, like wearing a seatbelt or even fighting in a war. Governments have no choice about a lot of what they do. They have to make continuity an absolute priority: They cannot just stop providing border security for a few weeks. Nor can they apply one set of rules to one citizen and another set of rules to another just on a whim.

And their slowness is not always a bad thing—for example, when you're deciding whether to go to war or whether to convict somebody of a crime on disputed evidence. James Q. Wilson might be engaging in hyperbole when he says of the American government that "it is not hyperbole to say that the constitutional order is animated by the desire to make the government 'inefficient.'"[14] But he is right to argue that citizens have deliberately constrained governments' freedom of action in all sorts of ways to prevent them from riding roughshod over their peoples. Joseph Nye says that Americans do not really want their state to work too well: "There is something special about government. It has coercive power, so it is essential that you have a healthy skepticism of it."[15]

WHY THIS TIME COULD BE DIFFERENT

There have been dozens of attempts to fix government in recent decades. George W. Bush claimed to have a "management agenda" based on his reading of Peter Drucker. Al Gore had a plan to "reinvent government." Ronald Reagan appointed the Grace Commission to reduce government waste. Jimmy Carter championed lean government. These plans have invariably come to nothing or run out of steam. So why do we think that the public sector may now be on the verge of radical change? Why after so many disappointments might it be different this time?

The most obvious reason is the fiscal crisis: Governments in many places are running out of cash in the same way that the Swedes did two decades ago. The other reason also goes back to the Nordics: Government could be done much better.

There is lots of room for efficiency improvements. A succession of governments have managed to trim the state without embracing any big ideas. They have just turned the tap off. That was how Canada did it a decade ago and, for all the rhetoric about the Big Society, it is broadly the way that David Cameron's government has gone about it in Britain: With their budgets cut, local councils have suddenly found that they can share facilities without the public noticing much. The "cuts" that so worry public-sector unions are puny compared with the sort of pruning that regularly takes place in the private or voluntary sectors. (One of us attended a private dinner in Paris where a group of French businesspeople listened politely to a politician complaining about the fact that his department had had to reduce its costs by 5 percent in real terms. Then one businessman pointed out that he had knocked out a fifth of his costs in a little over two years—and not, he acidly noted, just in real terms. The politician shut up.) It does not take a business genius to tell you that contracting fifty-five separate companies to work on healthcare.gov, the Web site at the center of Obamacare, was not a clever idea.[16] And forcing tax-dodging citizens to pay their taxes or making better use of government's procurement power is just common sense. For instance, Britain's National Audit Office claims that the NHS could save £500 million, or well over $800 million, a year by bundling its buying power: There is no need for hospital trusts to buy twenty-one different forms of A4 file paper and 652 different kinds of surgical gloves.

Still, improving your purchasing of A4 paper or surgical gloves can only get you so far. Serious reformers also need to change both what the state tries to do and how it goes about doing it. In the next chapter we will look at the deep philosophical questions about what we believe the state should do. In this chapter we will focus on whether the state can do what it already does better. And here, things are finally beginning to change.

Globalization and technology, the forces that have transformed the private sector, are beginning to transform the public sector too, spreading more efficient versions of government. To show how, we will focus on the part of Leviathan that is both most associated with government sluggishness and most likely to bankrupt it: health care.

The prospect of ever more sick people demanding ever more health care haunts governments everywhere. About half of American adults already have a chronic condition, such as diabetes or hypertension, and as the world becomes richer the diseases of the rich are spreading. But health care is slow to change. Whereas America's overall labor productivity has increased by 1.8 percent annually for the past two decades, the figure for health care has declined by 0.6 percent each year, according to Robert Kocher of the Brookings Institution and Nikhil Sahni, until recently of Harvard University.[17] There are also powerful interest groups that make a comfortable living out of the current high-cost model. Five of the seven largest lobbying organizations in Washington, D.C., are run by doctors, insurance companies, or drug firms.

THE HEART OF THE MATTER

One of the most striking things about comparing modern statecraft with modern management is how parochial statecraft can be. Globalization rules the corporate world: Managers are constantly learning from one another. Governments can learn too but they tend to do it in phases—Fabianism before and after the First World War, privatization in the 1980s. Now there is another surge of ideas, with some of the most interesting coming from the most unexpected places.

Just as Detroit used to sneer at Japan's tinny cars, American doctors associate Indian hospitals with backwardness and dirt. The Indian government spent just 1 percent of its GDP on health care in 2012. India is chronically short of medical staff: It has just 1.6 doctors, nurses, and midwives for every 1,000 people, below the 2.5 level the World Health Organization recommends, let alone the dozen that is the norm in America and Britain. India's infant mortality rate is three times higher than China's and seven times higher than the United States'. Yet when it comes to rethinking health care, India is one of the most innovative places in the world, typified by Devi Shetty, an entrepreneur who has built a chain of hospitals from nothing and a man whom America's surgeons may one day remember in the same way that American engineers think of Kiichiro Toyoda.

Shetty is India's most celebrated heart surgeon, famous for performing the country's first neonatal heart surgery on a nine-day-old baby and for counting Mother Teresa among his patients. But his greatest claim to fame lies in applying Henry Ford's management principles to health care. Shetty's flagship Narayana Hrudayalaya Hospital in Bangalore, India's technology capital, has 1,000 beds compared with an average of 160 beds in American heart hospitals. Shetty and his team of forty-odd cardiologists perform about six hundred operations a week in a veritable medical production line: No Western hospital comes close. Like Henry Ford, whom Shetty repeatedly cites as an inspiration, he holds that economies of scale and specialization can radically shave costs and improve quality. The sheer number of patients allows his surgeons to acquire world-class expertise in particular operations, while the generous backup facilities allow them to concentrate on their specialty rather than wasting their time on administration. Surgeons perform an average of four hundred to six hundred operations a year compared with one hundred to two hundred in the United States; Shetty himself has performed more than fifteen thousand heart operations. Richer patients pay more so that poorer ones can get heart operations for free, but the fees are far lower because of that scale: The hospital can perform open-heart surgery for $2,000 compared with about $100,000 in America. Yet the success rate is as good as in the best American hospitals. And Shetty is trying to bring ever more Indians into his system, sending "clinics on wheels" to nearby rural hospitals to test for heart disease and setting up a health-insurance scheme with various local self-help groups that covers 2.5 million people for a premium of about eleven cents a month each and generates about a third of his patients. Despite catering to so many poor people for practically nothing, the whole enterprise produces healthy profits.

Shetty's empire is spreading. His group has built three other hospitals next to the heart clinic—a trauma center, a 1,400-bed cancer hospital, and a 300-bed eye hospital—that share central facilities such as laboratories and blood banks to drive economies of scale. It is also establishing "medical cities" in other parts of India. Shetty plans to increase the number of beds he has at his disposal by 30,000 over the next five years, making Narayana the largest private-hospital group in India and giving it more bargaining power when it negotiates with suppliers, thus driving down costs further. Shetty, who trained at Guy's Hospital in London, also wants to take his ideas abroad. He has established video and Internet links with hospitals in India, Africa, and Malaysia so that his surgeons can give advice. And he is building a 2,000-bed hospital in the Cayman Islands that will offer Americans heart operations for less than half of what they would pay in the United States.

Shetty is one of a group of Indian entrepreneurs who are focusing on applying mass production to health care. LifeSpring Hospitals has reduced the cost of delivering a baby to forty dollars, a fifth of the cost at comparable local hospitals. The Aravind Eye Care System offers surgery to about 350,000 patients a year, around 70 percent of the number of eye operations offered by Britain's NHS, for 1 percent of the cost. Operating rooms have at least two beds, so surgeons can swivel from one patient to the next. Aravind has exported its training model to about thirty developing countries. Meanwhile, another Indian eye outfit, VisionSpring, a social enterprise, uses a franchising model to provide retailers in thirteen countries with what is in effect an eye business in a bag: all the equipment they need to diagnose and correct farsightedness.

A decade or so ago these Indian pioneers would have been nothing more than an interesting sideshow to health-care reformers in the West. Today their ideas are gaining traction as governments everywhere look to save money. Reform, a British think tank dedicated to reforming the basic building blocks of the welfare state and with close ties to Downing Street, has championed Shetty and Aravind. Clayton Christensen of the Harvard Business School, perhaps the world's most respected writer on innovation, thinks the public sector will be upset by what he calls "mutants"—new organisms spinning out of it. The point about the mutants is that they come from anywhere.

Christensen's mutants can dethrone powerful producer groups. The Indian health-care revolution is not only about mass production. It is about rethinking the role of doctors. For the past century health care has been centered on doctors—no operation can be performed and no prescription filled without them. They run the medical profession and they have done very well out of their position: In America almost half the people in the richest 1 percent are medical specialists, a fact that somehow escaped the Occupy Wall Street movement. To get that trusted role in society, doctors require a lot of training: A minimum of seven years, not counting four years spent in university. In America more than 80 percent of graduates leave medical school with debt, owing an average of $150,000.

Doctors' central (and lucrative) role in the health-care system is now under threat.[18] Patients are not as happy to sit and listen to a man whose sometimes outdated advice they can second-guess on the Internet. Meanwhile, people who have not qualified as doctors, ranging from nurses to smart machines, can do a lot of the more routine work, especially for the chronic diseases, which, according to McKinsey, eat up 60 percent of global health-care spending. Physician's assistants in America can do about 85 percent of the work of a general practitioner, according to James Cawley of George Washington University. But doctors are keen to defend their patch. When America's Institute of Medicine called for nurses to play a greater role in primary care in 2010, the American Medical Association, the main doctors' lobby, poured cold water on it: "Nurses are critical to the health care team, but there is no substitute for education and training." The Confederation of Medical Associations in Asia and Oceania, a regional group of doctors' lobbies, wants "task shifting" limited to emergencies.

In fact, task shifting is exactly what needs to be done—and India will play an outsized role in this revolution for two reasons. First, it has no real choice other than to give nondoctors a bigger role: Britain has 27.4 doctors for every 10,000 patients. India has just six. Second, its health care is so rudimentary that it is a tabula rasa. It can experiment. Aravind employs six "eye-care technicians" for every surgeon in order to perform the many jobs that do not require a surgeon's training. More than 60 percent of the company's workforce consists of "village girls" who admit patients, keep medical records, and generally help doctors. L.V. Prasad Eye Institute hires and trains high-school graduates to work as "vision technicians" who do some of the work of optometrists. India's health ministry has proposed a new three-and-a-half-year degree that would let graduates deliver basic primary care in rural areas. That was immediately blocked by India's doctors. But a pilot program of rural health-care workers in India—the type that the health ministry and Shetty want to expand—found that the workers were perfectly able to diagnose basic ailments and prescribe appropriate drugs.

India is also the command center of the other great attack on medical inflation: the soaring cost of medical devices. Not far from Dr. Shetty's hospital, General Electric is pioneering an innovative new design-cum-manufacturing technique that is reducing the cost of medical equipment by up to 90 percent. The company's Mac 400—a handheld electrocardiogram (ECG) machine—is a good example. The ECG sells for one hundred dollars, half the cost of a conventional ECG, and provides ECG tests for just one dollar per patient. GE has reduced the cost by getting rid of all the unnecessary bells and whistles that add to the cost of traditional ECG machines. The multiple buttons have been reduced to just four. The bulky printer has been replaced by a simple ticket machine. The whole thing is small enough to fit into a small backpack. GE is now taking these "Indian" devices into the United States, particularly into rural areas.

Ideas are not just traveling in one direction. Many emerging countries are looking at Britain's NHS as a possible model for their own countries. A single-payer system (where the government offers to cover everyone) has several attractions to big countries like China, India, Mexico, and South Africa, which currently have patchy health-care systems and large groups of unemployed people (who cannot be reached by insurance). Emerging governments are also enthusiastic about using general practitioners to act as gatekeepers and prevent patients from clogging up hospital waiting rooms or pestering specialists. Niti Pall, a doctor from Birmingham, has set up a social-enterprise company with former NHS colleagues to deliver around 150 primary-care practices to Indian cities, modeled on British GP services.[19]

The flow of ideas is not limited to health care. For instance, when it comes to welfare, Brazil is now playing the same role that India is in hospitals. That is mainly thanks to Bolsa Família, a successful "conditional cash transfer" system that gives money to poor families, provided that they do things, such as sending their children to school or taking them for health checks. The program is cheap, about 0.4 percent of GDP, but it has had a big effect on inequality because it encourages people to change their behavior.[20] The Bahia state government has created Citizen Assistance Service Centers that offer a range of public services, from issuing IDs to providing medical help, in convenient places such as shopping malls or on trucks that travel to remote places: welfare states on wheels, as it were.

Maybe India's heart hospitals and Brazil's welfare trucks will deliver less than they promise. But they both symbolize the biggest change of all: the importance of public comparison. The leader here has been the Programme for International Student Assessment (PISA) standards in education. One British minister privately calls PISA the single biggest instrument for reforming schools. For all its faults—and measuring the quality of China's schools by focusing on Shanghai was certainly one—it shows people in America, Britain, and France that their schools are much worse than those in Finland, South Korea, Japan, and Canada. The Finns saw the whole world beating a path to their door when they came out on top. American parents now know that their children are almost exactly as good at math as Slovakian ones are, even though their government spends twice as much on schools as the Slovakians do. That seems a reasonable point to raise with America's teachers' unions. An American reformer, Amanda Ripley, used the PISA rankings as the starting point for her influential 2013 book, *The Smartest Kids in the World and How They Got That Way*, following American teenagers who spent a year on exchange programs in Finland, South Korea, and Poland (which has recently leapfrogged over America in the PISA rankings). Ripley's American students were surprised by how hard their host students worked, how little they relied on calculators, and how strictly the schools followed tests. None of the smart-kid countries thought it was clever or compassionate to coddle students who underperformed, as America does.

Citizens are beginning to understand that other governments are doing some things much better. Ideas are crossing borders—and they are getting there partly thanks to the other great force that reshaped the private sector and is beginning finally to have an impact on the public sector: technology.

FIXTHESTATE.COM

Asked to talk about how technology affects productivity, Peter Thiel, the venture capitalist who backed Facebook, draws a simple graph on his whiteboard: input on the y-axis, output on the x-axis. He then dabs on two blobs. The private sector goes in the bottom right: You put in relatively little and get out a lot. Government goes in the top left: a lot of input and very little output. Thiel, a prominent libertarian whose passions include "seasteading" and space travel, may be unsympathetic to the public sector, but his chart is not a bad guide to the past forty years or so. Technology has lamentably failed to change the public sector. Billions have been spent on new computers with, outside the armed forces, very little impact on efficiency. In 1958, when the first primitive computers were being deployed, it cost the

UK tax authorities about £1.16 to collect £100 of tax. Today, with computing power cheap and ubiquitous, it costs £1.14.[21]

Many of the worst technological foul-ups have involved health care: The rollout of Obamacare turned into a debacle because the Web site was plagued by glitches. Only six people succeeded in signing up for Obamacare on the site's first day in operation. For the past twenty years, health departments have spent fortunes on PCs, without fundamentally changing the way they work: Most of the new gadgets were in effect slightly faster typewriters or virtual filing cabinets. They certainly did little to reduce paperwork. America's semiprivate insurance system involves far more form filling than Europe's nationalized ones. Technology in the form of new drugs has simply meant more expense. Dreams that robots and machines could remove human error have proved equally unfounded: Patients want to talk to real people.

But the maxim that people always overestimate the effect of a technology in the short term but underestimate it in the long term may well apply to the public sector. Take those robots. Just as drones have helped the armed forces, machines will allow doctors to be more precise, making incisions more neatly than human hands can—and even to do it at long distance: As long ago as 2001 doctors in New York used robotic instruments under remote control across the Web to remove the gall bladder of a (rather brave) woman in Strasbourg. Or take those banks of computers and jumbles of health records. Just as computers are now allowing companies to make connections and target services at consumers ever more accurately, so "Big Data" could also allow health departments to personalize medicine.

The biggest change maker of all, however, is the Internet. Naming and shaming is gradually coming to health care in the same way it has to education, with doctors' organizations and public hospitals playing the same role as teachers' unions, denouncing any attempt to assess their performance as simplistic. To the rest of us it does not seem un-reasonable to know how much money a hospital spends, how quickly it deals with its cases, and what the chances of somebody coming out of it alive are. That is the reason why Sweden's health registries are likely to spread.

The Internet is also making monitoring chronic diseases much easier. Already tiny sensors attached to your body, or inside it, can report to your doctor (or his computerized surrogates) your insulin level—and flag problems. That not only means you need to see your doctor far less often; it also reduces the chances of a chronic condition drifting into an emergency. In Britain a randomized trial of remote monitors examined six thousand patients with chronic diseases: Ad-missions to the emergency room dropped by 20 percent and mortality plummeted by 45 percent. The Montefiore Medical Center in New York has reduced hospital admissions for older patients by more than 30 percent by using remote monitors to check patients.

The monitoring revolution plays into what some call the self-help revolution, a movement that is well summed up in a slogan coined by disability-rights activists, "No decision about me without me." Alco-holics Anonymous has a superb record of helping people deal with al-coholism. Now the Internet is spawning the creation of hundreds of new groups, such as PatientsLikeMe, that help people who suffer from serious physical illnesses swap information and social support. Again the savings from making patients more responsible for their own health are enormous: A study by the Wolfson Institute of Preventive Medicine found that about 43 percent of British cancer cases were caused by "lifestyle and environmental factors." The fewer heavy smokers and drinkers there are in a society, the cheaper its health-care bills.

More generally, Web-based collaboration is allowing people to do

for themselves what government used to do for them. Finland has created a digital platform so that volunteers can help digitize the national
library; the Danish government has opened up its tax records so that
outside academics can work on problems like inequality that the state
would otherwise have to pay for itself. Estonia has coordinated a remarkable attempt to rid the country of unsightly junk: Volunteers
used GPS devices to locate over ten thousand illegal dumps and then
unleashed an army of fifty thousand people to clean them up. FixMy
Street.com allows Britons to report potholes in the road or burned-out
streetlamps. Boston has an app that allows Bostonians to take a photograph of a problem—offensive graffiti or a hole in the road—and
send it to the city with the GPS data attached, which then generates
a work order for the public-works crew. Another app, SFpark, helps
drivers in San Francisco find parking spaces ("Circle less and live
more"). Manor, a town in Texas, has launched "Manor Labs," which
rewards locals when their suggestions for improvement are taken up.
Prizes include a ride-along with the police or a chance to be mayor for
a day. These reforms frequently prove self-perpetuating: When the
mayor of Washington, D.C., Vincent Gray, asked Washingtonians to
produce new "apps for democracy," he received forty-seven Web,
iPhone, and Facebook apps in thirty days.

This is only the beginning of a huge "Copernican revolution" (to
borrow a phrase from Matthew Taylor, one of Tony Blair's advisers)
that is putting the user at the center of the public-sector universe. The
current centralized state has been shaped by the idea that information
is in short supply: It derives its power from the fact that it knows lots
of things that ordinary people do not. But information is now one
of the world's most abundant resources: available in huge quantities
and accessible to anyone with a computer or a smart phone. As Eric
Schmidt, Google's chairman, and Jared Cohen, who worked for Hil-

lary Clinton, point out in *The New Digital Age*, this changes the nature of the relationship between individuals and authority. The top-down state may become more like a network that can mobilize the energies and abilities of thousands or even millions of well-informed citizens—or "prosumers," as one cyberguru, Don Tapscott, has called them.

There is another side to this. A more networked state will surely expect those newly empowered citizens to take more responsibility for their behavior. Government will increasingly nudge people in the same way that private insurers do. Discovery Group, a South African firm, uses smart cards to monitor how often people go to the gym and what sort of food they buy. It is not hard to imagine Lee Kuan Yew doing that. Why not chivvy parents to get their children to school on time? Why not expect homeowners to protect their property? The most telling example of the new emphasis on responsibility is rubbish collection. A few years ago most of us threw our rubbish in the bin and forgot about it. Now we divide it up into different categories according to whether it can be reused.

THE JOY OF PLURALISM

As globalization and technology begin to change the balance between the government and the governed, some people think they can see a clear pattern. One is Tony Blair: "The modern Western state was created in the era of mass production and command and control, where governments told you what to do and provided everything. Modern life is about choice—and the state, even if it pays for something, should not be the only choice." He argues that creating "a post-bureaucratic state" with a small center and a multitude of public and private providers should be a particular cause for the center-left to embrace. "In every other walk of life a citizen gets services from bodies that are anxious for their business. We have to open up the state to transparency and competition, or else anyone who is rich enough will pay to opt out." Blair has no truck with the idea that the public sector is bound to keep growing. The key, he thinks, lies in breaking the state down into smaller and more innovative units, like charter schools in America and academies in Britain. "As more and more choices are made by consumers, not politicians, we will shrink the state," he predicts.[22]

This is all very much a work in progress, as Blair admits. But if you look at each of the main assumptions behind the old state, they are beginning to be challenged. The desire to control everything is giving way to pluralism, uniformity to diversity, centralization to localism, opacity to transparency, and *immobilisme*, or the resistance to change, to experimentation. The state is beginning to move in each case (though it could move a lot faster). We will look at each in turn, starting with pluralism.

As we have already seen in Sweden, there are huge gains to be had from a government being agnostic about who delivers a public service. It does not have to be the state. That may sound commonsensical; but inside government "the purchaser-provider split" is revolutionary because it injects competition into the state's vital organs. States have, in fact, always thought like this in emergencies: When the British army was about to be marooned at Dunkirk in 1940, no trade unionist questioned whether it was right to outsource the job of rescuing the troops to a flotilla of private boats. And many overtly left-wing governments in continental Europe, including those in France and Germany, have long used private hospitals to look after public patients. New Zealand and Australia increasingly treat senior civil servants as high-powered executives who are in the business of striking performance deals with competing providers. In the mid-1970s the American public sector—federal, state, and local combined—devoted 40 percent of all outlays to government workers. Today that share has fallen to 29 percent.[23] The split is also producing a new class of global companies that specialize in providing public services, like Britain's Serco Group, which runs prisons at home, driver licensing in Canada, and air-traffic-control centers in the United Arab Emirates.

There are two objections to pluralism. One is ideological: There are still many on the left who care more about how a service is provided than about whether it is any good. But the Left will eventually have to decide whether it is on the side of the minority of public-sector workers or the majority of citizens. The serious objection is practical: The purchaser-provider split does not always work as smoothly as people would have hoped. Contracting things out can make life even more complicated. You need new managers to choose the providers and a layer of regulators to check that they do that right. The new British Rail is broken into a hundred different pieces—different companies run different regions and own different bits of the infrastructure—so that it is hard to know whom to blame if anything goes wrong (which it frequently does). One reason why American health care is such a mess is that so much of it is contracted out: The state ends up paying for a lot of it—most obviously through tax breaks—but seldom directly. Collaboration with the private sector can be messy. Some of the worst abuses by American forces in Iraq were by private-security firms. And measurement is hard to do well. How do you stop a school from weeding out difficult pupils in order to boost its results? The wrong measurement system can be fatal. In Britain's Stafford Hospital between 400 and 1,200 more people died between 2005 and 2008 than actuarial science would have predicted because the managers were so obsessed with hitting targets that they routinely neglected patients.[24]

But these are reasons to make the system work better, not to abandon it altogether. Contracts need to be written properly and contractors supervised vigilantly.[25] Measurement systems need to be designed sensitively. Citizens need to be given as much information as possible about how the various contractors are performing, as they are in Sweden. Governments are getting better at using things like performance-related pay to control private companies: The British government has made 10 percent of Serco's income from running Doncaster Prison conditional on reducing recidivism by 10 percent. The best regulators of the public sector are citizens themselves: This argues for giving them more information about what is going on and more choice about where "their" money is spent.

THE CHARM OF DIVERSITY

The second big change, not unrelated to the first, is that the state is becoming less uniform. It is increasingly prepared to tolerate different sorts of organizations within the "public sector," organized according to different sorts of principles and staffed by different sorts of people.

The most striking example of institutional diversity is in education. In America there are about five thousand charter schools educating about 1.5 million students. These charter schools vary from "back to basics" academies to progressive schools to vocational schools. In Britain half the schools are largely autonomous "academies." The government is pushing the academy model further. Groups of parents and teachers can establish "free" schools, which are, in essence, publicly funded educational start-ups.

Diversity of schools within the public sector is a good thing in itself. If there are technical schools for the technically minded and "fame" schools for the theatrical, it increases the likelihood that you will find one that suits your child. It also means that there are many more ideas. In America the Knowledge Is Power Program (KIPP) schools have introduced longer school days, longer school weeks (with classes on Saturday), and longer school years. Sometimes these experiments will fail badly: Some charter schools have been disasters. But on the whole these educational "mutants" have a good record of promoting systemwide improvements as well as generating new ideas. In Sweden districts with a higher proportion of pupils at free schools have better average achievement across the whole district.[26] The biggest improvement is in noncharter schools. In Britain academies are not only producing better results but also boosting the performance of adjacent schools, according to a recent report from the London School of Economics.[27]

Governments are also keener to experiment when it comes to talent. Australia's government has introduced almost Singaporean levels of pay for its senior civil servants. The Australian equivalent of the cabinet secretary earns about £500,000 a year, twice as much as his British equivalent. It also has an impressive record of recruiting outsiders for top jobs and "laundering" them into their new positions with lower-level appointments. Britain is also doing a little better at importing highfliers from outside the civil service. Gordon Brown tried belatedly to create something called GOATs (Government of All the Talents) by bringing in centrist businesspeople like Mervyn Davies of Standard Chartered Bank to help run departments. David Cameron has appointed a Canadian, Mark Carney, to run the Bank of England. David Higgins, an Australian, has held a succession of senior positions: running the government regeneration agency, heading the Olympic Delivery Authority, and at the moment running Network Rail.

Governments are also keener on working with voluntary groups. Code for America is a "mash-up" of the Peace Corps and Teach for America. The organization keeps a talent bank of techies (known as Coders) who want to help solve social problems. It then identifies problems that need tech-based solutions and appoints members of its bank to work with government officials to produce innovative solutions. The list of Coder-created solutions is a long one: A Web site in Boston that identifies snow-bound fire hydrants, another Web site in Honolulu that identifies failing batteries in the local tsunami warning system, a GPS system that tells parents if the school bus is running late, a walker's guide to the murals in Philadelphia.

This is beginning to change government career structures. The days when you joined a government department after university and climbed the greasy pole to the top are coming to an end. Career civil servants increasingly go to the private sector on secondment. Private-sector figures increasingly go in and out of the civil service. But the transition from a self-contained machine to a fluid network is still a long way off.

TOWARD THE LOCALITIES

It is notable how many of the best recent ideas have come from local government rather than central government. The great centralizing passion of the midtwentieth century has played itself out.

Around the world local governments are reasserting themselves, upending national politics, and scrambling old ideological divisions in the process. Local governments have some of the most vivid figures, such as Rahm Emanuel in Chicago and Ron Huldai in Tel Aviv. They also have some of the great ideological cross-dressers: In London Boris

Johnson, a conservative, embraced what he called "an entirely communist scheme" of bike sharing while his predecessor, "Red" Ken Livingstone, introduced the entirely free-market scheme of road pricing. Local politicians are increasingly leaping over national politicians in the public mind. People not only trust them far more but are often more interested in what they have to say as well. On one visit to China Bill Clinton found himself in a radio studio with the mayor of Shanghai. Two-thirds of incoming calls were for the mayor rather than the global superstar.[28]

Localism has paid off particularly well in two places. The first is America: The paralysis in Washington, D.C., has given ambitious local politicians no choice but to step in. "Local elected officials are responsible for doing, not debating," Michael Bloomberg has said. "For innovating, not arguing. For pragmatism, not partisanship." Minnesota and Massachusetts pioneered the "welfare to work" ideas that became Bill Clinton's welfare reforms. Massachusetts pioneered the health-care reforms that Barack Obama took national. Indeed, it is an interesting comment on the relative merits of central and local government that Mitt Romney opposed the health-care reforms as a national candidate that he had pioneered as a Massachusetts governor.

The second place localism has paid off especially well is the emerging world. Reforming governments have frequently used local governments as laboratories of reform: Look at the role of Shenzhen or Guangdong in China in the 1980s or the role of special economic zones in the Middle East today. Dubai alone has 150 economic zones, such as the International Financial Centre, which uses the English legal system to resolve commercial disputes, and the Jebel Ali Free Zone, which is one of the world's largest and most efficient ports. India and China are so gigantic that they cannot avoid giving a good deal of self-determination to provinces that contain as many as one hundred million people. Bill Antholis of the Brookings Institution argues that "local leaders are increasingly running much of India and China, which are home to a third of all humanity, from the bottom up." In some cases that has led to disaster and corruption. But there are also stars. For example, Narendra Modi, the chief minister of Gujarat, may have some unpleasant sectarian baggage, but he has taken advantage of his freedom to adopt the most business-friendly policies in India and turn Gujarat into India's leader in manufacturing and exports. A large number of businesspeople would like him to repeat this trick on the national scale.

There are good reasons to expect localism to play an even bigger role in the future. Cities everywhere are becoming more important. The proportion of the world's population that lives in them has grown from 3 percent in 1800 to 14 percent in 1900 to more than 50 percent today. It could reach 75 percent in 2050: In the developing world more than one million people move to cities every five days. Some cities are veritable behemoths: Chongqing, where Bo Xilai had his power base, sits at the heart of a region of thirty million people, six times the population of Denmark and about the same as the population of Canada. Cities are also the locus of the knowledge-economy: Parag Khanna of the New America Foundation, a think tank, calculates that forty city-regions produce two-thirds of the world's economic output and an even higher share of its innovations. Gerald Carlino of the Federal Reserve Bank of Philadelphia notes that the denser the city, the more inventive: The number of patents per head rises by an average of 20 percent to 30 percent for each doubling of the number of employed people per square kilometer.

Cities are also bypassing their national governments and forming relations with one another: San Francisco has formed a close relationship with Bangalore, India's IT powerhouse, and Detroit with Pune, its auto capital. The same is true of states: Jerry Brown has been particularly active in forging relations between California and local Chinese authorities. Ideas are also leaping from one local government to another without going through the medium of national governments: Over three hundred cities have introduced bike-sharing programs, for example. The old world, where the most important global relations were between national governments or capital cities, is being replaced by a much more networked world in which successful mayors and governors weave ever-more-complicated webs of relationships with one another.

A LITTLE EXPERIMENTATION

The final curse of the old state that we hope the Fourth Revolution will dispel is in a sense the sum of the others: *immobilisme*. Has anything happened to change the resistance to change? It is hard to chart a change of mind, but we would argue that if you take all the various things we have described above, something is beginning to move.

Out of despair in some cases, hope in others, bureaucrats and politicians are beginning to think differently. The presumption that the state should do it all; the love of uniformity; the urge to centralize everything: You can find examples from all the way around the Western world of these old credos beginning to break down. They may not amount to much individually but together they amount to something rather big. Bit by bit a new model is emerging. We are living through changes just as dramatic as the ones associated with Hobbes and Mill and the Webbs, though nobody has yet succeeded in putting this Fourth Revolution into memorable words and clothing it in a distinctive philosophy.

That is largely because this part of the revolution is driven from below—by mayors experimenting, by parents demanding better schools, by ideas seeping across borders. The people at the top have changed a bit. There is a new accent on innovation. The Nordic fashion for setting up policy labs, like Denmark's MindLab and Helsinki's Design Lab, is spreading. The Obama administration has created a new Office of Social Innovation and Participation to find clever ideas being produced by social entrepreneurs and "bring them into the Oval Office."[29] There is a willingness to be more pragmatic. As Barack Obama said in his first inaugural speech, "the question we ask today is not whether our government is too big or too small, but whether it works."[30] But it is patchy. Obama, the self-styled pragmatist, has persistently opposed voucher schemes, such as the one that was so popular among the black citizens of Washington, D.C.

This will change: Governments, even America's, have little alternative than to find things that work quickly. But it will happen a lot sooner if politicians begin to make this set of organizational changes into something bigger. Looking back, one notable part of the three previous revolutions was the ability of a few leaders to pick out a handful of principles that drove all the others. The Victorian liberals succeeded because they seized on a few big ideas, such as careers open to talent and open competition, and built them into the heart of the state. The Fabians succeeded for the same reason. Today's reformers also need to pick out a handful of central ideas. It is to those ideas that we will now turn.

CHAPTER NINE

WHAT IS THE STATE FOR?

IN THE INTRODUCTION to *Democracy in America* (1835) Alexis de Tocqueville argued that "a new science of politics is indispensable to a new world." Tocqueville had a catholic definition of the "science of politics." *Democracy in America* examined the standard fare of political science, such as the nature of federalism and the organization of parties, but what really fascinated him was not so much the organization of the state as its animating spirit. How had the twin principles of democracy and equality taken over as the organizing principles of modern life? And why had America made so much better a job of moving with the times, creating a new "science of politics . . . for a new world," than Tocqueville's France?

This book has argued that there have been three new "sciences of politics" since the dawn of the modern era, sciences that have all proved indispensable for three new worlds: the politics of the sixteenth and seventeenth centuries that emphasized sovereign power; the politics of the eighteenth and nineteenth centuries that emphasized individual liberty (and a good deal of Tocquevillian democracy); and the politics of the twentieth century that emphasized social welfare. Our

Fourth Revolution is an attempt to reimagine the science of politics in the light of new technology and new political pressures.

In the last chapter we looked at the mechanics of the Fourth Revolution. What is being done around the world to make the state more efficient? The barriers to progress that William Baumol and others identified have been weakened. But we can get only so far with purely pragmatic reforms: Vested interests will always be able to frustrate pragmatic reformers if they continue to hold the moral high ground. It is the animating ideas that determine the workings of the state in much the same way that operating systems determine the workings of computers. The crisis of the state is more than an organizational crisis. It is a crisis of ideas.

The social contract between the state and the individual needs to be scrutinized in much the same spirit that Hobbes and Mill reexamined it. The twentieth century has seen the state adding a succession of ideals to the Hobbesian ideal of order and the Millian ideal of liberty: We have ended up with far broader concepts of what equality means and what citizenship entitles one to. Much too broad. The state has become bloated and overwhelmed. Even if it were run by the world's most efficient technocrats, the state would still be a gigantic mess: supersized by ambition and pulled hither and thither by conflicting aims. Worse, the state is also becoming an enemy of liberty.

The revolution that most inspires us is thus the one most firmly rooted in liberty. Western government needs to recapture the spirit of the great eighteenth- and nineteenth-century liberals: the Founding Fathers in America; John Stuart Mill and Thomas Babington Macaulay in Britain; Alexis de Tocqueville and Nicolas de Condorcet in France. There are similarities between the bloated patronage-driven state of the early Victorian era and the entitlement-driven state of our own period. Our Leviathan is just as out of tune with the spirit of the

Internet age as the early-Victorian state was with the railway age: It sucks up huge amounts of resources but fails to exploit the productivity-boosting capacities of modern technology; it clings to the old world while losing contact with the most vigorous elements in commercial society; and its democratic core has been weakened by empire building and vested interests. The liberals then championed the cause that needs to be championed now. That cause is freedom.

THE POLITICS OF FREEDOM

The nineteenth-century liberals put freedom at the heart of the state and the individual at the heart of society. For them the point of the state was not to promote equality or fraternity or any of the other shibboleths of the French Revolution. It was to give the individual the maximum freedom to exercise his God-given powers and achieve his full potential. That was not just a good in itself; it was a way to harness the whirlwind of progress.

The classical liberals thought that the essence of freedom lay in freedom from interference from others. "The only freedom which deserves the name," Mill memorably declared, "is that of pursuing our own good in our own way."[1] They did not think that the state should disappear: Mill in particular recognized that freedom for the pike could be death for the minnows if the pike was not forcefully restrained. They were also willing to compromise freedom in the interests of other values like justice. But they insisted that there was a certain minimal area of personal freedom that the state had no right to violate: a realm of self-determination that had to be preserved from outside bullying. The exact size of this island was a matter of intense debate. So was the content of the list of rights that had to be guarded in the name of liberty. But they all agreed on the basic list: freedom of opinion (including freedom of religion), freedom of private life, freedom of expression, and freedom of property. If the state invaded these basic liberties, it was abusing its power and engaging in despotism.

Their claim was first and foremost a moral claim: People have a right to live their lives according to their own lights. They exercise their humanity when they are instruments of their own rather than other people's wills. This is why Immanuel Kant thought that "paternalism is the greatest despotism imaginable." But their liberalism was also a practical one. Socialists have justified interfering with freedom on the grounds of promoting the common welfare. The liberals believed that this was a false trade-off. Not only was individual liberty perfectly compatible with economic progress and social harmony, but it was also a precondition for it. Adam Smith argued that economic progress was the result of self-seeking individuals entering into contracts with one another. Mill argued that civilization could advance only if people were given the maximum freedom to think as they wished. That is why Gladstone busied himself saving candle ends and cheese parings in the cause of the country. The classical liberals worried that people might forget about the real meaning of freedom. Even if the state is doing something that you might approve of—like taxing the rich to help the poor—you must recognize that it is diminishing freedom and that every little assault on freedom adds up to one big assault. This was best put by Macaulay in his review of Robert Southey's *Colloquies on Society* in 1830. Southey had presented an idealized view of the role of the British state before the dissolution of the monasteries. The great historian lacerated the book:

> He conceives that the business of the magistrate is, not merely
> to see that the persons and property of the people are secure

from attack, but that he ought to be a perfect jack of all trades, architect, engineer, schoolmaster, merchant, theologian, a Lady Bountiful in every parish, a Paul Pry in every house, spying, eaves-dropping, relieving, admonishing, spending our money for us, and choosing our opinions for us. His principle is . . . that no man can do any thing so well for himself, as his rulers . . . can do it for him, that a government approaches nearer and nearer to perfection, in proportion as it interferes more and more with the habits and notions of individuals.

Macaulay put forward a very different liberal vision:

It is not by the intermeddling of Mr Southey's idol, the omniscient and omnipotent state, but by the prudence and energy of the people, that England has hitherto been carried forward in civilization. . . . Our rulers will best promote the improvement of the people by strictly confining themselves to their legitimate duties; by leaving capital to find its most lucrative course, commodities their fair price, industry and intelligence their natural reward, idleness and folly their natural punishment; by maintaining peace, by defending property, by diminishing the price of law, and by observing strict economy in every department of the state. Let the government do this— the people will assuredly do the rest.

Since Macaulay's day the rest that the people would "assuredly do" has shrunk. In some cases that is because the concept of liberty has been stretched—or perverted. Communist ideologues routinely justified despotism in the name of "real" freedom. But more generally it has been through a mixture of stealth and popular demand. It is interesting to imagine what Macaulay would have made of the scope of government in modern Britain. A state police force keeps a permanent watch on citizens through thousands of CCTV cameras. A secret state monitors every communication. The state as schoolmaster dictates the curriculum of every school in the country and runs 90 percent of them. The state as nanny gives instructions on how to climb up ladders or dispose of rubbish. The state as broadcaster pumps out television and radio programs twenty-four hours a day.

The gradually diminishing importance of liberty in the West has worried some libertarians and a few philosophers, like Isaiah Berlin, but has barely caused a squeak of protest from the wider public. Quite the reverse. Britons, for instance, like "Auntie," as the BBC is sometimes known, and feel safer because of security cameras. This arguably would have worried Macaulay and Mill even more. For the old classical liberals, the nexus of big government and mass democracy was a frightening prospect. Democracy, they warned, was not much of an advance on monarchical tyranny if it simply transferred the power of oppression from the few to the many. The Founding Fathers drew up a Bill of Rights and created a Supreme Court in order to limit what the state could do, even when it was backed by the wishes of the majority. Tocqueville, haunted by the fear of soft despotism, emphasized the importance of devolving power from the center to the localities: That was one reason for his fascination with the United States. Macaulay focused on the importance of selecting the best and brightest for high offices through a program of high-quality education and rigorous examinations: The elite civil service would act as a barrier on the power of the legislature.

In many ways what the old liberals feared has come to pass. People have voted again and again for the state to do more. Liberty has suffered. But it is not as if either democracy or the state looked any better for it. Democracy has grown rather shabby—the subject of our conclusion. As for the state, it is stuck in a paradox: Government, backed by the general democratic will, has never been more powerful; but in this bloated, overburdened condition, it also has seldom been as unloved or inefficient. Freedoms have been given up, but the people have not gotten much in return.

THE LEVIATHAN PARADOX

Merely adding up all the polls showing declining trust in government around the West does not do justice to the contempt voters now feel for their rulers. The "Old Corruption" of the eighteenth century inspired some of the world's greatest satire. Where would James Gillray, William Hogarth, and Jonathan Swift have been without rotten boroughs and political graft? The spirit of satire lives on. The New York *Daily News* reacted to the shutdown of Washington in 2013 in Hogarthian fashion by calling Congress the HOUSE OF TURDS, which was itself a play on *House of Cards*, which, like *Veep* and *The Thick of It*, depicts Western politicians as either crooks or imbeciles or a foulmouthed mixture of the two. But what would the great eighteenth-century satirists have made of a world in which two sober political analysts had to produce a second edition of a book called *It's Even Worse Than It Looks* because things got so much worse so quickly? Or in which a supposedly serious magazine put Beppe Grillo and Silvio Berlusconi on its cover under the headline SEND IN THE CLOWNS and was then inundated with complaints—from clowns? Or in which one candidate for a congressional seat in Delaware, Christine O'Donnell, admitted to "dabbling" in witchcraft and made her opposition to masturbation a key part of her campaign, a position that put her in apparent conflict with Anthony Weiner, a mayoral candidate in New York (and now one of the country's best-known politicians)?

All this has turned politics into a form of comic entertainment: It is telling that anybody who wants to be president now has to appear on Jon Stewart's show. But it is laughter with a poisonous edge. The tidal wave of hostility is making government more difficult. Coalition governments are becoming the rule: In 2012 only four of the OECD's thirty-four countries had governments with an absolute majority in parliament. And paralysis is becoming ever more common. The American Congress has not passed a proper budget on time since 1997. Belgium spent 541 days without a government in 2010–11. The Western state is in the throes of a midlife crisis.

OVERLOAD AND ITS DISCONTENTS

Throughout this book we have referred to the state as Leviathan, a power-hungry monster. But the modern state is also like Augustus Gloop, the greedy boy in *Charlie and the Chocolate Factory*: It is being punished by its own deepest instinct, by being given too much of what it craves—too many obligations, too much power. It has drunk too much from the chocolate river.

The overfeeding is the work of both the Left and the Right. The main culprit is the Left (as we have argued throughout this book), which has repeatedly reinterpreted the concepts of equality, fraternity, and liberty to justify overstuffing the state. Equality of opportunity has become equality of results. Fraternity has become about entitlements that we are all due, not responsibilities that we all have. And that has ended up changing the idea of liberty in much the same way that both Mill and Isaiah Berlin feared. People no longer associate it with freedom from external interference but rather with freedom from social scourges, such as ignorance or want.

This has practical consequences. So many of the things that the state does badly are ones where it is charged with pursuing impossible dreams. The more it fails to meet its impossible targets, the more it resorts to micromanagement to make up for its failures. Examining the problem of why so many government programs are either ineffective or counterproductive, one of the twentieth century's greatest economists, Ronald Coase, put it this way:

> An important reason may be that government at the present time is so large that it has reached the stage of negative marginal productivity, which means that any additional function it takes on will probably result in more harm than good. . . . If a federal program were established to give financial assistance to Boy Scouts to enable them to help old ladies cross busy intersections, we could be sure that not all the money would go to Boy Scouts, that some of those they helped would be neither old nor ladies, that part of the program would be devoted to preventing old ladies from crossing busy intersections, and that many of them would be killed because they would now cross at places where, unsupervised, they were at least permitted to cross.

The progressive agenda has become self-defeating. Each new government department, program, or entitlement makes it harder for the state to focus on its core functions. When private businesses expand they frequently enjoy economies of scale. Such savings are less common in government—and problems of coordination and bureaucratic bloat are far more common in a sector that does not face the disciplines of losing customers or facing bankruptcy. It has also tipped progressive politics into a vicious spiral: the state gets ever bigger because voters want ever more from it, but voters lose confidence in the state as soon as it begins to weigh heavily on their lives, which means they then demand even more. The very forces that drive the expansion of the state simultaneously undermine the state's claim to authority. It creates a constant feeling of frustration and fear. Ordinary citizens worry that they will not get the pensions or medical care that they have been counting on.

But the overfeeding has not been the work of only the Left. The Right can be just as guilty of Gloopism. Look, for instance, at the growth of the security state in the wake of September 11. Here too was something that the voters wanted. And here too the voters have suffered from getting their desires satisfied. The balance between liberty and security has shifted dramatically in a way that may not have advanced security but has certainly diminished liberty. Until recently it was assumed that the evils of the security state were confined to "over there," to Guantánamo, Abu Ghraib, and extraordinary rendition. But the disclosures from two whistle-blowers, Bradley Manning and Edward Snowden, have revealed a veritable secret Leviathan, capable of classifying more than ninety-two million documents in one year and giving 1.8 million people "top security" clearance, including Manning, a lowly private in his early twenties with a record of emotional instability.[2] And who was in charge of all this? The authority to monitor the private conversations of American citizens (and non-American citizens, like Angela Merkel) has come from secret judicial orders issued by a secret court based on a secret interpretation of the law. Admittedly that was monitored by a Senate committee, but the supervising politicians were also bound by more oaths of secrecy: The head of America's intelligence service felt comfortable lying to Congress about whether the spying that Snowden revealed was going on.

This is symptomatic of the overload from both left and right. Nobody knows exactly what is going on. Each new government department or government program stretches thinner the ability of citizens and their representatives to monitor government's behavior and correct its failures and abuses. Government is like a bloated conglomerate—think of ITT in its 1960s heyday—that is involved in so many different lines of business that the top executives have very little idea what is going on further down the organization. Look at the scandals that swirl around the Obama White House, from tapping Merkel's mobile phone to singling out conservative groups for extra scrutiny on their taxes, and the real scandal is that Obama's lame excuse (how could he know what the two million people he employs are doing?) might be true. Jonathan Rauch puts this sense of alienation well in *Demosclerosis*. The American government, he says, "probably has evolved into about what it will remain: a sprawling, largely self-organizing structure that is 10% to 20% under the control of the politicians and voters and 80% to 90% under the control of the countless thousands of client groups."[3] His words could equally well describe Whitehall or Brussels.

When a business is out of control, it tends to lose money and run up debts. The British government has run a budget surplus only six times since 1975. The U.S. government has run a surplus in only five of the fifty-two years since 1960.[4] In the twenty-five years from 1965 to 1980 the annual federal deficit topped 3 percent of the nation's gross domestic product just twice. In the past twenty-five years it has done so thirteen times. An astonishing number of countries are running debts that are equivalent to more than 100 percent of GDP; and as we saw in the last chapter, even that ratio is achieved only by burying all sorts of liabilities and obligations in the footnotes.

Very little of this borrowing is to finance investment. From Baltimore to Brasilia, it feeds entitlements. George Bernard Shaw once quipped that politicians can always rely on Paul's vote if they give him money that they steal from Peter. This understates the problem with democracy because Paul is an old man and Peter is either a child or unborn.

LIGHTENING THE BURDEN

All this amounts to a state that is not working, whatever your political starting point. Our starting point is liberal: We want the state to be smaller and individuals to be freer. But we are not libertarians. Even in its current lopsided form, the modern state has a lot to be proud of. Those Americans who regard government as the work of the devil forget that Uncle Sam won the Second World War, built a huge interstate highway system, put a man on the moon, laid the foundations of the Internet, and discovered dozens of life-transforming drugs. Germans have even more reasons to be grateful to a government that dug their country out of the ruins of Nazism, banished political extremism from the heart of Europe, and helped create an industrial powerhouse. We believe that the state has certain vital functions—not just providing a night watchman but also helping provide infrastructure. One reason why India has fallen behind China is that India's state has been so inept at building roads and providing schools. Chile has pulled ahead of Argentina not just because it has a smaller state, but also because it has a strong state. We also believe that shrinking the state needs to be tempered by pragmatism. Leaving everybody to buy their own health care might sound appealing to free-market sorts, but Europe's single-payer systems are clearly more efficient than America's jumble of private insurance systems, as well as fairer.

"The State is the most precious of human possessions," Alfred Marshall wrote in *Industry and Trade* in 1919, "and no care can be too great to be spent on enabling it to do its special work in the best way: a chief condition to that end is that it should not be set to work, for which it is not specially qualified, under the conditions of time and place." But over the intervening years we have done little else but set government to work on new jobs, many of which it is not specially qualified to tackle, and all of which, when added together, constitute an overwhelming burden.

Imposing such a burden on the state has created two pressing dangers. The first is that government will collapse under its own weight. A small but strong state is preferable to a large but weak state, not just because a large state intrudes into our lives and costs us lots of money but also because it usually fails to do its basic job. The second is that a bloated government encourages popular discontent. Bernard Baruch, who worked as an adviser to both Woodrow Wilson and FDR, liked to tell people to "vote for the man who promises least; because he'll be the least disappointing." Since Baruch's time people have been voting for the candidates who promised the most, and the possibility that disappointment will turn into fury is huge.

How can governments go about lightening the burden? We argued in the last chapter that better management and cleverer use of technology might help slim Leviathan: Even if it stuck to delivering the same services that it does at the moment, a state that behaved more like Google and less like the old General Motors would certainly be smarter and might well be leaner. But you also need to chop away at what the state tries to do.

There are three areas where Leviathan begs for unburdening: first, selling things that the state has no business owning by reviving privatization, an old cause of the Right; second, cutting the subsidies that flow to the rich and well connected, an old cause of the Left; and third, reforming entitlements to make sure that they are targeted to people who need them and sustainable in the long term, an old cause of everybody who cares about the health of the state.

Different states have different opportunities: Nigeria has more to gain from attacking crony capitalism than Scandinavia does while China has more to gain from selling off state assets than Britain does. To give our prescriptions some focus, we will concentrate on the world's best-known government—in Washington, D.C.

LET SOMEBODY ELSE USE THE SILVER

The first cause is privatization, the most striking bit of unfinished business from the half revolution of the 1980s in conservative eyes. Thirty years after Margaret Thatcher sold off British Telecom in 1984 it is remarkable how much "family silver" (to borrow a phrase from one of her aristocratic critics, Harold Macmillan) the state continues to own in the form of companies, buildings, and land. Selling off the family silver is not only an excellent way to reduce the debt that is crushing so many countries. It is also a good way to manage the silver better.

State capitalism is not just a Chinese trait. At the end of 2012 the OECD's thirty-four member governments owned, either completely or largely, more than two thousand companies with a combined workforce of more than six million people and a collective value of $2 trillion, the same as the global hedge-fund industry. Governments continue to own large chunks of "network industries" such as transportation, electricity, and telecom, on the grounds that they constitute both public goods and strategic national assets: Private companies might use their market power to extort consumers or exclude the poor, and foreign investors might buy them to gain a beachhead in a foreign country. In fact, insofar as these objections make sense they can be dealt with by regulation rather than ownership.

America is less out and proud about its dirigiste tendencies than France, where the government owns €60 billion worth of shares in the likes of Renault and France Telecom. But Uncle Sam is a closet state capitalist. Why, for instance, does it own Amtrak, which manages to stumble from crisis to crisis despite controlling one of the most lucrative commuter railway lines in the world? One answer is that America started by owning relatively few of the big, obvious assets that were the first to be privatized in Europe: Both its telecoms and its utilities were run by the private sector. So America missed out on the privatizing wave of the 1980s and 1990s that swept over other sorts of assets. Other countries have privatized their post offices, prisons, and airports. America has not—and it shows. Airports look an especially tempting target for sale: much shoddier and worse managed than their privatized equivalents in Europe and Asia.

America's underused portfolio of land and property is particularly extensive. The Government Accountability Office estimates that the government owns more than 900,000 buildings worth "hundreds of billions" of dollars. At least 45,000 of these are underused or unneeded. Add government buildings that are in needlessly expensive places, like central Washington, and you have an even bigger portfolio: If France can summon up the gumption to lease out a defense-ministry building on the Place de la Concorde and move its occupants to less plush offices on the outskirts of Paris, then America can do the same. The Department of the Interior oversees 260 million acres through the Bureau of Land Management and other agencies. It makes sense for some of this land to stay in the public sector: America's national parks are one of the glories of the country. But why own agricultural land? It is just an excuse for subsidy and bureaucracy. America's shale-gas revolution has taken place almost entirely on private land, even though the state owns much of the best prospects: The Green River Formation—the biggest source of shale oil in the world—is on federal land. The Institute for Energy Research calculates that developing federal shale could contribute $14.4 trillion to the economy by 2050.[5]

America is hardly alone in having an untapped treasure trove of public property. Dag Detter, who helped mastermind much of Sweden's privatization program, suspects that in many advanced economies the market value of government-owned commercial property alone exceeds the national debt. Taken as a whole, OECD governments could well be sitting on land and buildings worth $9 trillion. But the American Right in particular seems unusually sluggish in thinking about privatization. Ignorance is one reason. America's government, especially at the local level, has no idea what it owns. Another reason is obduracy: When Barack Obama suggested selling the Tennessee Valley Authority, an electricity company that played an iconic role in the New Deal, prominent Republicans protested. It would be unfair to compare American public land with Greece, where a twenty-year-long effort to create a proper account of the land has gotten nowhere largely because so much has been built on with politicians' connivance; but the nexus between Republican congressmen, ranchers, and the Department of the Interior is not a healthy one. The heirs of Reagan could do with a little of his vim.

CRONY CAPITALISM BY THE POTOMAC

If privatization is the American Right's great blind spot, subsidies for the wealthy is the Left's. Dismantling the web of handouts for the rich and powerful should be at the very top of progressive America's agenda—in the same way that royal patronage was the great enemy for John Stuart Mill. So far the Left has concentrated on trying to raise taxes in the name of redistribution. It would be much better to focus on dismantling the welfare state for America's plutocrats. There are two rich targets. The first is crony capitalism: all those subsidies for well-connected industries. The second is the personal tax system, which, as we have seen, is massively distorted by aid to the rich. Fixing these things would simultaneously slim Leviathan and help it focus its energies on people who actually need its help.

Crony capitalism represents the most egregious example of Olson's law. If market capitalism provides a way of turning private benefits to the public good, as Adam Smith argued, crony capitalism provides a way of turning public goods to private gain, lining the pockets of the powerful, undermining economic competitiveness, and misdirecting resources on a huge scale.

The industry with the longest history of sucking at the udder of the state is agriculture. The U.S. Department of Agriculture distributes between $10 billion and $30 billion in cash subsidies to farmers each year (the particular amount fluctuates with the market price of crops and the frequency of disasters).[6] The payments are heavily tilted toward the big producers: The largest 10 percent of farmers received 68 percent of all commodity subsidies in 2010.[7] The beneficiaries include some of America's biggest companies, such as Archer Daniels Midland, and some of its richest individuals, such as Ted Turner, as well as some people who don't farm at all but who own land that was once deemed agricultural.

It is hard to tell what is the most harmful consequence of all this. Farm subsidies transfer money from the average taxpayer to the rich. They distort the economy by encouraging the overfarming of land. They ruin the environment. They hurt the poor of the emerging world whose products are shut out. They wreck the prospects of a global trade deal. And they engender waste and corruption. The sugar industry, which has helped build America's obesity epidemic, has a particularly tawdry history with Congress, but still the politicians keep feeding the lobby. The 2008 farm bill added a new sugar-to-ethanol subsidy under which the government buys "excess" imported sugar that might put a downward pressure on inflated sugar prices and sells it to ethanol producers. It is as if the Corn Laws had never been repealed.

The Cato Institute, which has studied this problem in detail, has dug up a delightful quotation from an ornery congressman in 1932. He pointed to the perversity of the Agriculture Department spending "hundreds of millions a year to stimulate the production of farm products by every method, from irrigating waste lands to loaning and even giving money to the farmers, and simultaneously advising them that there is no adequate market for their crops, and that they should restrict production."[8] The only things that have changed today are that the millions are billions and that the associated bureaucracy has swollen beyond reason. The U.S. Department of Agriculture employs over one hundred thousand people and costs around $150 billion per year.

The best excuse that America's agriculture lobby can come up with is that Europe's farmers are even more cosseted. It does not need to be that way. New Zealand ended its farm subsidies completely in 1984, despite the fact that it is four times as dependent on agriculture as the United States. The change produced fierce resistance at first, but farmers soon adapted and prospered: Farmers have boosted productivity, developed niche markets such as kiwifruit, and diversified into nonfarm income. Are we really supposed to believe that America's farmers are less independent and innovative than their New Zealand rivals?

If agriculture is the grand old man of crony capitalism, then the financial-services industry is the flashy new kid on the block. The industry now employs more lobbyists than any other: four per congressman. Wall Street has all but dug an underground passage to the treasury: Four of the past seven treasury secretaries had close ties to investment banks. Luigi Zingales of the University of Chicago's Booth School of Business (who left Italy in 1988 because he felt his country was being destroyed by cronyism) calculates that the implicit subsidy that comes from banks being too big to fail is worth $34 billion a year.[9] Two other economists, Thomas Philippon and Ariell Reshef, argue that between a third and a half of the huge increase in Wall Street pay has come from rents rather than productivity improvements.[10] The fact that private-equity people can treat their income as capital gains is particularly disgraceful. And like agriculture, all this special treatment for finance creates red tape (witness Dodd-Frank) and distorts capitalism: Ever more finance is now being constructed in "dark pools" beyond the reach of regulators.

There are innumerable other examples of rent-seeking special interests. If the government stopped subsidizing the production of fossil fuels, it could save $40 billion over the next decade.[11] Spending on lobbying in Washington has more than doubled in the past fifteen years. The Supreme Court's 2010 *Citizens United* decision has given companies carte blanche to spend freely on influencing elections. And America is hardly unique. Whitehall is also becoming far too close to various industries. The days when British mandarins retired to their country houses and crosswords are long gone. Over the past decade eighteen former senior ministers and civil servants have taken jobs with Britain's biggest three accountancy firms, whose work includes helping businesses minimize their tax bills and lobby the government.

For progressives of all sorts this is a huge missed opportunity. The battle against crony capitalism is older than America itself: The Boston Tea Party was a protest against the East India Company, which was using its political connections in London to subsidize its tea. The Democratic Party would not only save the state a lot of money if it were to campaign against crony capitalism. It would also become a champion of the future in much the same way that British radicals did in the nineteenth century by taking on the systems of "outdoor relief for the upper classes" in the form of Corn Laws and patronage. Fully 77 percent of Americans believe that too much power is in the hands of the rich and large corporations.[12]

An even bigger target for "True Progressives"[13] is all the state spending that is sprayed at well-off individuals. America's tax system, as we have already seen, is riddled with loopholes and exemptions, collectively worth $1.3 trillion, or 8 percent of GDP. Most countries indulge the rich in this way, but America takes the indulgence to new levels—for example, by setting the limit for tax relief on mortgages at $1 million or allowing people to claim especially generous health-insurance packages. If the mortgage relief were limited to $300,000, it would cut the deficit by $300 billion. Alternatively, the government could just set an overall limit: Allowing taxpayers to claim their deductions at a rate of 15 percent would save $1 trillion over ten years.

Indeed, all these exemptions could be phased out relatively painlessly, especially if the proceeds were used both to close the deficit and to lower tax rates. That is the great bargain (together with entitlement reform) that Barack Obama has inched toward making with congressional Republicans, only for both sides to retreat to their shells at the last moment. Once again simplification is a good in its own right because it brings light to something that is too often shrouded in darkness. A "tax expenditure" does not appear as public spending, so very few Americans know how much money their state is spending on the rich and the powerful.

TRIMMING ENTITLEMENTS

The biggest problem that governments face is the explosion of entitlements, which have risen relentlessly since the Second World War and are due to rise even more relentlessly in the next few years, thanks to the aging of the population. Fixing the entitlement crisis will not only save the state from insolvency. It will also preserve the social contract that is at the heart of the welfare state. The state was supposed to look after people when they suffered from problems that were no fault of their own; instead, it is increasingly lavishing money on rich baby boomers who have already spent much of their lives gorging themselves at the great welfare-state buffet.

Here the American example is particularly interesting because it displays three things. The first is that entitlements are the heart of the matter: They have risen from less than half of federal spending twenty years ago to about 62 percent in 2012. The second is that problems can easily spiral out of control. The federal debt is already much too high at 73 percent of GDP in 2012 (general government gross debt is

103 percent), but it will reach 90 percent of GDP in 2035 if current policies continue.[14] The combination of an aging population and rising health-care costs is pushing the cost of basic entitlements such as Social Security (pensions), Medicare (health care for the elderly), and Medicaid (health care for the poor) ever upward. The third is more cheerful: The system can be restored to solvency through implementation of a relatively gentle set of reforms.

The federal government's biggest obligation is Social Security, which cost $809 billion in 2012, or 5 percent of GDP. The number of beneficiaries will grow by 1.5 million a year for the next two decades: This will increase the cost of benefits to 5.9 percent of GDP in 2031. But this can be fixed by changing the rules. The biggest gain would come from increasing the retirement age from sixty-five. At the moment the average 65-year-old retiree can look forward to another 19.5 years of life, compared with 12.7 years for men and 14.7 years for women in 1940 (five years after the system was set up in 1935). The retirement age is set to rise to 67 in 2022, with provisos. That date should be brought forward and the age increased to 70 and indexed to life expectancy, as happens in Sweden. That would also boost GDP by 1 percent, according to the Congressional Budget Office, because more people would be working. The benefits should also rise in line with price inflation rather than wage inflation. And ideally there would be some element of social insurance rather than social assistance, like the Singaporean model, where the state provides a minimum but people are allowed to pay in more savings.

An even bigger cost is Medicare, currently 3.6 percent of GDP and set to rise to 5.6 percent in 2035. This too needs to be aligned with demography: The eligibility age should rise to sixty-seven from sixty-five. As for rising medical costs, we have argued that there are good reasons to think that you can reverse these by rearranging hospitals (like India's Dr. Shetty), using frugal equipment (like the kit that GE is producing around the corner from Shetty), and letting more of the work be done by nondoctors, gadgets, and technology. However, a truly radical America would leapfrog over the muddle of Obamacare and pluck ideas from both new Asia and old Europe.

The European idea is a single-payer system, broadly along the Swedish model. It may sound socialist to Tea Party fundamentalists, but it would provide universal coverage in a transparent way and cost considerably less than the current confused mess (with its mixture of public provision and strings of private insurers). It would be clear how much the state was spending and on what, so the taxpayer would be less likely to end up paying for, say, cosmetic surgery for people who don't think they are good-looking enough. A single-payer system would need to be combined with an independent medical board to evaluate the cost-effectiveness of medicines, similar to Britain's National Institute for Health and Care Excellence (NICE) (which in effect rations care), and with small charges to patients to discourage overuse. The Asian idea, again from Singapore, is to introduce some form of hypothecated tax to pay for this, allowing people to build up accounts through its Medisave system. Again Singapore always insists that a small payment be made for each operation, and it means-tests people to determine how much subsidy they get for some procedures.

Most people would accept that the state should provide a basic minimum to all its residents in terms of a pension and health care. But there are also other entitlements that raise trickier questions about equity. Here Europe is a much greater offender than America: The continent has gotten into the habit of dishing out universal perks, such as free bus passes and winter fuel allowances, regardless of people's ability to pay. The answer in most cases is means testing: Sir Mick and Sir Elton should be deprived of their bus passes forthwith.

Another answer is to make individuals pay more if they gain more from public investment than society at large. A student who goes to university gains a colossal advantage in the job market. Why should poorer taxpayers subsidize that?

On the core welfare bill—providing money and services for the needy and unemployed—the West does not have to follow Lee Kuan Yew's model of tough love to save a lot of money. Three policies suggest themselves. One is conditionality. Latin American countries tie people's benefits to adopting good habits, such as sending their children to school or having checkups at health clinics. More rich countries could copy that, tying payouts to people's willingness to invest in skills and education. The second is the reform of disability. In America enrollment in Social Security's disability-insurance program has increased from 1.7 percent of the working-age population in 1970 to 5.4 percent. Americans have taken to enrolling in disability systems when their unemployment pay runs out, spurred on by doctors who have been broadening the definition of disability. But disability is a terrible trap. America's disability systems do not devote any effort whatsoever to getting people back to work: They were designed in an era when ill people did not get better. It would be far better if they were targeted at retraining people. Denmark now grants disability benefits only if people's ability to work is permanently impaired and if they cannot even accept flexible work options.

The third cause is transparency. At the moment welfare is distributed through many different systems: In America the earned-income tax credit comes from a different source than housing aid, which is paid separately from aid to mothers with young children. The idea proposed in Britain of a single check that shows how much a person is getting from the state is the right approach. (It also allows room for the government to impose a cap. It should be impossible for a fit person to live off welfare and earn more than somebody who has a lowly paid job.) If the same were also done for the various government subsidies for the rich, then it would be obvious how much people were getting.

Entitlement reform has to involve some element of increased responsibility from the beneficiaries. The idea that a public service should be free sounds attractive. But it has not worked in practice. People should be expected to pay something—even a token amount—for medical services to demonstrate that there is no such thing as a free lunch. People should also be obliged to engage in retraining after a certain amount of time on the dole. The social-welfare system was created at a time when the majority of people worked in repetitive manufacturing jobs: Unemployment pay was meant to tide them over until they could find another job doing much the same as they had done in the past. But today's economy is going through a particularly disruptive phase: Information technology is reordering entire industries and globalization is redividing labor. Workers need to upgrade their skills if they are to have a chance at getting new jobs.

This might sound hard-hearted or judgmental. But it is actually in the spirit of the original welfare state. In his blueprint for the welfare state in 1942, Britain's William Beveridge worried that the new welfare state would collapse if it subsidized idleness or tolerated abuse. He applied strict time limits to the amount of time that could be spent on the dole. He imposed means tests to make sure that the rich did not claim benefits that were intended for the poor. It is better to be hard-hearted than soft-headed. It is also better to be fair to future generations than to impoverish them in order to cosset the current generation. Governments have repeatedly shifted the cost of funding existing entitlement programs onto future generations (who have no say in the matter). The idea of borrowing from future generations might have made sense when populations were growing and everybody knew their children would be richer than they were. Now that this is no longer true it looks a lot more risky, especially as the money being borrowed by Uncle Sam at the moment is not to finance infrastructure or build schools: It is going in tax breaks to crony capitalists and welfare payments. There is nothing progressive about that.

WAKE UP, MAGGIE

Is all this feasible? There is very little proposed above that has not already been put into practice by other governments. But individual reforms will work best if they are part of a general reengineering of the American state. Positive reforms, like negative abuses, tend to be self-reinforcing. A Congress that was prepared to deal with entitlements and clean up the tax system would also be far more likely to introduce sunset clauses for new regulations and take a tough look at defense programs. Reform is as much about changing mentality as about redesigning structure.

That inevitably prompts another question. Reagan and Thatcher embarked on something slightly similar, and they certainly changed the debate. But they still managed only a half revolution. Why would this time be different? The opportunity now is greater—much more similar to the Victorian revolution—in two ways.

The most important is the information revolution. The classical liberals were in tune with the industrial revolution. They represented a new class, hungry for change and convinced that history was on their side. Dramatic improvements in communications through the development of the railroad and the mail system suddenly made a leaner, more efficient Leviathan possible: Rather than just selling an office to a placeholder and hoping for the best, you could monitor a civil servant's performance by visiting him to check what he was doing. The information revolution has also upset society, creating a class of consumers who are used to immediate gratification, democratizing information, and, as we have seen, making it easier to reform the core functions of government, like education, health, and law and order.

The second reason has to do with competition. The nineteenth-century liberals saw life as a matter of competition red in tooth and claw. In the 1980s people feared the Soviet Union, but only for its missiles, not its economic prowess. Now, as we have seen, there is a real threat from the East. Asian companies are outcompeting the West not just in brawn work but also in brain work. And Asian politicians have created a new model that is in many ways leaner and more efficient than the decadent Western model. Competition may give politicians the courage to reform the machinery of government.

We consequently have a golden opportunity to complete the revolution of the 1980s—to reform government from the ground up and put liberty at the heart of the state's relations with its citizens. But is democracy up to the task? A couple of decades ago people in the West were confident that democracy was not only "the worst form of government except all those other forms that have been tried from time to time," in Churchill's immortal phrase, but also the best form of government: much more capable of solving the world's most pressing problems than any of its rivals. Today many people are having second thoughts. Democracy seems to be responsible for the problem of bloat. Politicians bribe their way into office with other people's money and voters put off difficult decisions. Democracy is also becoming increasingly dysfunctional as the West confronts the problem of scarcity. Can a democratic system really confront hard choices? Can it deal with scarcity as well as abundance? The West's greatest advantage in the battle with the Asian alternative is increasingly looking like a handicap.

The conclusion will argue that democracy remains a huge advantage for the West: For all its messiness it forces the state to respond to people's worries as well as allowing it to tap their talents. But democracy also needs to be reformed if it is to work properly: prevented from indulging its worst instincts and encouraged to express its best. The case for limiting government is not only a case for extending liberty. It is also a case for restoring democracy to its full potential.

CONCLUSION

THE DEMOCRATIC DEFICIT

"DEMOCRACY NEVER LASTS LONG," said John Adams, America's second president. "It soon wastes, exhausts and murders itself. There never was a democracy yet that did not commit suicide."[1] This gloomy reflection, penned in 1814, might sound odd coming from one of the fathers of the first democratic nation. But for Adams and his generation democracy was far from being a self-evident answer to the riddle of politics. Democracy had all but disappeared from the world when the Macedonians defeated the Athenians in 322 B.C. (A few Swiss cantons did not make for a great political movement.) Europe's great experiment with unfettered people power, in the form of the French Revolution, had soon led to bloodshed and tyranny. Adams's great worry, however, was about human nature itself: "It is in vain to say that democracy is less vain, less proud, less selfish, less ambitious, or less avaricious than aristocracy or monarchy. It is not true, in fact, and nowhere appears in history. Those passions are the same in all men, under all forms of simple government, and when unchecked, produce the same effects of fraud, violence, and cruelty."[2] The secret of good government lay in checking human passions, not unleashing them.

Many of the leading thinkers of Adams's day shared these worries.

To be sure, as educated gentlemen, they had all read Thucydides's great *History of the Peloponnesian War*—and Pericles's funeral oration that listed the virtues of democracy: How it enshrined the principle of individual equality; how it drew on the talents of all citizens rather than a privileged (and often decadent) few; how it inculcated respect for political institutions and a willingness to defend those institutions in battle. But they had also read Plato's counterblast in *The Republic*. Plato worried that the masses were moved by emotion rather than reason and by short-term self-interest rather than long-term wisdom. Democracy thus became a "theaterocracy," with the vulgar hordes gawping at professional politicians on the stage and voting for the ones who produced the prettiest speeches and the juiciest promises.

To these classical doubts the architects of our Second Revolution added a special worry: that democracy might crush the greatest of all political virtues, individual liberty. In America, Adams and his fellow Founding Fathers erected all sorts of defenses against the tyranny of the majority. Senators were appointed for six-year terms to make sure they focused on the long term—George Washington famously likened the Senate to a saucer into which you pour your coffee to cool it. Supreme Court justices had jobs for life. The Bill of Rights listed individual rights that no government could breach. In Britain, John Stuart Mill fretted about the tendency of "masses to predominate over individuals." The ethos of the democratic age was a collectivist one: Majorities crushed minorities into conformity by a combination of moral pressure and legal regulations. Mill was particularly worried that dissenters would censor themselves out of fear of standing out from the crowd or losing their jobs.[3] In France, Tocqueville was equally worried about "soft despotism" and the idea that democratic societies might reduce individuals to the same level of insignificance—all equal, but all slaves to the overmighty state, lulled into a condition of mindless conformity: "It is not at all tyrannical, but it hinders, restrains, enervates, stifles, so much that in the end each nation is no more than a flock of timid and hardworking animals with the government as its shepherd."[4]

For Adams, Tocqueville, and Mill, democracy was a powerful but imperfect mechanism: something that needed to be designed carefully in order to harness human creativity but also to check human perversity, and then kept in good working order. Today few people ask such basic questions about the strengths and weaknesses of the democratic order. A few political theorists produce excellent books—Larry Siedentop's *Democracy in Europe* springs to mind—but for the most part popular discussion about the subject is threadbare. In the vacuum a dangerous paradox is emerging. On the one hand, voters have scant respect for the governments that democracy has landed them with: To varying degrees, they loathe their leaders and regard them as corrupt and inefficient. On the other hand, they assume that democracy is beyond criticism, a permanent feature of political life. They hate the practice, but never question the theory.

That situation is unlikely to last. Adams was right: The threat to democracy comes from within—if not from the temptation to commit suicide, then at least from the temptation to waste and exhaust itself. Democracy has become too sloppy and self-indulgent over the recent decades of prosperity: It is overloaded with obligations and distorted by special interests. In the nineteenth century liberals combined reform of the machinery of state with reform of the system of representation; they got rid of rotten boroughs and extended the franchise to ever wider segments of the population. Their modern descendants should take the same approach: Trim the state and revitalize democracy.

AFTER 1,000 YEARS, ONE GOOD CENTURY

For Western democracy, like the Western welfare state in general, the twentieth century was a triumph. In 1900 not a single country had what we today would consider a democracy: a government created by elections in which every adult citizen could vote. In 2000 Freedom House classified 120 countries covering 63 percent of the world population as democracies. When representatives of more than 100 countries gathered at the World Forum on Democracy in Warsaw in 2000 to proclaim that "the will of the people" is "the basis of the authority of government," the mood was one of celebration. America's State Department declared that "at long last democracy is triumphant."

But the triumph had not been straightforward. Seventy years before, communism and fascism had been on the rise. When Spain temporarily restored parliamentary government in 1931, Mussolini had likened it to returning to oil lamps in the age of electricity. In 1941 Franklin Roosevelt had worried that it might not be possible to shield "the great flame of democracy from the blackout of barbarism," a fear repeated during the cold war. But democracy had eventually won. The great heroes of the late twentieth century were heroes of democracy: Think of Nelson Mandela leading the peaceful transition to majority rule in South Africa or Václav Havel constructing the velvet revolution in the Czech Republic. In the introduction to *Democracy in America* Tocqueville argued that "the effort to halt democracy appears as a fight against God himself."[5] Substitute the word "history" for "God" and by 2000 that was a statement of conventional wisdom.

Yet today things look very different: Democracy's advance has come to a shuddering halt. Freedom House notes that there is one fewer democracy in the world today than in 2001. Democracy has fared particularly poorly on what might be called its frontiers, where countries are in flux and history is being made. Horrified by the chaos that their potential democratic freedoms were creating (and unwilling to accept Donald Rumsfeld's blithe "Stuff happens" explanation for the looting and burning in liberated Iraq) a worrying number of countries have rejected democracy for strongmen.

Indeed, the story of democracy in the twenty-first century has been a story of hopes dashed and promises cheated. After the collapse of the Berlin Wall everyone assumed that the losing side would embrace democracy. In the 1990s Russia took a few drunken steps in that direction under Boris Yeltsin. But on the very last day of the twentieth century Yeltsin resigned and handed power to Vladimir Putin: a postmodern czar who has been both prime minister and president twice and who has neutered the opposition, muzzling the press, cowing his mainstream opponents, and putting his most persistent critics in prison. The disappointment was even greater in the Middle East. The invasion of Iraq in 2003 was supposed to usher in democracy; instead it brought chaos—and eventually a Putinesque strongman. The collapse of Hosni Mubarak's regime in Egypt in 2011 revived the hope of spreading democracy to the Middle East. But Egypt's elections were won not by liberal activists (who were hopelessly divided into myriad Pythonesque parties) but by Mohamed Morsi's Muslim Brotherhood, which then tried to manipulate the constitution while allowing the economy to disintegrate—so much so that many cheered when the army deposed Egypt's first democratically elected president and killed or imprisoned thousands of members of the Muslim Brotherhood. Today only three of the twenty-two members of the Arab League can claim to be democratic—and even Tunisia, Libya, and Iraq all have serious flaws.

Meanwhile, some of the most important recruits to the democratic camp are losing their luster. The African National Congress, which has ruled South Africa since 1994, is increasingly corrupt. Jacob Zuma, the current president, has used his office to accumulate a huge personal fortune, including spending R200m ($20 million) of public money on a house. Recep Tayyip Erdogan, Turkey's prime minister, has marginalized his opponents, imprisoned journalists, and treated his critics with contempt. Viktor Orban, Hungary's prime minister, has behaved in such a high-handed manner that the European Commission has repeatedly censured him.

These setbacks are all significant in themselves. But they are given even more significance by two developments. The first was the subject of chapter 6: the rise of the Beijing consensus with its emphasis on top-down modernization and meritocratic selection. We have argued that this model is more vulnerable than it looks, but it has been much easier for other countries to turn their backs on democracy when the world's fastest growing big economy is proudly undemocratic. And the other development is undeniable: Democracy is suffering from serious problems in its traditional heartland.

IN SERIOUS NEED OF A MAKEOVER

In both the United States and the European Union, all the vanity, pride, selfishness, ambition, and avariciousness that Adams feared have been on full display. Democracy's flaws are being revealed in its two great champions, but in very different ways. America's problems stem from the fact that it exemplifies too many of democracy's vices; by contrast, the European Union has exhibited too few of the virtues.

One of the few things that Americans agree on nowadays is that their political system is a mess. This mess is becoming increasingly costly. The Peterson Foundation calculates that, since 2010, fiscal uncertainty—i.e., gridlock—might have slowed America's GDP growth by one percentage point and stopped the creation of two million jobs. The mess is also taking a toll on America's image—and by extension democracy's image—abroad. Politics used to stop at the water's edge. No longer: Democrats lustily accused George W. Bush of being a warmonger. Now Republicans equally lustily accuse Barack Obama of being an appeaser. All this vexes America's allies and even its rivals. For one of China's most powerful men, who follows Washington closely and likes spouting Tocqueville, the idea that politicians would want to run down their own foreign policy is one of the most puzzling things about America.

Why is this happening? Some of America's problems come from the fact that its democracy is too democratic, too prone to the emotions that vexed Plato and Mill. The wrangles over the budget that have recently taken America to the verge of defaulting on its debts twice have come about in part because politicians have done what the voters wanted them to do. Many Democrats do not want to cut spending at all, just as many Republicans do not want to raise taxes an iota. America is a polarized country, and Washington's theaterocracy merely reflects that. However, Washington's problems have been exacerbated by three structural quirks.

The first is a strength that is in danger of becoming a weakness. America's checks and balances continue to fulfill their main function of preventing the tyranny of the majority but at a great cost in terms of efficiency and even justice. Did the founders really mean to make it so easy for a senator from Wyoming (population 576,412) to frustrate the will of the people, at least as defined by senators representing the other 315 million people? As for the idea that filibusters and other delaying mechanisms would force parties and "factions" to reach compromise, that also seems outdated now that modern American politics is in the grip of an ideological fever. In 2010 Mitch McConnell, the Senate Republican leader, said that "the single most important thing we want to achieve is for President Obama to be a one-term president." The *National Journal* calculates that the current Congress is the most ideologically polarized ever, with the most ideologically liberal Republican senator more conservative than the most conservative Democrat. At a time when the degree of ideological overlap between the parties is zero, the filibusters, delays, and other procedural quirks in Congress, which were supposed to be used only as a last resort, are now used on the smallest pretext. In the six decades between 1949 and 2008, a mere sixty-eight presidential nominees were blocked by the Senate. Between January 2009 and November 2013, when the Democrats finally changed the filibuster procedure, seventy-nine of Barack Obama's nominees were blocked, forcing the president to appoint people while the Senate was in recess (itself something of an abuse of power).[6] Obama struggled to get Republican senators to let him appoint Chuck Hagel as his defense secretary, even though Hagel was both a decorated military veteran and a former Republican senator. Even allowing for the 2013 reform, the American political system continues to give extraordinary power to individual politicians to gum up the works. It remains what Francis Fukuyama has dubbed a "vetocracy."

Mill and Tocqueville would have been nervous about fiddling with the checks and balances that were designed to protect liberty. The other two structural problems, gerrymandering and money politics, even though they find some protection in the Constitution, seem far more alien to any idea of liberty. Indeed, they reek of the Old Corruption.

Gerrymandering is simply a modern name for rotten boroughs. The fact that so few congressional seats are contestable, together with a system of closed party primaries, entrenches extremism: All that matters to most politicians is that they appeal to the most powerful interest groups in their parties. That hands disproportionate amounts of power to special interests, like California's prison officers, who can focus their firepower on one party, and ideological zealots, who can ignore the middle ground. But the deeper problem is simply that gerrymandering is unfair. Weirdly drawn districts create the impression that American democracy is a crapshoot designed by insiders for their own benefit. The problem will persist as long as politicians are allowed to set their own electoral boundaries. The most useful thing would simply be to hand over redistricting to an independent commission, which happens in some states already.

The third problem is money. If America's politicians are increasingly divided by ideology, they are united by the pursuit of the greenback. In the 2012 election Barack Obama spent $1.1 billion on running for president and Mitt Romney spent $1.2 billion. The total cost of presidential and congressional elections combined was almost $6.3 billion, twice the figure in 2000.[7] Senate and congressional candidates spend their lives dialing for dollars in order to pay for the spin doctors, image mongers, and political consultants who get them reelected. Washington, D.C., is home to almost 12,000 lobbyists (more than 20 for every member of Congress), who cost their clients $2.4 billion in 2012.[8] These lobbyists are not only responsible for obvious sins like getting sweetheart deals for their clients. They also add to the complexity of legislation: The more convoluted a law is, the easier it is to smuggle in special privileges. It is all very good defending this political expenditure as a constitutionally protected exercise in free speech. But it creates the impression that American democracy is for sale; that the rich have more power than the poor; that favors are being exchanged and deals being done. No matter how often American politicians and donors insist that nothing is being traded, any study of human psychology, not to mention any DVD of *The Godfather,* suggests that "gifts" create obligations and expectations on both sides.

The doublespeak in defending such practices is all rather grotesque, but the problems of American democracy are at root those of good democracy gone bad. Teddy Roosevelt would be horrified by the influence of money and special interests, but he would also sense the political opportunity that lies in cleaning out America's Augean stables. By contrast, the European Union's problems are much deeper. The EU never had very much democracy to begin with—and certainly has no mechanisms for producing a Teddy Roosevelt to clean the system up.

The EU began as a project of elites. Having seen their continent all but destroyed by popular passions, Europe's leaders wanted to design a machine that would keep those passions under control. As the union has become more substantial, they have made a few halfhearted attempts to fix Europe's "democratic deficit," but "halfhearted" is the word. The main symbol of that democracy, the European parliament, is widely ridiculed as a vehicle for time servers and protest parties. Symptomatically, the union's most consequential decision of the postwar era—the introduction of the euro in 1999—was taken without any democratic input whatsoever. Europe's leaders considered getting popular approval for the 2007 Lisbon Treaty, which consolidated power in Brussels, but in a move that recalled Bertolt Brecht's line about "dissolving the people and electing another" it gave up when the people started voting the wrong way. During the darkest days of the euro crisis, the European Central Bank expanded its balance sheet by 3 trillion euros—a number almost as large as Germany's entire

GDP. That was probably the right thing to do, but it was done without consultation. Brussels will soon claim the power to inspect and veto national budgets. Again that seems logical, but it is hard to see where the democratic mandate for it comes from.

Europe's antidemocratic dynamic is also poisoning the national democracies below it. At the height of the euro crisis Italy and Greece were bullied and shamed into replacing democratically elected governments with technocratic leaders in the form of Mario Monti and Lucas Papademos. The European Union is becoming a breeding ground for populist parties that claim to speak for "the ripped-off, lied-to little people" against the arrogant and incompetent elites. Geert Wilders, the leader of Holland's Party for Freedom, rails against "this monster called Europe." Marine Le Pen, the leader of France's National Front, likens the EU to the old Soviet Union, doomed to collapse "under the weight of its own contradictions." Greece's Golden Dawn is testing the question of how far democracies can tolerate Nazi-style parties. A project that was designed to tame the beast of European populism half a century ago is actually poking it back into life.

FROM DEMOCRATIC DYSFUNCTION TO DEMOCRATIC DISTEMPER

The European Union is an extreme example of the deeper problem of "representative democracy," which has worked through the medium of nation-states. National voters elect representatives from national parties to national office and those representatives pull the levers of national power. Now that modus operandi looks a little dated. It is under threat from above and below, often for good reasons.

From above, globalization is changing national politics profoundly.

National politicians have surrendered ever more power, for example over trade and financial flows, to what might be loosely called global capitalism. They have either pooled sovereignty in various supranational bodies, like the World Trade Organization or indeed the European Union, or they have handed power across to technocrats, notably central bankers, in order to gain the confidence of the markets. There is a compelling logic to much of this: How could a single country deal with a problem like climate change? And there has also been a noble element of self-restraint: If you are a national politician the best way to resist the Siren's song of printing money is to tie yourself to the mast—and let Janet Yellen do it for you.

There are equally powerful challenges from below—from breakaway nations, such as the Catalans and the Scots, from Indian states, from Chinese provinces, from American city mayors. They are trying to reclaim powers they surrendered to national governments during the great age of centralization. There are also a host of what Moisés Naím calls "micro-powers," everything from NGOs to lobbyists, which are disintermediating traditional politics. The Internet is lowering barriers, making it easier to organize and agitate; in a world where people are now used to choosing and voting with a click, parliamentary democracy, where elections happen only every few years, looks increasingly anachronistic. Douglas Carswell, a British member of Parliament, likens traditional politics to HMV, a chain of British record shops that went bust, in a world where people are used to buying music through iTunes.[9]

The biggest challenge from below comes from the voters themselves. Plato's great worry about democracy—that citizens would "live from day to day, indulging the pleasure of the moment"—has proved prescient. One rough gauge of the public's lack of interest in the long term in America is public-sector capital spending: It fell from 5 percent of GDP in the mid-1960s to about 3 percent in the 2000s. Now that things have gotten tougher, voters have merely gotten more cynical about politicians, perhaps the most extreme example coming in Iceland, where the ironically named Best Party won enough votes in 2010 to co-run Reykjavik's City Council (which is tantamount to co-running Iceland) on the promise that it would betray its promises and be openly corrupt. Membership in the mainstream national parties has collapsed, in Britain's case from 20 percent of the voting-age population in the 1950s to just 1 percent today. Political parties are finding it harder to win majorities: In 2012 only four of the OECD's thirty-four countries had governments with absolute majorities in parliament.

Such cynicism might be healthy if people wanted little from the government. But they continue to want a great deal. The result can be a toxic and unstable mixture: dependency on government on the one hand and disdain for government on the other. The dependency forces government to overexpand and overburden itself while the disdain robs government of its legitimacy and turns every setback into a crisis. Democratic dysfunction goes hand in hand with democratic distemper.

CAPITALISM, GLOBALISM, AND DEMOCRACY

These failures raise a big question: Is democracy really the wave of the future? Democracy's claim to inevitability rests on two assumptions, neither of which John Adams would have rushed to accept. The first is that democracy is a universal creed: All you need to do is to remove tyranny and democracy will put down roots. The second is that democracy and capitalism are twins: Free choice in politics can only flourish alongside free choice in economics. These assumptions were at the heart of Fukuyama's famous essay on "The End of History" in 1989. But over the past decade and a half they have both been tested and found wanting.

Democracy may be a "universal aspiration," as Tony Blair and George W. Bush and others have insisted, but it is a culturally rooted practice. It was invented in ancient Greece and rediscovered from the mid-nineteenth century onward in Western Europe. Western countries almost invariably introduced the mass franchise only after they had already introduced sophisticated political regimes with powerful legal systems and entrenched constitutional rights—and they did so in cultures that cherished notions of individual rights. Even then they were plagued by serious problems. Half of Europe surrendered to authoritarianism in the 1920s and 1930s. From that perspective it is not surprising that democracy wilted so quickly in Russia and Egypt.

The link between liberal democracy and liberal capitalism is also far from automatic, a problem economists have been much quicker to recognize than politicians. James Buchanan and other "public choice" theorists worried that democratic politicians would always pander to their electorates—and thus build up deficits and underinvest in infrastructure—a worry that has been proven spectacularly accurate. Dani Rodrik argues that modern nation-states confront a trilemma: They cannot simultaneously pursue democracy, national self-determination, and economic globalization. In the postwar period they sacrificed globalization in the name of democracy and national determination. In Rodrik's view they are increasingly sacrificing democracy and national determination in the name of globalization.

There is also the problem of the inequality that capitalism inevitably creates. Louis Brandeis, the great American Supreme Court judge, once pronounced that "we can have a democratic society or we can have great concentrated wealth in the hands of a few. We cannot have both." The golden age of Western democracy was arguably during the long postwar boom when inequalities of income were relatively compressed and nation-states offered full employment and expanding welfare provisions. Democracy has seemed less golden when so many of the spoils have gone to the top 1 percent. As our colleague Philip Coggan has pointed out, this contradiction, like many others, was manageable in the era of more, when the economy was growing and it was easy for both governments and their citizens to borrow. But the 2007–8 financial crisis stopped that: In an era of less, democracy is under more pressure.

That does not mean that it is on the verge of collapse, let alone that Chinese-style authoritarianism is coming to a town hall near you. Democracy is an extraordinarily adaptive system: It created welfare states in the early twentieth century as people got the vote. It still provides people with a peaceful way of kicking the bums out and recruiting new talent from high and low. It reinforces human rights and encourages innovation. Perhaps, most fundamentally people want it, so the chances are that the Chinese will follow the Taiwanese and the South Koreans: As they get richer, they will demand more freedoms. But that is no excuse for doing nothing in the West, or being complacent about the damage that the demons now stalking Western democracy could do. Once again there is a risk. By allowing their democracies to decay, Western governments have let down their own people. But just as with the bigger question of the state itself, there is also an opportunity.

RETOOL AND REVISE

The argument we made earlier about fixing the machinery of state also applies to the machinery of democracy. There is a host of practical things that publicly spirited democratic politicians of all persuasions should want to get on with. We have already mentioned several, like forcing American politicians to accept boundaries set by an independent commission, not gerrymandered by themselves. European countries also have obvious problems to fix. Spain gives too much power to its provinces; Italy has far too many MPs (who are paid far too much) and two equally powerful chambers. Britain has outsourced its electoral boundaries to a commission, but its system still gives Scots greater voting clout than the English in Westminster, even though the Scots now have their own parliament.

But reformers need to embark on a grander project. The key to reviving the democratic spirit lies in reviving the spirit of limited government. The great problem of the West is not just that it has overloaded the state with obligations it cannot meet; it has overburdened democracy with expectations that cannot be fulfilled. This book has repeatedly demonstrated the truth of Plato's two great criticisms of democracy: that voters would put short-term satisfaction above long-term prudence and that politicians would try to bribe their way to power—as they have done by promising entitlements that future generations will have to pay for. A narrower state, especially one that constrained itself by various self-denying ordinances, would be a more sustainable one.

Again, whenever people have looked hard at the problems of democracy, they have focused on self-restraint as part of the solution. Limited government was the centerpiece of the American Revolution.

"In framing a government which is to be administered by men over men," James Madison argued in The Federalist Papers, "the great difficulty lies in this: you must first enable the government to control the governed; and in the next place oblige it to control itself." America's Founding Fathers put a lot of thought into doing that: hence all those checks and balances. Limited government was also integral to the relaunch of democracy after the Second World War. For Reinhold Niebuhr, Carl Friedrich, and the postwar constitution builders, it was crucial that governments controlled themselves. The United Nations Charter (1945) and the Universal Declaration of Human Rights (1948) established rights and norms that countries could not breach even if majorities wanted to do so. The German Federal Republic, partly written by Friedrich, was modeled on America's.

These checks and balances were based on a fear of tyranny—of greedy kings and power-mad dictators. The danger to democracy's health today, at least in the West, comes in three more subtle forms. The first is that the state will keep on expanding, gradually reducing liberty. The second is that the state will surrender ever more power to special interests—something that gets easier when the state sprawls. The third danger is that the state will keep making promises it cannot fulfill—either by creating entitlements it cannot pay for or by committing itself to unreachable goals, such as abolishing terrorism or ending poverty, that end up in bloated failure. In all these areas the state is overextending itself and overtaxing its democratic credentials. It is time to put the "liberal" back into "liberal democracy": to persuade both voters and governments to accept restraints on the state's natural tendency to overindulge itself.

What sort of restraints does this mean in practice? One part is fairly obvious. Governments can exercise self-restraint by putting on a straitjacket—as the Swedes did by pledging to balance their budget over the economic cycle and vowing to fund their entitlements properly (with pensions linked to life expectancy). The biggest restraint of all, and one that is overdue throughout the West, is the introduction of sunset clauses. At the moment laws and regulations are like vampires: Once created, they are impossible to kill. A system whereby each law expired after ten years, including the self-denying ordinances we have advocated here, would force government to keep themselves under control.

The other two ways for politicians to restrain themselves rely on making much better use of the two forces that currently undermine representative democracy. The pressures from above and below—from globalization on the one hand and assertive voters on the other—are here to stay. National politicians need to find a way to bring these forces into balance by handing over some powers to technocrats and others to Naím's "micro-powers."

On the economic front, handing some decisions to technocrats (or committees of the great and good) makes sense. Giving control of monetary policy to independent central banks has been a success: It reduced inflation rates in the West from 20 percent or more in the 1980s to almost nothing today. Giving control of fiscal policy to independent commissions could help to bring entitlements under control. In recent years the best chance of restoring fiscal sanity to the United States was provided by the (Alan) Simpson and (Erskine) Bowles commission, which included politicians from both parties and recommended reforming the tax code to reduce basic rates but also eliminate or cut various exemptions, like the mortgage interest deduction: Sadly it was blocked.

Surely several of these restraints, especially the outsourcing of some decisions to third parties, just increase the threat of technocracy? Yes, they do. But that risk can be reduced if such delegation is done sparingly, with only a few big decisions being eligible and the delegation is open and transparent. Voters know that central bankers set their interest rates and they can read their minutes online. And another way to limit any drift toward technocracy is to push more power in the opposite direction, down toward the voters—especially toward local government.

A consistent theme throughout this book has been that government is best when it is close to the people to whom it is accountable (city mayors regularly get double the approval ratings of national politicians) and when it works with the grain of technology. E-communities such as Britain's Mumsnet encourage "nonpolitical" people to take an interest in political problems such as food labeling and child-care policies. The Finns, who are looking at ways to restrain their government from spending too much, have also experimented with lots of ways to devolve power and harness e-democracy. Decisions about pension systems might be handed to technocrats (subject to parliamentary approval). But decisions about the local community center might be decided by "liquid democracy." Some of California's reforms also fit this pattern, calling in technocratic fixers for some problems, such as gerrymandering, while trying to widen democracy by opening up primaries to all comers. Tocqueville made a perfect case for local democracy: "Local institutions are to liberty what primary schools are to science; they put it within the people's reach, they teach people to appreciate its peaceful enjoyment. . . . Feelings and opinions are recruited, the heart is enlarged, and the human mind is developed by no other means than the reciprocal influence of men upon each other."[10]

UNITED AT THE END

The Fourth Revolution is about many things. It is about harnessing the power of technology to provide better services. It is about finding clever ideas from every corner of the world. It is about getting rid of outdated labor practices. But at its heart it is about reviving the power of two great liberal ideas.

It is about reviving the spirit of liberty by putting more emphasis on individual rights and less on social rights. And it is about reviving the spirit of democracy by lightening the burden of the state. If the state promises too much, it creates distemper and dependency among its citizens; it is only by reducing what it promises that democracy will be able to express its best instincts, of flexibility, innovation, and problem solving. This is a fight that matters enormously. Democracy is the best safeguard for basic rights and basic liberties. It is also the best guarantee of innovation and problem solving. But fighting against its worst instincts will be tough.

The three revolutions we have chronicled in this book have all been enormously hard fought. The revolutionaries had to question long-cherished assumptions and dream up a very different world, often in the face of stern opposition from people at the very heart of the state. Hobbes defined a world in which power was justified not by God or lineage but by its ability to solve the problem of public order. The great nation builders of early modern Europe had to take on lords spiritual and temporal who were jealous of their privileges. They also had to create an administrative machine in a world in which travel was difficult and educated bureaucrats in short supply. Mill imagined a world in which power was constrained by individual liberty. The great reformers of the eighteenth and nineteenth centuries did prolonged battle with the forces of Old Corruption that gained so much from the old order. Beatrice Webb rethought the assumptions of her childhood about the evils of state intervention. The early twentieth-century socialists were furious institution builders, creating the modern welfare state, with its schools, hospitals, and unemployment pay, against the background of extreme suspicion.

Yet each one of these revolutions brought huge rewards. Early modern Europe became the most dynamic continent in the world. Victorian England created a liberal state that provided better services at lower cost than Old Corruption, oversaw the transition to mass democracy with little disruption, and ruled a vast empire very cheaply. The welfare state provided millions of people with tangible securities in a world that could be horrifically harsh.

The Fourth Revolution will be no easier: The half success of the Reagan–Thatcher reforms shows that. It will force many Westerners to rethink two things that are widely regarded as self-evident goods: the welfare state and the practice of democracy. But that is only because they have become self-destructive of late: The welfare state has sprawled and democracy has become self-indulgent, tawdry, and, too often, corrupt. Convincing people that a narrower state which offers fewer benefits will be a stronger one will be hard; so will imposing self-denying rules on democracy. There will be plenty of opportunities for demagoguery on the part of special interests. Parliamentarians will not give up their rotten boroughs easily; crony capitalism will fight hard for its subsidies.

But reformers should push ahead, clinging to the three great undeniables of their cause. The first is that the cost of inaction is high—just as it would have been if early modern Europe had refused to build state machines or if early-twentieth-century Europe had declined to provide services for its poor. Unreformed, the modern welfare state will stagnate under its own weight: It is already failing to help the people who need its support most, lavishing its largesse on cosseted vested interests. And democracy will waste away just as John Adams predicted. The second undeniable is the opportunity. The rewards for pressing ahead with the Fourth Revolution will be dramatic: Any state that harnesses the most powerful innovative forces in society will pull ahead of its peers. And, finally, they have history on their side: This revolution is about liberty and the rights of the individual. That is the tradition that propelled first Europe and then America forward. The West has been the world's most creative region because it has repeatedly reinvented the state. We have every confidence that it can do so again, even in these difficult times.

ACKNOWLEDGMENTS

In this book we are rude about public-sector productivity and complain about the fact that a few people take a lot of credit for the work of others. This is of course deeply hypocritical. It has taken a depressingly long time for two journalists to produce this relatively short book, and we have as usual relied too often on the hard work of others whose only reward is to be mentioned here and then blamed when anything goes wrong.

Our biggest debt is to *The Economist*—for giving us permission to use bits of published articles, for providing us with employment, and for affording us such a superb vantage point to examine this subject. All our colleagues have been incredibly tolerant of us, even allowing for the fact that one of us is, in many cases, their boss. But we would particularly like to single out the following people who have helped us directly, with research, proofreading, picture selection, jacket design, and, possibly most difficult of all, taking the authors' photograph: Sheila Allen, Mark Doyle, Celina Dunlop, Rob Gifford, Graeme James, Robert Banbury, and Tom Nuttall. We would also like to thank Ed Carr, Emma Duncan, and Zanny Minton Beddoes for reading the book in draft form, and improving it considerably. We also drew on the work of Simon Cox, Simon Long, Anne McElvoy, Michael Reid, Ed McBride, and Helen Joyce. And we would like to apologize to Caroline

Carter, Patsy Dryden, Georgia Grimond, Daniel Franklin, and Anne Foley, whose lives were too often disrupted by what happened.

Other friends generously read the book, gave us advice on it, or put up with our coming to stay with them to write it, including Jesse Norman, Victor Halberstadt, Donella Tarantelli, Charles and Juliet Macdonald, Anne Applebaum, and Anne Bernstein. Whenever we tired of our subject or felt the lure of short-term gratification, the kindly but stern figure of Gideon Rachman appeared, whip in hand, to keep us on the straight and narrow.

We have been extremely lucky to have kept the same two editors—Scott Moyers in New York and Stuart Proffitt in London. In a world where publishers seem to pay ever less attention to detail, they are a wonderful exception. We would also like to thank Akif Saifi, Yamil Anglada, Mally Anderson, and Tracy Locke at The Penguin Press in New York, as well as Sarah Watson in London. And, as usual, this book would not have happened without our agent, the incomparable Andrew Wylie.

As before, though, the main burden of this book fell on our families—on our wives, Fev and Amelia; on parents, uncles, and aunts who found Christmases, birthdays, and holidays disrupted; and on our children. In more perfect families, it is possible that Ella and Dora Wooldridge and Tom, Guy, and Eddie Micklethwait would have wholeheartedly embraced the idea of our writing this book. Had they been born with the social purpose and discipline of, say, Sydney and Beatrice Webb, they would not have moaned about their father's retreating to his shed or being late to pick them up, nor would they have looked forlornly on our computers as decent game consoles that had been hijacked for a malign purpose. Nevertheless, we love our children a lot; and when the Fourth Revolution happens, it will happen to them. So we have dedicated this book to them.

NOTES

INTRODUCTION

1. "Politics and the Purse," Daily Chart, *The Economist*, September 19, 2013.
2. Alexander Hamilton, "The Federalist Number One," in *The Federalist Papers*, Clinton Rossiter, ed. (New York: New American Library, 1961), p. 1.
3. Boyd Hilton, *A Mad, Bad, and Dangerous People? England 1783–1846* (Oxford: Oxford University Press, 2006), p. 558.
4. Vito Tanzi and Ludger Schuknecht, *Public Spending in the 20th Century: A Global Perspective* (New York: Cambridge University Press, 2000), p. 6, and "Economic Outlook," OECD, January 2013.
5. Neil King and Rebecca Ballhaus, "Approval of Obama, Congress Falls in New Poll," *Wall Street Journal*, July 24, 2013. Based on a *Wall Street Journal*/NBC poll in July 2013.
6. Francis Fukuyama, "The Middle-Class Revolution," *Wall Street Journal*, June 28, 2013.
7. Gurcharan Das, *India Grows at Night: A Liberal Case for a Strong State* (New York: Allen Lane, 2012).
8. The outstanding value of domestic bonds stood at $70 trillion; government bonds accounted for 61 percent of that. "Bond Markets," Financial Markets Series published by TheCityUK, London, October 2012.
9. "Working-Age Shift," *The Economist*, January 26, 2013.
10. Two canny optimists are Martin Wolf ("The Reality of America's Fiscal Future," *Financial Times*, October 22, 2013) and Lawrence Summers ("The Battle over the US Budget Is the Wrong Fight," *Financial Times*, October 13, 2013).
11. Ezra Klein, "The U.S. Government: An Insurance Conglomerate Protected by a Large, Standing Army," *Ezra Klein: Economic and Domestic Policy, and Lots of It* (blog), WashingtonPost.com, February 14, 2011.

12. Merkel used these numbers in remarks to the World Economic Forum in January 2013.

13. John Maynard Keynes, *The End of Laissez-Faire* (London: Hogarth Press, 1927). This was first delivered as a lecture at Oxford University in 1924.

CHAPTER 1
THOMAS HOBBES AND THE RISE OF THE NATION-STATE

1. One of us (AW) was a colleague of Finer's when he was writing his book and still recalls with awe the diminutive man's determination to scale the mighty mountain he had fixated upon and his enthusiasm for discussing his findings of the day over lunch, tea, dinner, and late-night drinks.

2. Virginia Woolf, "Mr Bennett and Mrs Brown," in *The Hogarth Essays* (London: Hogarth Press, 1924).

3. It is not clear whether *Leviathan* was published in late April or early May. The books started being noticed in bookshops in May.

4. George Will, *Statecraft as Soulcraft: What Government Does* (New York: Touchstone, 1983), p. 30.

5. A. P. Martinich, *Hobbes: A Biography* (New York: Cambridge University Press, 1999), p. 2.

6. Noel Malcolm, *Aspects of Hobbes* (Oxford: Clarendon Press, 2002), pp. 2–3.

7. O. L. Dick, ed., *Brief Lives* (Oxford: Oxford University Press, 1960), p. 604.

8. Ibid., p. 12.

9. Alan Ryan, *On Politics: A History of Political Thought from Herodotus to the Present* (London: Allen Lane, 2012), pp. 445–46.

10. Geoffrey Parker, *Global Crisis: War, Climate Change and Catastrophe in the Seventeenth Century* (New Haven, CT: Yale University Press, 2013), p. xix.

11. Ibid., p. 64.

12. Niall Ferguson, *Civilization: The Six Killer Apps of Western Power* (New York: Penguin Books, 2012).

13. "Think how far Christendom once extended and how many lands are now lost to the victorious Turk, who holds North Africa and the Balkans and has besieged Vienna," Louis Le Roy, a French philosopher, wrote in 1559. "Meanwhile, as though in answer to Mohammedan prayers, Europe is soaked in her own blood." John Hale, *The Civilization of Europe in the Renaissance* (New York: Athenaeum, 1993), pp. 6–7.

14. Ibid., p. 42.

15. Rondo Cameron, *A Concise Economic History of the World: From Paleolithic Times to the Present* (New York: Oxford University Press, 1997), p. 86.

16. Ferguson, *Civilization*, pp. 73–74.

17. Francis Fukuyama, *The Origins of Political Order: From Prehuman Times to the French Revolution* (London: Profile Books, 2011), p. 124.

18. Charles Tilly, "Reflections on the History of European State Making," in Charles Tilly, ed., *The Formation of National States in Western Europe* (Princeton, NJ: Princeton University Press, 1975), p. 42.

19. Charles Wilson, *Profit and Power* (New York: Springer, 1978), p. 2.

20. Malcolm, *Aspects of Hobbes*, p. 8.

21. Daron Acemoglu and James Robinson, *Why Nations Fail: The Origins of Power, Prosperity and Poverty* (New York: Crown, 2012), p. 233.

22. Étienne Balázs, *La bureaucratie celeste: Reserches sure l'economie et la societe de la Chine traditionelle* (Paris: 1968), quoted in David Landes, *The Wealth and Poverty of Nations: Why Some Are So Rich and Some So Poor* (New York: W. W. Norton: 1998), p. 57.

23. Jonathan Spence, *The Search for Modern China* (New York: W. W. Norton, 1999), pp. 122–23.

24. Samuel Huntington, *The Clash of Civilizations and the Remaking of World Order* (New York: Simon & Schuster, 1996), p. 70.

25. Jonathan Israel, *Radical Enlightenment: Philosophy and the Making of Modernity* (Oxford: Oxford University Press, 2001), pp. 2–3.

26. John Locke, Second Treatise on Civil Government, 1690.

27. Steve Pincus, *1688: The First Modern Revolution* (New Haven, CT: Yale University Press, 2009), p. 371.

28. Ibid., p. 8 and passim.

29. Thomas Paine, *Common Sense*, 1776, Project Gutenberg e-book.

30. Ryan, *On Politics*, p. 534.

31. Paine, *Common Sense*.

CHAPTER 2
JOHN STUART MILL AND THE LIBERAL STATE

1. John Stuart Mill, *Autobiography* (Project Gutenberg e-book, 2003), p. 5.

2. Ibid., p. 34.

3. Ibid., p. 52.

4. Ibid., p. 156.

5. W. D. Rubinstein, "The End of 'Old Corruption' in Britain 1780–1960," *Past and Present* 101, no. 1 (November 1983): p. 73.

6. Peter G. Richards, *Patronage in British Government* (London: George Allen & Unwin, 1963), p. 23.

7. Boyd Hilton, *A Mad, Bad, and Dangerous People? England 1783–1846* (Oxford: Oxford University Press, 2006), p. 558.

8. Martin Daunton, *State and Market in Victorian Britain: War, Welfare and Capitalism* (Woodbridge: Boydell Press, 2008), pp. 73-74.

9. The Northcote-Trevelyan Report of the Organization of the Permanent Civil Service, vol. 1, November 23, 1854. Reprinted in Report of the Committee on the Civil Service, 1966–68 (chaired by Lord Fulton).

10. Ibid., p. 108.

11. Ibid., p. 109.

12. John Stuart Mill, "Reform of the Civil Service," *Collected Works of John Stuart Mill*) vol. 18 (Toronto, 1977), p. 207.

13. David Vincent, *The Culture of Secrecy: Britain 1832–1998* (Oxford: Oxford University Press, 1998).

14. Michael Sandel, *Democracy's Discontent: America in Search of a Public Philosophy* (Cambridge, MA: Belknap Press, 1998), p. 156.

15. *Democratic Review*, 1838, vol. 1, issue 1, p. 6.

16. Alan Ryan, *On Politics: A History of Political Thought from Herodotus to the Present* (London: Allen Lane, 2012), p. 695.

17. Mill, *Autobiography*, p. 97.

18. A. V. Dicey, *Lectures on the Relation Between Law and Opinion in England During the Nineteenth Century* (London: Macmillan, 1920), pp. 430–31.

19. Oxford University Commission: Report of Her Majesty's Commissioners Appointed to Inquire into the State, Discipline, Studies and Revenues of the University and Colleges of Oxford (London, 1852), p. 149.

20. Quoted in Simon Heffer, *High Minds: The Victorians and the Birth of Modern Britain* (London: Random House, 2013), p. 445.

21. Gladstone speech at Saltney, Cheshire, October 26, 1889.

22. Michael Dintenfass and Jean-Pierre Dormois, *The British Industrial Decline* (London: Routledge, 1999), p. 14.

23. Bentley B. Gilbert, *The Evolution of National Insurance in Great Britain: The Origins of the Welfare State* (London: M. Joseph, 1966), p. 61.

24. From a speech in July 1854, quoted in G. S. Boritt, *Lincoln on Democracy* (New York: Fordham University Press, 2004), p. 64.

CHAPTER 3
BEATRICE WEBB AND THE WELFARE STATE

1. Bertrand Russell, *The Autobiography of Bertrand Russell, 1872–1914*, vol. 1 (London: Allen & Unwin, 1967), p. 107.

2. Quoted in W.H.G. Armytage, *Four Hundred Years of English Education* (Cambridge: Cambridge University Press, 1970), p. 174.

3. Norman and Jeanne MacKenzie, eds., *The Diary of Beatrice Webb*, vol. 2, *1892–1905: All the Good Things of Life* (Cambridge, MA: Harvard University Press, 1984), p. 63.

4. George Bernard Shaw, *Man and Superman*, quoted in A. E. Dyson and Julian Lovelock, *Education and Democracy* (London: Routledge & Kegan Paul, 1975), p. 270.

5. Granville Eastwood, *Harold Laski* (London: Mowbray, 1977), p. 4.

6. Vito Tanzi, *Government Versus Markets: The Changing Economic Role of the State* (Cambridge: Cambridge University Press, 2011), p. 126.

7. Quoted in Robert Skidelsky, *Keynes: A Very Short Introduction* (Oxford: Oxford University Press, 2010), p. 46.

8. Nicholas Timmins, *The Five Giants: A Biography of the Welfare State* (London: HarperCollins, 1995), p. 25.

9. Christian Caryl, *Strange Rebels: 1979 and the Birth of the 21st Century* (New York: Basic Books, 2013), p. 54.

10. Martin van Creveld, *The Rise and Decline of the State* (Cambridge: Cambridge University Press, 1999), p. 361.

11. Quoted in John Samples, *The Struggle to Limit Government* (Washington, D.C.: Cato Institute, 2010), p. 24.

12. Jim Sidanius and Felicia Pratto, *Social Dominance: An Intergroup Theory of Social Hierarchy and Oppression* (Cambridge: Cambridge University Press, 1999), p. 196.

13. R. H. Tawney Papers, "The Finance and Economics of Public Education," London School of Economics, a lecture given in Cambridge, February 1935, p. 5.

14. Barry Goldwater, *The Conscience of a Conservative* (Portland, OR: Victor Publishing, 1960), p. 15.

15. John Micklethwait and Adrian Wooldridge, *The Right Nation: Conservative Power in America* (New York: Penguin, 2004), p. 63.

CHAPTER 4
MILTON FRIEDMAN'S PARADISE LOST

1. John Micklethwait.
2. The author should state clearly that he is not absolutely sure that the conversation happened in a sauna. The two boys did stay with Fisher, they did meet Milton Friedman, and they had a sauna. Whether it was all at the same time is unclear. He remembers it as being in a sauna. His traveling companion, now a major general, confirms the conversation took place but is not so sure it was in a sauna. It was a very long time ago.
3. Daniel Stedman Jones, *Masters of the Universe: Hayek, Friedman, and the Birth of Neoliberal Politics* (Princeton, NJ: Princeton University Press, 2012), p. 55.
4. Buchanan and Tullock did not teach at Chicago, but they were educated there.
5. Angus Burgin, *The Great Persuasion: Reinventing Free Markets Since the Depression* (Cambridge, MA: Harvard University Press, 2012), p. 192.
6. Ibid., pp. 90–91.
7. Ibid.
8. Daniel Yergin and Joseph Stanislaw, *The Commanding Heights: The Battle Between Government and the Marketplace That Is Remaking the Modern World* (New York: Simon & Schuster, 1998), p. 147.
9. Burgin, *Great Persuasion*, pp. 206–7.
10. Ibid., p. 207.
11. Ibid., p. 154.
12. Jones, *Masters of the Universe*, p. 180.
13. R. H. Tawney, *Equality* (New York: Capricorn Books, 1961), p. 163.
14. Brian Watkin, *The National Health Service: The First Phase and After: 1948–1974* (London: Allen & Unwin, 1978), p. 155.
15. Paul Addison, *No Turning Back: The Peacetime Revolutions of Post-War Britain* (Oxford: Oxford University Press, 2010), p. 38.
16. Quoted in John Samples, *The Struggle to Limit Government* (Washington, D.C.: Cato Institute, 2010), p. 54.
17. Richard Sander and Stuart Taylor, *Mismatch: How Affirmative Action Hurts Stu-*

dents It's Intended to Help, and Why Universities Won't Admit It (New York: Basic Books, 2012).

18. A. H. Halsey, ed., Department of Education and Science, *Education Priority*, vol. 1, *Problems and Policies* (London: HMSO, 1972), p. 6. Cf. A. H. Halsey, "Sociology and the Equality Debate," *Oxford Review of Education* 1, no. 1 (1975), pp. 9–26.

19. The phrase came from Reyner Banham, an architectural historian.

20. Christian Caryl, *Strange Rebels: 1979 and the Birth of the 21st Century* (New York: Basic Books, 2013), p. 183.

21. Charles Moore, *Margaret Thatcher: The Authorized Biography*, vol. 1, *Not for Turning* (London: Allen Lane, 2013), p. 315.

22. Caryl, *Strange Rebels*, p. 160.

23. Yergin and Stanislaw, *Commanding Heights*, p. 107.

24. Moore, *Margaret Thatcher*, p. 245.

25. Ibid.

26. Ibid., p. 352.

27. Charles Moore, "The Invincible Mrs. Thatcher," *Vanity Fair*, November 2011.

28. Yergin and Stanislaw, *Commanding Heights*, p. 123.

29. "Bruges Revisited," the text of the speech delivered in Bruges by Margaret Thatcher on September 20, 1988 (London: Bruges Group, 1999).

30. Hendrik Hertzberg, "Walking the Walk," Talk of the Town, *New Yorker*, February 4, 2013.

31. Manmohan Singh, quoted in Patrick French, *India: An Intimate Biography of 1.2 Billion People* (London: Allen Lane, 2011), p. 164.

32. Caryl, *Strange Rebels*, p. 326.

33. Clive Crook, "Special Report on the Future of the State," *The Economist*, September 20, 1997. Crook, to his credit, demolished the idea that the state would wilt away.

34. "Taming Leviathan," *The Economist*, March 17, 2011, p. 5.

35. Milton Friedman, "The Euro: Monetary Unity to Political Disunity?" Economists Club, *Project Syndicate*, August 28, 1997.

36. Richard Carter, "Friedman: 'Strong Possibility' of Euro Zone Collapse," *EUObserver*, May 17, 2004.

37. Stephen D. King, *When the Money Runs Out: The End of Western Affluence* (New Haven, CT, and London: Yale University Press, 2012), pp. 49–50.

38. Burgin, *The Great Persuasion*, p. 223.

CHAPTER 5
THE SEVEN DEADLY SINS—AND ONE GREAT VIRTUE—
OF CALIFORNIA GOVERNMENT

1. Some of the material in this chapter is based on a section in "Taming Leviathan," a special report in *The Economist*.
2. Troy Senik, "The Radical Reform That California Needs," *The Beholden State: California's Lost Promise and How to Recapture It*, Brian Anderson, ed. (Boulder, CO: Rowman and Littlefield, 2013), p. 77.
3. "Taming Leviathan," *The Economist*, p. 5.
4. Jon Ungoed-Thomas and Sarah-Kate Templeton, "Scandal of NHS Deaths at Weekends," *Sunday Times*, July 14, 2013.
5. William Baumol and William Bowen, *Performing Arts: The Economic Dilemma* (Cambridge, MA: MIT Press, 1966).
6. Regents of the University of California, Budget for Current Operations, 2012–13. For the 1990–91 figure see "UC Budget Myths and Facts," Chart on Per Student Average Expenditures of Education, http://budget.universityofcalifornia.edu/files/2011/11/2012-13_budget.pdf/?page_id=5.
7. Mancur Olson, *The Logic of Collective Action: Public Goods and the Theory of Groups* (Cambridge, MA: Harvard Economics Studies, 1965), p. 36.
8. This term was popularized by Angela Davis: see "The Prison Industrial Complex": CD-ROM, Ak Press, 1999.
9. "Fading Are the Peacemakers," *The Economist*, February 25, 2010.
10. Troy Senik, "The Worst Union in America," in Anderson, *Beholden State*, p. 199.
11. "Enemies of Progress," *The Economist*, March 17, 2011.
12. Senik, "The Worst Union in America," pp. 203–5.
13. Mark Niquette, Michael B. Marois, and Rodney Yap, "$822,000 Worker Shows California Leads U.S. Pay Giveaway," Bloomberg, December 10, 2012.
14. Michael Marois and Rodney Yap, "Californian's $609,000 Check Shows True Retirement Cost," Bloomberg, December 13, 2012.
15. Perry Anderson, "An Entire Order Converted into What It Was Intended to End," *London Review of Books*, February 26, 2009.
16. William Voegeli, "The Big-Spending, High-Taxing, Lousy-Services Paradigm," in Anderson, *Beholden State*, p. 27.
17. "California Reelin'" *The Economist*, March 17, 2011.
18. Joel Stein, "How Jerry Brown Scared California Straight," *Bloomberg Businessweek*, April 25, 2013.

19. Edward McBride, "Cheer Up" (special report on American competiveness), *The Economist*, March 16, 2013.

20. James D. Hamilton, "Off-Balance-Sheet Federal Liabilities" (working paper no. 19253, National Bureau of Economic Research, July 2013).

21. National Center for Policy Analysis, "America's True Debt: The Fiscal Gap" (issue brief no. 101, September 7, 2011), available at http://www.ncpa.org/pub/ib101.

22. Interview with Micklethwait, Buenos Aires, October 9, 2013.

23. "Boundary Problems," *The Economist*, August 3, 2013.

24. All the numbers in this segment are from "For Richer, for Poorer," Zanny Minton Beddoes's special report on the world economy in *The Economist*, October 13, 2012, especially from "Makers and Takers."

25. Beddoes, "Makers and Takers" *The Economist*, October 12, 2012.

26. Richard Reeves, " 'The Pinch': How the Baby Boomers Stole Their Children's Future by David Willetts," *Guardian*, February 6, 2010.

27. Dennis Jacobe, "One in Three Young U.S. Workers Are Underemployed," *Gallup*, May 9, 2012.

28. Don Peck, "How a New Jobless Era Will Transform America," *Atlantic*, March 1, 2010.

29. Nicolas Berggruen and Nathan Gardels, *Intelligent Governance for the 21st Century: A Middle Way Between West and East* (Cambridge: Polity, 2013), p. 26.

30. Gavin Newsom, *Citizenville: How to Take the Town Square Digital and Reinvent Government* (New York: Penguin Press, 2013), pp. 80–81.

31. Dennis Kavanagh and Philip Cowley, *The British General Election of 2010* (New York: Palgrave Macmillan, 2010), p. 327.

32. Quoted in "Staring into the Abyss," *The Economist*, July 8, 2010.

33. Luigi Zingales, *A Capitalism for the People: Recapturing the Lost Genius of American Prosperity* (New York: Basic Books, 2012), p. xiii.

34. Joel Stein, "How Jerry Brown Scared California Straight," *Bloomberg Businessweek*, April 25, 2013.

CHAPTER 6
THE ASIAN ALTERNATIVE

1. Graham Allison and Robert D. Blackwill, with Ali Wyne, *Lee Kuan Yew: The Grand Master's Insights on China, the United Sates and the World* (Cambridge, MA: MIT Press, 2013), p. xv.

2. Ibid., p. vii.

3. Quoted in Michael Barr, "Lee Kuan Yew's Fabian Phase," *Australian Journal of Politics & History*, March 2000.

4. Ibid., p. 128.

5. "Taming Leviathan," *The Economist*, March 19, 2011, p. 9.

6. Joshua Kurlantzik, *Democracy in Retreat: The Revolt of the Middle Class and the Worldwide Decline of Representative Government* (New Haven, CT: Yale University Press, 2013), p. 79.

7. Allison and Blackwill, *Lee Kuan Yew*, p. 27.

8. Ibid., p. 32.

9. Ibid., p. 120.

10. Ibid., p. 113.

11. Ibid., p. 34.

12. Ibid., p. 25.

13. "New Cradles to Graves," *The Economist*, September 8, 2012.

14. "Asia's Next Revolution," ibid.

15. "Widefare," *The Economist*, July 6, 2013.

16. Francis Fukuyama, "The End of History," *National Interest*, Summer 1989.

17. Joint news conference in Washington, D.C., October 29, 1997.

18. Fukuyama, "The End of History."

19. Kurlantzik, *Democracy in Retreat*, p. 201.

20. Ibid., p. 7.

21. Bertelsmann Foundation, "All Over the World, the Quality of Democratic Governance Is Declining" (press release), November 29, 2009.

22. Jim Krane, *Dubai: The Story of the World's Fastest City* (London: Atlantic Books, 2009), pp. 137–38.

23. "Taming Leviathan," *The Economist*, p. 8.

24. Interview with John Micklethwait, Davos, January 2013.

25. Kurlantzik, *Democracy in Retreat*, p. 142.

26. Lant Pritchett, "Is India a Flailing State: Detours on the Four-Lane Highway to Modernization," Kennedy School of Government, working paper, May 2009.

27. Allison and Blackwill, *Lee Kuan Yew*, p. 15.

28. Interview with John Micklethwait, March 5, 2013.

29. Dexter Roberts, "Is Land Reform Finally Coming to China?," *Bloomberg BusinessWeek*, November 20, 2013.

30. Jiang Xueqin, "Christmas Comes Early," *Diplomat*, November 24, 2010.

31. Timothy Beardson, *Stumbling Giant: The Threats to China's Future* (New Haven, CT: Yale University Press, 2013), p. 73.

32. David Shambaugh, *China Goes Global: The Partial Power* (Oxford: Oxford University Press, 2013), p. 188.

33. Paul Mozur, "China Mobile's Profit Growth Eases," *Wall Street Journal*, April 22, 2013.

34. Richard McGregor, *The Party: The Secret World of China's Communist Rulers* (New York, HarperCollins, 2010).

35. Shambaugh, *China Goes Global*, p. 69.

36. Kurlantzik, *Democracy in Retreat*, p. 128.

37. "Leviathan as a Minority Shareholder: A Study of Equity Purchases" by the Brazilian National Development Bank (BNDES) 1995–2003, Harvard Business School, working paper.

38. Adrian Wooldridge, "The Visible Hand: A Special Report on State Capitalism," *The Economist*, January 21, 2012. An OECD paper in 2005 noted that the total-factor productivity of private companies is twice that of state companies. A study by the McKinsey Global Institute in the same year found that companies in which the state holds a minority stake are 70 percent more productive than wholly state-owned ones.

39. Shambaugh, *China Goes Global*, p. 254.

40. Beardson, *Stumbling Giant*, p. 99.

41. Jagdish Bhagwati and Arvind Panagariya, *Why Growth Matters: How Economic Growth in India Reduced Poverty and the Lessons for Other Developing Countries* (New York: Public Affairs, 2013), p. xvii.

42. Off-the-record interview with Adrian Wooldridge, November 2011.

43. "Social Security with Chinese Characteristics," *The Economist*, August 11, 2012.

44. Nicolas Berggruen and Nathan Gardels, *Intelligent Governance for the 21st Century: A Middle Way Between West and East* (Cambridge: Polity Press, 2013), p. 45.

45. Richard McGregor, *The Party: The Secret World of China's Communist Rulers* (New York: HarperCollins, 2010), p. 31.

46. Daniel A. Bell, "Political Meritocracy Is a Good Thing (Part 1): The Case of China," *Huffington Post*, August 21, 2012.

47. Ibid.

48. Tom Doctoroff, *What Chinese Want: Culture, Communism, and China's Modern Consumer* (New York: Palgrave Macmillan, 2012), pp. 105 and 127.

49. He Dan and Huang Yuli, "NGOS Get Boost from Shenzhen Register Reforms," *China Daily*, August 21, 2012.

50. "Taming Leviathan," *The Economist*, March 17, 2011, p. 1.

51. Ibid., p. 11.

52. Ivan Zhai and Echo Hui, "Beijing Steps Up Centralisation of Power to Control Provincial Leaders," *South China Morning Post*, July 5, 2013.

53. Pranab Bardhan, "The Slowing of Two Economic Giants," *New York Times*, July 14, 2013.

54. David Barboza, "Billions in Hidden Riches for Family of Chinese Leader," *New York Times*, October 25, 2013.

55. Beardson, *Stumbling Giant*, p. 194.

56. McGregor, *The Party*, p. 140.

57. Andrew Jacobs and Dan Levin, "Son's Parties and Privilege Aggravate Fall of Elite Chinese Family," *New York Times*, April 16, 2012.

58. Rupa Subramanya, "Economics Journal: Why Do We Accept Political Dynasties?" *Wall Street Journal*, February 15, 2012.

59. Thomas Friedman, "Our One-Party Democracy," *New York Times*, September 8, 2009.

60. Martin Jacques, *When China Rules the World* (London: Penguin, 2010), p. 168.

61. Interview with Wang Jisi, *Asahi Shumbun*, June 12, 2010.

62. Zhang Weiwei, "Meritocracy Versus Democracy," *New York Times*, November 9, 2012; Zhang Weiwei, "China and the End of History," *Globalist*, March 5, 2013.

63. Bhagwati and Panagariya, *Why Growth Matters*, p. 207.

64. "Asia's Next Revolution," *The Economist*, September 8, 2012.

65. OECD (2013), "Education at a Glance 2013: OECD Indicator," OECD Publishing, http://dx.doi.org/10.1787/eag-2013-en.

66. Interview with Dominique Moïsi with John Micklethwait, January 18, 2013.

CHAPTER 7

THE PLACE WHERE THE FUTURE HAPPENED FIRST

1. Jo Blanden, Paul Gregg, and Stephen Manchin, "Intergenerational Mobility in Europe and North America," Centre for Economic Performance, London School of Economics, April 2005.

2. Anders Böhlmark and Mikael Lindahl, "Independent Schools and Long-Run

Educational Outcomes: Evidence from Sweden's Large Scale Voucher Reform," (CESifo Working Paper Series No. 3866, Institute for the Study of Labor, Bonn, June 29, 2012).

3. Alan Downey, "Mind the Gap," in *Reform: The Next Ten Years*, Nick Seddon, ed. (London: Reform Research Trust, 2012), p. 125.

4. James Manyika et al., "Disruptive Technologies: Advances That Will Transform Life, Business, and the Global Economy," McKinsey Global Institute, May 2013, p. 42.

5. "Where Have All the Burglars Gone?" *The Economist*, July 20, 2013.

6. "The Curious Case of the Fall in Crime," ibid.

7. "Age Shall Not Wither Them," *The Economist*, April 7, 2011.

8. Lynn Hicks, "Older Entrepreneurs Find New Niche in Startups," *USA Today*, March 11, 2012.

CHAPTER 8
FIXING LEVIATHAN

1. Gerald F. Davis, "The Rise and Fall of Finance and the End of the Society of Organizations," *Academy of Management Perspectives*, August 2009, p. 30.

2. Ludwig Siegele, "Special Report on Start-ups," *The Economist*, January 18, 2014, p. 13.

3. Ken Auletta, *Googled: The End of the World as We Know It* (New York: Penguin Press, 2009), p. 15.

4. Don Tapscott and Anthony D. Williams, *Macrowikinomics: Rebooting Business and the World* (New York: Portfolio / Penguin, 2012), p. 253.

5. Chris Anderson, *The Long Tail: Why the Future of Business Is Selling Less of More* (New York: Hyperion, 2006), p. 5.

6. Nicholas Bloom and John Van Reenen, "Measuring and Explaining Management Practices Across Firms and Countries," *Quarterly Journal of Economics* 122, no. 4 (November 2007).

7. Gavin Newsom, *Citizenville: How to Take the Town Square Digital and Reinvent Government* (New York: Penguin Press, 2013), p. 9.

8. Bruce Katz and Jennifer Bradley, *The Metropolitan Revolution: How Cities and Metros Are Fixing Our Broken Politics and Fragile Economy* (Washington, D.C.: Brookings Institution Press, 2013), pp. 176–77.

9. "Old School Ties," *The Economist*, March 10, 2012.

10. Ibid.

11. McKinsey & Company, "The Economic Impact of the Achievement Gap in America's Schools," April 2009, available at http://mckinseyonsociety.com/downloads/reports/Education/achievement_gap_report.pdf.

12. Philip K. Howard, "Fixing Broken Government" (seminar for the Long Now Foundation, San Francisco, January 18, 2011).

13. In U.S. dollars at constant prices since 2000.

14. James Q. Wilson, *Bureaucracy: What Government Agencies Do and Why They Do It* (New York: Basic Books, 1989), p. 326.

15. "Taming Leviathan," *The Economist,* March 17, 2011.

16. "Whoops," *The Economist,* November 2, 2013.

17. "Squeezing Out the Doctor," *The Economist,* June 2, 2012.

18. Ibid.

19. "How to Sell the NHS," *The Economist,* August 3, 2013.

20. Marcelo Neri, a local economist, told us that Bolsa Família accounts for 17 percent of the narrowing in inequality since 2001.

21. TaxPayers' Alliance, "New Research: The Cost of Collecting Tax Has Barely Fallen in over 50 Years," May 20, 2012, available at http://www.taxpayersalliance.com/home/2012/05/cost-collecting-tax-barely-fallen-50-years.html.

22. Interview with John Micklethwait, quoted in "Taming Leviathan," *The Economist,* March 19, 2011, p. 11.

23. John D. Donahue and Richard J. Zeckhauser, *Collaborative Governance: Private Roles for Pubic Goals in Turbulent Times* (Princeton, NJ: Princeton University Press, 2011), p. 9.

24. Bernard Marr and James Creelman, *More with Less: Maximizing Value in the Public Sector* (London: Palgrave Macmillan, 2011), p. 18.

25. Ibid., p. 55.

26. Anders Böhlmark and Mikael Lindahl, "The Impact of School Choice on Pupil Achievement, Segregation and Costs: Swedish Evidence" (IZA Discussion Paper no. 2786, May 2007), available at http://ftp.iza.org/dp2786.pdf.

27. Stephen Machin and James Vernoit, "Changing School Autonomy: Academy Schools and Their Introduction to England's Education" (Centre for the Economics of Education discussion paper no. 123, April 2011), available at http://cee.lse.ac.uk/ceedps/ceedp123.pdf.

28. Benjamin R. Barber, *If Mayors Ruled the World: Dysfunctional Nations, Rising Cities* (New York: Yale University Press, 2013), pp. 84–85.

29. William D. Eggers and Paul Macmillan, *The Solution Revolution: How Business, Government, and Social Enterprises Are Teaming Up to Solve Society's Toughest Problems* (Boston: Harvard Business Review Press, 2013), p. 15.

30. Marr and Creelman, *More with Less*, p. 3.

CHAPTER 9
WHAT IS THE STATE FOR?

1. John Stuart Mill, *On Liberty* (1859) (Oxford: Oxford World's Classics series, 1998), p. 17.

2. Figures are from the Director of National Intelligence's report to Congress on Security Clearance Determinations for Fiscal Year 2010, September 2011.

3. Jonathan Rauch, "Demosclerosis Returns," *Wall Street Journal*, April 14, 1998. Note that the quote does not appear in *Democsclerosis* the book.

4. Christopher DeMuth, "Debt and Democracy" (working paper presented at the Legatum Institute, May 21, 2012).

5. Joseph R. Mason, "Beyond the Congressional Budget Office: The Additional Economic Effects of Immediately Opening Federal Lands to Oil and Gas Leasing," Institute for Energy Research, February 2013, available at http://www .instituteforenergyresearch.org/wp-content/uploads/2013/02/IER_ Mason_Report_NoEMB.pdf.

6. Chris Edwards, "Agricultural Subsidies" (Washington, D.C.: Cato Institute, June 2009), available at http://www.downsizinggovernment.org/agriculture/ subsidies.

7. "The Agriculture Reform Act of 2012 Creates Jobs and Cuts Subsidies," Democratic Policy and Communications Center, June 13, 2012, available at http:// www.dpcc.senate.gov/?p=issue&id=163.

8. Edwards, "Agricultural Subsidies."

9. Luigi Zingales, "How Political Clout Made Banks Too Big to Fail," *Bloomberg View*, May 29, 2012.

10. Thomas Philippon and Ariell Reshef, "Wages and Human Capital in the U.S. Financial Industry: 1906–2006," *Quarterly Journal of Economics* 127, no. 4 (November 2012).

11. Hamilton Project, *15 Ways to Rethink the Federal Budget* (Washington, D.C.: Hamilton Project, 2013).

12. "Public Views of Inequality, Fairness and Wall Street," Pew Research Center, January 5, 2012, available at http://www.pewresearch.org/daily-number/public-views-of-inequality-fairness-and-wall-street/.

13. "True Progressivism" was a creed put forward in *The Economist*, October 13, 2012.

14. Statistics come from the Congressional Budget Office, "The 2013 Long-Term Budget Outlook," September 17, 2013.

CONCLUSION:
THE DEMOCRATIC DEFICIT

1. "Letter to John Taylor of Carolina, Virginia," in George W. Covey, ed., *The Political Writings of John Adams* (Washington, D.C.: Regency Publishing, 2000), p. 406.

2. Ibid.

3. "Civilization," (1836) in John Stuart Mill, *Dissertations and Discussions* (New York: Cosimo, 2008), p. 172.

4. Alexis de Tocqueville, *Democracy in America* vol. II, 1840, George Lawrence, tr., J. P. Mayer, ed. (London: Fontana Press, 1994), p. 692.

5. Ibid., p. 12.

6. "Dropping the Bomb," *The Economist,* November 30, 2013.

7. The Center for Responsive Politics, http://www.opensecrets.org/bigpicture/.

8. Ibid.

9. Douglas Carswell, "iDemocracy and a New Model Party," The Spectator.com, July 15, 2013.

10. Tocqueville, *Democracy in America*, p. 63.

INDEX

INDEX

AVAILABLE FROM PENGUIN

God Is Back
How the Global Revival of Faith is Changing the World
John Micklethwait and Adrian Wooldridge

It is a given that the global rise of faith will have dramatic and far-reaching effects in this new century. Religious civil wars are reshaping the world. Many factors have helped spark this international revival in religion, including the failure of Communism and the rise of globalism. The esteemed journalists who are the authors of *God Is Back*, argue that religion and modernity can thrive together, and explain how the same American ideas which created our unique religious style can be applied everywhere to channel the rising tide of faith away from volatility and violence.

PENGUIN BOOKS

AVAILABLE FROM PENGUIN

The Right Nation
Conservative Power in America
John Micklethwait and Adrian Wooldridge

The Right Nation is not "for" liberals, and it's not "for" conservatives. It's for any of us who want to understand one of the most important forces shaping American life. How did America's government become so much more conservative in just a generation? Conservative positions have not prevailed everywhere, of course, but this book shows us why they've been so successfully advanced over such a broad front: because the battle has been waged by well-organized, shrewd, and committed troops who to some extent have been lucky in their enemies.

PENGUIN BOOKS